# THE SPY
# WITHIN

# THE SPY WITHIN

*Larry Chin and China's
Penetration of the CIA*

## TOD HOFFMAN

Hanover, New Hampshire

For information about permission to reproduce
selections from this book, write to:
Steerforth Press L.L.C., 45 Lyme Road, Suite 208,
Hanover, New Hampshire 03755

Library of Congress Cataloging-in-Publication Data
Hoffman, Tod.
The spy within : Larry Chin and China's penetration of the CIA /
Tod Hoffman. — 1st ed.
    p. cm.
Includes bibliographical references and index.
ISBN 978-1-58642-148-9 (alk. paper)
1. Jin, Wudai, 1922–1986. 2. Espionage, Chinese — United States
— History — 20th century. 3. Spies — United States — Biography.
4. Spies — China — Biography. 5. United States. Central
Intelligence Agency. I. Title.
E743.5.J44H64 2008
327.12092 — dc22
[B]
                                        2008024290


FIRST EDITION

I'm interested in what happens inside history, what history hides, what gets left out and what is forgotten.

— Henry Bromell, *Little America*

# Contents

# Prologue

Spies are ghosts.

A presence felt in the brush of an invisible eye peering over your shoulder. The déjà vu sensation that something is out of place as you stride down an unfamiliar street. A faint impression on a piece of paper.

They haunt the imagination of their pursuers, for whom every shadow is another trace hissing through their grip like fog. Every word uttered with conviction is exquisitely cryptic. Within every allegation lie contradictions. Just because a statement is true doesn't mean it is believable; just because it is believed doesn't make it true. Separating fact from lies and guesses and wishful thinking is like sluicing the soul out from the body. The effort takes its toll, leaves casualties.

Spies begin as one thing and end up another. So do those who chase them. The best possible outcome is rippled with tragedy. The mystery is never absolutely resolved.

This is a ghost story.

# — 1 —

# UNSUB

*Washington, DC, September 28, 1982*

Supervisory Special Agent I.C. Smith had traded his suit and tie for shorts and a T-shirt. He stepped out of the Federal Bureau of Investigation (FBI) headquarters compound on 10th Street needing a spell of strenuous activity to jolt the dissonant chords reverberating in his head into some kind of harmony. He had just received the news every counterintelligence officer outwardly dreads, but secretly hopes for. An accusation of espionage. Conveyed on a single sheet of paper letterheaded CENTRAL INTELLIGENCE AGENCY OFFICE OF SECURITY and rendered in the rigid, dispassionate tones that lend authority to official reports, it was maddeningly vague, with just enough specific detail to make it sound definite.

A Chinese male currently employed by US intelligence has, for a long period of time, been passing classified material to the People's Republic of China, it stated. The originator of the accusation is a source of unknown reliability. Nonetheless, the position of the source would allow him access to such information. Furthermore, the Central Intelligence Agency is confident the source is providing information he believes to be true. The suspect — the report concluded — is most likely an employee of the military, or perhaps the FBI, but is not likely a member of the CIA.

That last line was troubling. Unless the agency knew more than was written on that sheet of paper, how could its own people be exonerated from the outset?

It wasn't that the CIA had any more information. It was, however, obliged to admit having learned of the alleged penetration at least six months earlier. Despite the fact that the FBI has sole jurisdiction to investigate espionage cases on American soil, the CIA took the liberty — and the time — to conduct an internal inquiry of all agency personnel who fit the parameters set by the source and came up empty.

The bureau took umbrage at the apparent trespass, but an objective observer could understand, if not condone, the agency's reasoning.

Paul Moore, the FBI's senior China analyst between 1978 and 1998, allows, "CIA wanted to evaluate whether there was any substance to the allegation before they pass it over. They wouldn't want the FBI trampling around if there's a sensitive capability behind it."[1]

It was a matter of differing institutional cultures. The FBI is foremost a law enforcement service. While it certainly runs long-term collection operations in its counterintelligence program, when an American is alleged to be engaged in espionage within the United States, the bureau aims to definitively conclude an inquiry by apprehending a suspect and laying a charge.

The CIA is strictly in the business of collecting and analyzing foreign intelligence, with neither the power nor the inclination to arrest. Were a traitor in its midst, the agency's preference would be to handle things quietly — if not hush them up entirely — in accordance with how it perceives its more far-reaching objectives. Instead of prosecuting the offender, it might seek to manipulate him to some operational advantage — as an active double, for instance, or by surreptitiously feeding him disinformation intended to mislead and disorient the opposition.

Moreover, the CIA was loath to self-inflict the painful suspicion of infidelity among its employees, having only just emerged from a demoralizing experience of raging mistrust. As the laws of science decree every action sets off a corresponding reaction, so the laws of bureaucracy insist that each overreaction engenders a counter-overreaction. Nothing more clearly demonstrates this than the career of James Jesus Angleton, around whom a legend had been draped that long obscured the devastating failure of his life's work.

Angleton served as the CIA's counterintelligence chief from 1954 until he was unceremoniously fired in 1974 by Director William Colby, who said, "I couldn't find that we ever caught a spy under Jim . . . I'm afraid, in that respect, he was not a good CI Chief."[2] In what other respects might he be judged, one wonders?

The professional posture of the spy hunter admits the possibility that anyone could be a mole. This is different from the paranoid obsession that everybody *is* one. The former invigorates a rational examination of clues and circumstances in an effort to uncover a traitor. The latter assumes facts with disdain for evidence, and rationalizes the absence of proof as confirmation of intricate conspiracies too diabolical ever to be unraveled.

Angleton toppled toward obsession in 1963 when he became irredeemably sold on the wisdom of one particular defector, Soviet KGB major Anatoliy Golitsyn. Golitsyn came up with a brilliant ploy to embellish his importance in the eyes of his handlers. He asserted not only that Western intelligence was thoroughly penetrated by the Soviets, but also that the KGB would be sending over false defectors in his wake to discredit him and confuse its adversaries with disinformation.

When Yuriy Nosenko defected in 1964, Golitsyn pointed to him as proof of his claims. As journalist Tom Mangold presents the tale, "He further predicted that any Soviet sources who came later and supported Nosenko's bona fides would also be fakes. He said that the CIA officers who sided with Nosenko could possibly be moles themselves."[3]

Wholeheartedly supporting Golitsyn's theory, Angleton once bragged he had "knocked back" twenty-two Soviet defectors,[4] several of whom were subsequently executed, and proceeded to investigate forty senior CIA officers, fourteen of whom were active suspects,[5] all of whom were perfectly innocent. The net effect was to completely paralyze the agency's Soviet operations.

Following Angleton's dismissal, there was a backlash in the opposite direction, the effect of which was to desensitize the CIA to the possibility of penetration. By the 1980s, the agency's senior management was staffed by those who had witnessed Angleton's reign and fall. When cases went sour, they looked to other excuses — careless tradecraft, bad luck — before contemplating the possibility of a mole and initiating a traumatic and disruptive campaign to ferret him out.[6] With the allegation it was now sharing with the FBI, the CIA was undoubtedly relieved to pronounce its men absolved. The ball — more like a grenade — was tossed over to the bureau.

Responsibility for identifying the culprit was placed on I.C. Smith's China squad.

Gazing down the street, even preoccupied as he was, he retained the grim, insistent posture of a veteran cop. A big man, with a straight back and square shoulders, he had been with the bureau for nine years, before which he was on the beat back home in Monroe, Louisiana, a downtrodden little town where he was on a first-name basis with just about anyone who could be counted on to cause trouble.

Whenever he contemplated difficult decisions, Smith was in the habit of going for a run. It allowed him to consider a problem free of pent-up physical tension. Dashing south from headquarters to the National Mall, he made his way through the crowd of tourists and schoolchildren toward the Reflecting Pool, past the greatest concentration of museums and monuments in the United States.

"I always paid attention to the landmarks, but this time I didn't notice a single one. All I'm thinking about is who am I gonna give this case to," he recalls. "I knew right from this point that it wasn't a street case. It was going to be research, the drudgery of going through musty files. I had to choose a guy with a great ability to sit there, day in and day out."[7]

By the time he'd finished, cleaned up, and driven back across town to the Washington Field Office at Buzzard Point, he'd made up his mind.

Chinese is different. That's what all the old China hands say.

The FBI only got into the China business in earnest in 1971, when the first official delegation from the People's Republic took up residence at the United Nations in New York. This was followed, in 1979, by the opening of an embassy in Washington and consulates in New York and

San Francisco. Mixed in among the legitimate diplomats and support staff was presumed to be the mandatory intelligence contingent.

This being the height of the Cold War, the FBI's resources were overwhelmingly directed against the Soviets and East Bloc satellite targets. By the early 1980s, there were probably fewer than a hundred agents assigned to China nationwide. Those schooled in the textbook compiled from more than three decades of working the Soviets had to adapt to a new target that thought and behaved in a manner to which they were unaccustomed.

The Chinese method of gathering intelligence doesn't even look like espionage. An analogy used by the China-watchers supposes that the Chinese and the Soviets are both interested in analyzing the composition of the sand on a particular beach. The Soviets would send a submarine and, in the dead of night, land a platoon of collectors, who would gather several buckets of sand before disappearing as they came. China, on the other hand, would encourage people recruited for no other purpose to spend a day sunbathing at the beach and, upon returning home, shake the grains of sand that accumulated from their towels into a pail. Where the Soviets were aggressive and often heavy-handed, the Chinese are patient and cautious — subtle almost to the point of being imperceptible.

"The Chinese do not think in terms of hours, days or weeks, but in terms of decades. They are an ancient civilization. They are able to deal with the intricacies of long-term planning," insists Paul Redmond, the onetime head of counterintelligence for the CIA.[8]

China's collection efforts are more diffuse than those directed by Soviet bloc states, which were conducted under a formulaic protocol. If the aim was Western scientific knowledge, for example, the KGB or its local variant received tasking to get access to a specifically desired piece of information or equipment. In China, by contrast, the scientific community would employ its own wiles in pursuit of objectives it defined in the broadest possible terms. Thus, an American nuclear physicist from New Mexico might be courted by a professor teaching at a university in Guangzhou, while a chemical engineer from San Francisco could find himself buttonholed by a counterpart from Harbin.

It comes down to a different definition of what constitutes an effective intelligence program. The United States — and the Soviet Union, for that matter — emphasized recruiting a small number of agents and pushing them to produce large amounts of information. The Chinese rely on large numbers of people, each producing relatively small amounts of intelligence.

"Our way of doing things is much more secure and efficient," argues Moore. "China's way is much harder to detect. It also facilitates involving people who would otherwise be horrified at the thought of participating in hard-core espionage."[9]

Contacts are rarely coerced into collaborating. No harm is intended, they are reassured; China merely seeks a helping hand. In the interest of mutual friendship. Risk is discouraged. Tasking is generic, almost apologetic. Please, share with us whatever you can.

"If you don't ask your spy the hard questions, you let him keep his head down, you don't expose him," says T. Van Magers, who was among the original FBI agents assigned to the China squad, where he would spend some twenty-five of his thirty-three years' service. "'You give us what you can, what you think is important' — they'll leave it at that. They don't employ central tasking lists or that sort of direct objective out of Beijing. Because they don't stick their necks out to get a particular document or find the answer to a specific question, they don't draw attention to themselves."[10]

Many of the agents, like Magers, who got in on the ground floor of the program, became genuine Sinophiles. They immersed themselves in China — studied its history, read its literature, wondered at its art, familiarized themselves with its turbulent politics. Many learned to contort their Anglo tongues around the odd intonations of its language. They appreciated how working a target entails intimacy. A good intelligence officer is a student, open-minded and curious about his target. He reads everything. He studies the classified case files, past and present. He doesn't neglect to absorb the information in the public domain, paying attention to what journalists report and scholars hypothesize.

There was a visceral component to this job you had to ingest. It wasn't enough to be aware that the Chinese ate different food; you had to know how it tasted in your own mouth, what the texture was slipping down your own throat. Not enough to be told how a thing smells; you had to inhale it for yourself. You had to cultivate a feeling for the community in which the Chinese lived and the cultural tilt from which they saw the world. Maps sold in the United States depict North America at the center, with Europe to the east and Asia the west. Those sold in China have Eurasia at the fore, North America on the periphery.

The agents gathered frequently in Chinatown, usually at a restaurant where the owner or chef was someone's source, the information he provided being of less importance than that the food and drink be plentiful and the bill scarce. They manipulated their chopsticks with a native's dexterity, shoveling their rice with them, using them to gesture with the emphatic certitude of a maestro, clacking them in rhythm to the hushed tones and clipped phrases they affected in public. Their identity was an open secret, but circumstances could turn that to advantage: People knew where to go if they had something to report. Often this amounted to complaints against noisy neighbors or jealous gossip, but once in a great while you'd sift out a nugget of genuine intelligence.

With the CIA's trace info came an opportunity for the China hands to score a significant victory in the bureaucratic wars that underpin — and are frequently more vicious than — the spy wars, where managers engage in the close-quarters fighting for the budget and manpower by which they measure their status and exalt their worth. Capturing a certified Chinese spy would instantly elevate the program into the spotlight and confirm what they'd been insisting all along: that Chinese intelligence was ubiquitous and vigorously pursuing opportunities to acquire classified information in the United States.

"In my view," Smith contends, "we had to demonstrate the China threat, and the best way to do that was to build a prosecutable case."[11]

Nothing about Special Agent Tom Carson is flamboyant. He is a small-town Alabaman with the grace to think faster than he speaks. He spent his time inconspicuously but diligently following up leads, verifying records, meticulously noting any trace of intelligence he uncovered in the sundry files he worked, filling in blanks, doing the mundane chores that make up an investigator's day. Agents who thrive on the adrenaline promise of a climax aren't cut out for counterintelligence, where years of watching and monitoring and compiling often result in file drawers full of unanswered questions. Carson didn't succumb to frustration. He wouldn't let himself become careless and assume a room was empty because he couldn't hear a sound; he got down on his knees and checked under the bed. And for that he'd earned the respect of his colleagues and superiors.

Carson was at his battered metal desk in the bullpen he shared with the other members of the squad when Smith returned. He was summoned into his supervisor's office, the door closed.

Smith let him in on what he'd just learned. He asked Carson to take the case. Carson demurred. He was self-deprecating, suggesting other agents as better qualified. They went back and forth for half an hour, Smith explaining why he'd chosen Carson, Carson countering with why he'd made a mistake.

The real reason, he couldn't possibly articulate to his superior.

Carson had more than a decade in the field. He'd worked organized crime as well as Chinese counterintelligence in New York and DC. He understood how things would be. The pressure would be excruciating. The rewards nonexistent.

"Everybody from the president on down would have personal knowledge of the case. Everybody suddenly becomes an expert, with ideas on how to do things. And it ended up exactly that, and ten times worse." He heaves a sigh.[12]

In the end, Smith could have simply issued an order. That wasn't his way, nor was it Carson's to force a showdown. He relented, on the condition that he could pick his own team.

Smith agreed, but it was strictly need-to-know. That is to say, only those with a legitimate need were to know anything about the matter. For the moment, all Carson required was an alternate case agent to back him up and share the workload. Carson chose his jogging partner, Mark Johnson, the youngest member of the squad, with around six years' service. He was a lawyer and former navy fighter pilot from upstate New York whose sharp and restless nature could come off as abrasive, but Carson knew he could be counted on to do things right.

Carson opened a fresh file and labeled it unsub, FBI jargon for "unknown subject."

That this unsub was said to be a Chinese male working within the American intelligence community gave Carson some parameters by which to narrow the scope of his inquiries. There were only so many individuals who matched the description.

Furthermore, the profile fit the pattern with which China-watchers were familiar. Paul Moore has written, "Over the years, China has displayed a very strong preference for collecting as much intelligence as possible from individuals of ethnic Chinese heritage, and when it recruits agents, it almost invariably recruits ethnic Chinese. . . . The most common explanation . . . is that it feels more comfortable going after individuals with whom there is a shared culture, language and history."[13]

Carson's ability to run his investigation was handicapped by the CIA retaining sole access to the source. As a psychiatrist would doubt a second-hand diagnosis, an experienced investigator has an ingrained aversion to relying on someone else's judgment when it comes to evaluating a source. He cannot be comfortable without taking his own measure of the man. To see for himself if his eye twitches, or whether his jaw clenches, in reaction to a question. With every answer, he'd think of a succession of follow-ups. Removed from the spontaneous flow of a conversation, however, responses were bled of impact, like a punch connecting in slow motion. Moreover, he was constantly left wondering whether he was getting verbatim quotes from the source or a CIA intermediary's interpretation. Nuance is critical. People tend to confuse their own opinion with fact, supposition with truth, what's good for themselves with the greater good. To what extent this might have been happening, Carson had no way of evaluating.

He wasn't even privy to raw source material submitted by the handler; only secondary reports sanitized by agency analysts. When he pressed for further elaboration, he was stymied. Sensitivity of the source was cited.

Could the source respond to direct questions?

Yes, the agency conceded, thereby admitting that it was human rather than technical. The source's location, however, made it delicate. Arrangements were intricate and not open to flexibility. The bureau was invited to submit questions to be posed at the next opportunity, but it would take weeks, if not more, to get answers. The extended lags between question and answer were a slow water-drip torture to Carson. He wanted to finely dissect the source's accusation. How did he know the penetration was still active? Was he providing information regularly? How did he know the few details he was able to stipulate? What was his connection to the mole?

The CIA refused to hand over the reports of the internal investigation by which it had concluded that none of its employees were suspect.

Upset at their hindrance, Carson said, "Listen, I don't want to redo what you've done. But I'll bring every one of your members I have to down to our headquarters to sit down for an interview."[14] Technically, he could have tried, but practically it wasn't going to happen.

They've been cleared, he was told. But he resolved that he wasn't going to exclude CIA personnel from his investigation on its say-so alone.

For everything he might want to do, Carson had to devise a pretext to mislead from his true purpose, lest he inadvertently jeopardize the source. He was kept from interviewing possible suspects for fear that letting them know an FBI inquiry was under way represented an unacceptable level of exposure. After all, it could be the spy himself to whom he was speaking. Thus, he was restricted to reading files, trying to piece together from existing information something that ought to be reconsidered in the context of the spy's spectral presence.

There were very few Chinese in the FBI. Carson knew most of them personally. No indicators of problems were found in their files. The military was problematic because he couldn't ask to identify every Chinese officer with access to classified information without revealing that an investigation was under way.

About a month after passing along the initial trace, the CIA came forth with two additional pieces of intelligence, the latter being an indicator of how important an operative the UNSUB was. He had traveled to China aboard Pan Am airlines, leaving the United States on February 6, 1982, and departing Beijing on February 27. During his stay, a banquet was held in his honor, at which he was conferred the honorary rank of deputy bureau chief in the Ministry of Public Security by Vice Minister Li Wenchong.

Finally, Carson had a concrete lead to run down.

China was designated a criteria country, meaning travel — which had been completely prohibited until July 1969 — was strictly controlled. Unless they were going on official business, no government employee with a security clearance would be permitted to venture onto the mainland. The bureau would access the flight manifests from Pan Am for the appropriate dates and check the Chinese names against the employee rosters of the FBI, military intelligence, and CIA, then identify the spy. Piece of cake.

## New York, October 1982

At this point, Van Magers, then China squad supervisor at the New York Field Office, flew to headquarters to be indoctrinated into the case. Though it stopped over in San Francisco on its way to Shanghai and Beijing, Pan Am's China service originated at JFK International in New York. He would pursue this lead.

New York Field had the longest experience with the Chinese of any FBI office. It watched over the People's Republic's UN mission and investigated its intelligence service's efforts to recruit sources and exert influence within the city's large ethnic Chinese community. As it opened to the West, China was extremely sensitive to criticism emanating from overseas Chinese and tried to quell expressions of anti-Communist — which often meant pro-Taiwan — sentiments. Mostly this entailed propaganda — putting sympathizers in control of local community media, for example. It could also involve intimidation, such as letting shopkeepers know that they could be prevented from importing Chinese merchandise or threatening the families of outspoken critics who still resided on the mainland.

New York agents quickly determined that on the date specified — February 6 — there was no Pan Am flight scheduled to depart for China. There was, however, a return flight to the United States on February 27.

The first step taken by the New York case agent was to contact Pan Am security. He was informed that once a flight landed safely, the airline had no further need to know who had been aboard. Thus, the airline did not retain passenger manifests. Moreover, nothing was computerized. The only records Pan Am had relating to who had flown with it were flimsy, carbon-stained credit card slips. Kept only to ensure that payments were successfully processed, however, they did not identify where or precisely when a customer had traveled. Nonetheless, with no other lead to pursue, the agent spent days combing Pan Am's archives in northern New Jersey, fingering his way through box upon shoe-sized box of the smudged receipts.

He scribbled down possibles — that is to say, any Chinese-sounding names. But what of them? There was nothing to suggest the person had flown to Beijing or whether he might ever have worked for the government. He advised Washington Field that the effort was futile. He could spend months at it and never come up with anything. Moreover, what if the subject had paid cash?

Washington insisted he continue. And for a while he did, but ultimately he gave up.

One day, walking past Rockefeller Center, he looked in through a travel agency window and made eye contact with an attractive agent. He went in, introduced himself, and asked her about the complexities of airline booking and routing systems. She cheerfully took the time to explain and gave him a month-old copy of the *Official Airline Travel Guide*, a telephone-book-thick publication, updated monthly, that listed every scheduled flight cross-referenced with combinations of connections. This got him speculating about whether the UNSUB might have covered his tracks by catching a connection out of Paris or London or any one of a dozen hubs that served Beijing.

Another possibility came to mind: CAAC — Civil Aviation Authority of China, the national carrier — also flew in and out of JFK and San Francisco. The idea, however, was preposterous. Under no circumstances would an American government employee be authorized to fly CAAC. On the other hand, if his travel was arranged by Chinese intelligence, what would prevent them from just walking him aboard a CAAC flight undocumented? A check of airport logs showed that none of its aircraft had taken off on the sixth, either. A relief because, obviously, the FBI could never gain access to its records.

The CIA's Office of Security reviewed personnel records and accounted for the whereabouts of all Chinese employees during the period in question. Each one had an alibi. FBI did the same for its members and used discreet contacts within the military to verify whether any of its intelligence officers might have slipped into China. Everybody, without exception, checked out. So thoroughly, in fact, that nobody was suspicious enough even to warrant a preliminary investigation.

The bureau was coming to a dead end. Carson wondered whether the source was lying. The CIA remained confident that he was reporting accurately to the best of his ability. Still unaware who he was, the bureau was in no position to question his bona fides.

Was the CIA sharing everything? This constantly nagged at Tom. Or was he being told only enough to serve the agency's interests? What *were* its interests?

Carson and the New York agents were coming to the realization that the flight angle was pretty well exhausted. Some other course seemed warranted.

Tom undertook a painstaking review of all the data accumulated from the bureau's coverage of the Chinese embassy, a veritable fortress on Connecticut Avenue that backed onto Rock Creek Park. To set some parameters on the volume, he began with the month prior to the reported trip, and planned to continue through the month following. He was familiar with the embassy's routine from his normal duties, which involved keeping tabs on the consular affairs office, the section sheltering the highest concentration of intelligence personnel. He squinted over the daily contact logs on which watchers recorded all ins and outs, attentive to any extraordinary comings and goings. He stared at photographs they routinely snapped of passersby, trying to recognize one of the Chinese CIA or military officers whose pictures he'd seen when reviewing personnel files. Or, perhaps, to find one of his FBI colleagues. Were they running a source in place in the US government, you wouldn't expect the Chinese to have him saunter into their embassy in plain view, but you could never predict someone getting cocky or careless.

He read over the reams of transcribed phone conversations lifted off tapped lines, trying to decipher any nonchalant exchange that could be interpreted as code for something deceptive. It was enough to make one giddy. *The fat man sings in the shower. The eagle soars at night. These pretzels are making me thirsty.* Spies don't actually speak that way. Recognition signals, especially when used over the telephone, are scripted to sound like natural conversation. A query about family or banter about the weather. Comments so trivial listeners could never guess at an ulterior meaning.

It was already January 1983, nearly a year after the UNSUB's fateful trip, by the time Carson came across an incoming call placed on February 5, 1982, from a Chinese official who was at JFK. He was advising that his CAAC flight home was delayed by a snowstorm. He'd be leaving around five hours late. Carson did the math. With the time difference and crossing the international dateline, the delay would put this flight into Beijing on February 6, precisely as the source had reported.

Carson immediately advised New York of his discovery.

Checking at JFK, the New York agent confirmed that a storm had caused lengthy disruptions on that day and that CAAC had, indeed, left five hours behind schedule. He knew, without a doubt, that he had discovered the mystery flight on which the spy had flown.

With regard to the Pan Am confusion, it would be learned later, the American carrier shared facilities with CAAC in Beijing. The source had seen a Pan Am banner at the counter where the spy was supposed to have checked in to depart and, logically, assumed that was how he was returning home.

Putting aside the important question of how in the world an American government employee was able to fly CAAC, it was reasoned that he might have left the country undetected . . . but nobody gets back in without clearing US Customs.

New York approached local Customs and learned that passengers would have submitted declarations at the initial port of entry. A request was rushed to San Francisco Customs, CAAC's first stop, to pull the forms for its flight of February 27 — the return date provided by the source — and for several other proximal dates. It took time to process, putting Carson further on edge and under deepening pressure from headquarters. Eventually, the information was transmitted from the West Coast to the East.

There were twenty-three crew and thirty-nine passengers aboard CAAC Flight 983 on February 27. Only four were American citizens.[15] One passenger stood out from the rest. A Chinese male, American citizen. Resident of 4600 Duke Street, Apartment 1532, Alexandria, Virginia — a suburb south of Washington that was home to an inordinate number of federal government employees. Many of the FBI agents assigned to headquarters and the DC Field Office lived there. So did large numbers of the CIA officers posted at Langley, just a short commute up the Washington Memorial Parkway. And so did a battalion of the military and civilian personnel from the Pentagon, just five Metro Rail stops up the line.

New York Field ran his name through FBI indices. It came up as the subject of a Security of Government Employees file, which means the man was subject to a background check for the purpose of obtaining a security clearance.

Barely able to contain himself, Magers tried to call headquarters immediately over the STU-II, the securely encrypted phone system that would enable him to speak freely. But it was malfunctioning. Unable to divulge a name over an open line, Magers teletyped the information and told the desk supervisor to call up the appropriate file number, then "box and run" (deliver immediately).

A couple of hours later, Magers got a call back on the open line. The STU-II was still down. "You got him" is all that was said.

Washington ran the name by CIA. Is he yours?

No, they replied.

It was like pulling teeth. FBI rephrased, Was he *ever* yours?

CIA went back into their records.

They blanched. Yes, he was theirs.

He'd never came up during the agency's internal investigation because he was not currently employed there. He had retired back in July 1981. The source's assertion that the spy was a current government employee resulted from a ruse the spy was putting over on his Chinese friends. Anxious to uphold his status in their eyes, he'd never told them about his retirement and continued to pose as an active member of the American intelligence community.

The ghost spy had finally materialized.

Larry Wu-Tai Chin.

# PLANESMAN

Two critical details the source got wrong in reporting about the penetration of the US government — that the spy had flown Pan Am and that he was currently employed — ended up costing American authorities a full year. He had never intended to mislead. He had, as the CIA suggested, told the truth to the best of his ability.

Even today, the source is spoken of only furtively. Always with qualifiers — *alleged* and *purported* and *putative* — and the insertion of a measure of doubt — *if* — when not being disavowed outright. His existence has never been acknowledged by either the CIA or the FBI. He was, however, publicly exposed on September 1, 1986, in an Agence France-Presse bulletin announcing the defection of Yu Zhensan, described as being in his late thirties and the son of "veteran revolutionaries."[1] He was identified as chief of the Ministry of Public Security's (MPS) Foreign Affairs Bureau, or Waishiju, the section responsible for preventing penetrations of the Chinese government and running offensive operations against suspected foreign agents within China.

A report in the *Los Angeles Times* on September 5, 1986, quoted a US government official, whose name and affiliation were both withheld, as stating that this defector was the source who'd exposed Larry.[2] James Lilley, who had been sent to China as the first declared CIA officer (1973–1975) since World War II, and later returned as ambassador to the People's Republic (1989–1991), published an article in *The Wall Street Journal* on March 17, 1999, wherein he announced that Chin "was caught by a brilliant CIA penetration of the MSS [Ministry of State Security]."[3]

Of course the Chinese know the identity of the source. He's the one who'd disappeared from the ranks of the Ministry of Public Security just before Larry was arrested in 1985. He was code-named PLANESMAN by the bureau.

While they might not run the risk of awakening sleeping dogs now, Chinese intelligence was undoubtedly interested in locating him in the immediate aftermath of his departure. Initial reports rumored him to be in Taiwan, but local authorities denied any knowledge of him. Besides, China's intelligence service was very active there; it would be far too dangerous for his resettlement. The best guess was that he was under protection somewhere in the United States.

"*If* there is such a person, would the Chinese want to get rid of him as some sort of retaliation or as an example to others?" Moore asks rhetorically in explanation of the reticence. "You have to wonder whether you aren't just putting someone's neck on the line if you speak of it. That's a legitimate fear. Normally, the Chinese are not a forgive-and-forget regime. As long as you can see, from time to time, interest in locating whoever they think did them dirty, you have to assume the worst. So long as you don't know what they'll do, it's in everybody's interest not to take the situation casually. This was deeply embarrassing for the MPS.

"Remember, this is a police agency, with a police mentality," he adds ominously. "These are not your refined folks. The police have the idea that they own the territory. There's not much understanding for betraying your badge."[4]

Lilley relates a rather crude attempt by a Mr. Ge to learn PLANESMAN's whereabouts. Lilley first encountered Ge during his initial tour in Beijing, where Ge posed as an employee of the Diplomatic Services Bureau. He showed up at the beachside resort of Beidaihe, where Lilley was on holiday with his family in the summer of 1974. He treated them to an opera and showed them around. According to Lilley, "Mr. Ge was clearly different, more relaxed than most other Chinese . . . and I suspected he had an espionage role."[5] He smoked cigarettes out of a holder, wore a string bathing suit, and seasoned his English with American slang.

Eleven years later, Ge turned up in Washington at a reception for a visiting Chinese delegation at the residence of then vice president George Bush.

He approached Bush and demanded to know where the defector was. "As a gesture of friendship, we would like to be able to contact him."

The vice president didn't know what he was talking about and called over Lilley, who was then deputy assistant secretary of state for East Asian and Pacific affairs: "You handle this."

"You were asking after somebody," Lilley challenged.

Ge quickly dropped his inquiry.[6]

Looking back on the incident, Lilley says, "I think they wanted to identify him, maybe get across some hint that he'd be welcome to come back to the motherland. It's hard to second-guess them on this. I don't think they were going to try to kill him or anything. They always think they can seduce people back."[7]

There's a six-degrees-of-separation quality to the first generation of China's Communist leadership. Connect the dots and you find Yu Zhensan a mere three degrees from Chairman Mao Zedong himself.[8] His father was Yu Qiwei, who, in 1931, was reportedly married to Jiang Qing "after the fashion of militants of the period: without any ceremony or official certificate."[9] Jiang Qing would later become infamous after marrying Mao. Yu Qiwei was head of the Communist Party's clandestine propaganda department in Qingdao. His mother, Fan Jin, had served in the personal intelligence network of Communist Party stalwart and Prime Minister Zhou Enlai. Most significantly for his career prospects, with the untimely death of his father from a heart attack in 1958 at the age of forty-seven, Yu was taken under the wing of Kang Sheng, the notorious head of China's secret services. Kang was an indestructible survivor who managed to thrive at the paranoid heart of Chinese politics for fifty years, from the time he joined the Communist Party in 1925 until his death from cancer in 1975, at the age of seventy-seven.

According to French journalists Roger Faligot and Rémi Kauffer, Yu was Kang's adopted son.[10] While they acknowledge this rumor in their definitive English biography of Kang, *The Claws of the Dragon,* authors John Byron and Robert Pack claim that sources close to his family dismiss this relationship, saying they are unaware of Kang having ever adopted a son.[11] It has been intimated to me that Faligot and Kauffer are substantively correct about Yu's pedigree.

Kang Sheng's bond to Mao was clinched by more than polemics or politics. Kang had known Jiang Qing since she was a teen, when her mother came to work as a domestic for his father in Shanghai. The accepted wisdom is that they had a sexual relationship sometime during their long association. Jiang went on to become an actress. Years later, when she arrived at Communist headquarters at Yan'an during the Second World War, she succeeded in ingratiating herself with the leader, who, for his part, became infatuated with the glamorous young starlet. Kang willingly served as the conduit for their liaison, which solidified his standing with the chairman.

The opportunity to look out for the son of her former lover had obvious pragmatic appeal to Jiang. Here was a chance to get another potential ally into the ranks of the security service. He could prove a useful hedge against the unpredictable ebb and flow of Chinese politics, wherein the faction defining the correct orthodoxy one day could be marched to the gallows the next, as occurred in the late 1960s during the Cultural Revolution that Jiang herself helped initiate.

It also appealed to the extremely vindictive side of her nature. Here was the chance to undermine the woman for whom Yu Qiwei had jilted her. Here was the chance to influence Fan Jin's son in ways that Fan never could — even to supplant her in determining his future course.

In security work, Kang found the perfect outlet for his character: ruthless, cunning, and opportunistic. His career was marked by, and survival depended upon, myriad well-timed infidelities and betrayals. He cultivated favor with a succession of high officials, building self-serving alliances and viciously undermining potential rivals with deadly accusations of disloyalty. He had an acrobatic talent for vaulting from one faction to another, never planting himself so firmly behind any individual as to impede his next maneuver when shifting conditions dictated a change of stance. Byron and Pack write, "His opportunism may now seem recklessly transparent, but Kang acted with enough finesse to safeguard his reputation as a dedicated revolutionary. However insincere his support for any particular leader or policy, he always managed to convince his comrades that his uppermost priority was the Communist cause."[12]

He first joined the intelligence apparatus in 1930, when he was named to head the Communist Party's organization department in Shanghai. He would exercise influence over it, directly or indirectly, for the rest of his life. In 1933, he began a four-year stint in Moscow, where the NKVD (forerunner of the KGB) schooled him in more than "the simple technical details of arresting, torturing, and executing opponents — he discovered how to use panic as a means to suppress political dissent, how to turn the most ridiculously false confessions into potent tools, and how to silence enemies who might otherwise denounce him or attempt to oust him."[13]

Kang disregarded the likelihood that his tortures might elicit false confessions. He articulated the madness of his methods, saying that if "false evidence is what the criminals want to say, let them say it." He instructed an interrogator, "Ask ten thousand questions. Make it impossible for them ever to respond fully."[14] Such was the rationale underlying the security structure he built and presided over, based on guilt through innuendo, guilt by association, and guilt for daring to think anything but prescribed thoughts.

There was no underlying logic by which Kang's security apparatus could actually distinguish legitimate threats from the self-serving accusations he used to settle his own grudges or remove anyone he feared might undermine his position. So intimidating and skillful a manipulator was he that he could cause any and all elements of society to kowtow before him. He was, simultaneously, adept follower and careful instigator of the acceptable line. For him, loyalty was the most vaporous of qualities.

"I will not acknowledge tomorrow what I say today,"[15] he once remarked in what could serve as the most effective prescription for survival under the Maoist system.

As the protégé of such a man, Yu must have learned early to duck in order to avoid the sharpened scythe of politics that constantly spun just overhead. Peek up above the mass for a glimpse into the future and you got decapitated. Although he surely enjoyed some measure of protection, in the unpredictable world of the Chinese government those same bene-factors who could, in one circumstance, be held up as a shield, in another stood out as a target. When valued patrons fell hard from grace, one's own fate could suddenly be imperiled.

### Beijing, Winter 1981

Establishing the CIA station in Beijing in July 1973, Lilley, for all his familiarity with the language and landscape, found the working environ-ment nearly impossible. As he describes it, he was merely a channel for official communications, having no opportunity to conduct clandestine operations. Chinese citizens were forbidden from being in contact with foreigners, and the movement of diplomats was strictly monitored.[16] These were the waning days of the Cultural Revolution, and the country was only just beginning to look out from under one of the darkest periods in its recent history.

The Cultural Revolution was an explosive time of collective psychosis. Deeply frustrated from having been raised in abject poverty, periodically deteriorating into famine and starvation, under a pathologically repressive regime, China's youth were susceptible to being mobilized to violence. The government's exhortations to lash out, initially against teachers — who appear before students as the ultimate figures of authority — gave them the frenzied illusion that, finally, power was in their hands. Once sanctioned, the vicious attacks rose to a crescendo of euphoric madness. It was one of those terrifying moments when individuals, absolved of personal responsibility by the dictates of the regime, succumbed ecstati-cally to the fury of mob mentality.

In May 1966, the Cultural Revolution Small Group was formed, with Kang as adviser. Students were encouraged to condemn those who suppos-edly filled their heads with bourgeois ideas. They promptly launched their attacks, humiliating, beating, and sexually assaulting academics around the country. Styling themselves Red Guards, the defenders of Mao's leadership and Maoist thought, they were only too happy to comply when, in August, the chairman stood on Tiananmen Gate and instructed them to "smash . . . old culture."[17] Thus sanctioned, they went on to victimize writers, artists, and opera singers. They assailed them ruthlessly, forcing them into degrading self-criticism, driving many (even today, the numbers are only guessed at) to suicide. Far from satiated, they moved against private homes, burning books, slashing paintings, smashing records and anything else associated with culture.

The purges touched millions who were imprisoned or forcibly relocated to the countryside. The latter punishment was intended to purify the individual with a Spartan regimen of physical labor, rote memorization of Mao's dictums, and public self-criticism.

Not all of the terror was carried out by fanatical young Red Guards. The general anarchy was the perfect opportunity for the disposal of scores of bureaucrats and officials. Anyone whose Maoist credentials were blemished, who may have behaved in a nonconformist manner, who had uttered a derogatory word, or against whom somebody nursed a grudge, could be denounced, condemned to career-ending — if not life-ending — reprisals. Uttering a harmless comment could bring accusations of capitalist roadism, imperialist conspiratism, or a dozen other nonsensical smears that justified brutal beatings and cruel degradations. Mao himself had declared, "Who are against the great Cultural Revolution? American imperialism, Russian revisionism, Japanese revisionism, and the reactionaries."[18] That is to say, an inclusive laundry list of all the enemies of the chairman. Under the ensuing culture of suspicion, circumspection was the safest posture.

Only after Mao's death in 1976 could China proceed decisively along the path to recovery. The so-called Gang of Four, including Jiang Qing, were singled out for instigating the atrocities and put on public trial in 1980. They were officially accused of persecuting to death an estimated 34,800 people and of having framed and persecuted another 729,511. At the other end of the scale, estimates put the number killed between 1966 and 1976 at over 3 million, while a further 100 million people are said to have endured some degree of suffering.[19] Jiang's vindictive defiance in the courtroom and willful refusal to repent cast her as the villain for the regime, which still strictly delineated how far it could be called into question, and for a generation stunned by how easily its bloodlust was aroused. On January 25, 1981, she was sentenced to death, which was commuted to life under house arrest. She committed suicide in 1991.

Deng Xiaoping, who had been viciously struggled (in the euphemism of the day), humiliated, and stripped of his authority, emerged as the nation's preeminent political force. He had to tread a careful line between criticizing Mao's legacy and protecting the unassailability of the Communist Party's authority.

With his encouragement, China began to look outward for the tools of progress and economic advancement. Foreign visitors were admitted, and some of their ideas welcomed. With their arrival came more opportunities for intelligence gathering — on both sides. Western missions grew in size. Undoubtedly, their ranks included intelligence officers. Travelers, whether tourists or students on cultural exchanges or business people on scientific or trade delegations, were briefed prior to departure and debriefed upon their return as efforts were made to learn about the Middle Kingdom. And not exclusively from an intelligence perspective, but to understand more broadly how the state functioned, what one could expect in terms of the people's behavior and attitudes.

As subtle as the Chinese could be on foreign soil, their counterintelligence people were brazen on home turf. FBI agent Magers gives several examples of how closely he was monitored during a visit he made in 1997 on a diplomatic passport identifying him as a State Department official.

"I arrived on a full 747. My bags were the last two to come up the carousel — by around ten minutes," he says with a wink. "This is a clue. I was put in a room next to the elevators, pretty easy to run wires into. I came back from the embassy during the day and there was a man in a suit in my room. This is a clue."

Looking for souvenirs in the shopping mall beneath the Kempinsky Hotel, Magers was accosted by a Chinese man who, in a flurry of relatively unaccented English, inquired, "Hello, are you from the United States? I'm from Xian and am visiting Beijing to attend an art festival. I am staying at the apartment of a friend nearby. Would you like to go back to my friend's apartment, drink beer, and discuss the United States and China?"

Amused by the ham-fisted approach, Magers politely declined. "I didn't need to be the third part in a three-bagger," he laughs, noting how on that very same weekend in Beijing a British diplomat had been detained and a Chinese national who was hosting visiting Americans in his home at the behest of China International Travel Service was taken into custody.[20]

PLANESMAN was most likely recruited by the CIA about a year or so before he reported on the penetration. That is, just about enough time to have provided sufficient verifiable intelligence to establish a measure of confidence in his reliability. Otherwise his sketchy indicators might have been disregarded. Since he was in a position to know, even the barest intimation of a compromise was enough to chill the least credulous CIA operator.

Based on a general understanding of how Chinese intelligence operates, I piece together how the case developed. I imagine the episode began in winter.

Beijing turns brown in winter. Somewhere between sky and earth, the fresh snow picks up the sand blown in off the Gobi Desert by the harsh winds. Noxious coal, soot, carbon monoxide, and bacteria exude from all the activity that attends thirteen million spitting, snorting, hawking people pressed in too-close proximity to one another. The buildings. The streets. The stagnant, partially frozen puddles of slush. All brown, painted over with a slick, viscous coating as if an icy snail had slithered across everything. It's a setting fit for intrigue, every bit as much as John le Carré's dyspeptic Berlin or Graham Greene's sodden London.

The series of events that was to culminate with Larry Chin being identified as an infiltrator began when Yu Zhensan of the Ministry of Public Security was assigned a particular American target.

Every diplomat accredited by the Ministry of Foreign Affairs is subject to close scrutiny. Standard bureaucratic procedure. Among the multitude of forms that have to be completed as part of the process of assuring that the government will confer diplomatic status is a bio sheet, attach recent photo here, that is shared with the Ministry of Public Security under secret seal for its info. This American in question had presumed intelligence connections. That is to say, he was a spy. A covert CIA agent.

He may have been singled out because he was of Chinese ancestry. That would conform to the general pattern exhibited by Chinese intelligence, although Public Security was known to target non-Chinese on its home turf, particularly if it discovered something exploitable in their characters.

Much of the American's initial time in Beijing would have been spent walking and exploring. Preparing. Acquainting himself with the odd bends in the roads, the precise location of dim alleys that afforded quick detours to elude surveillance. He was averse to streets that ran too long between cutoffs. They gave him the awful sensation of being lured into the inner chamber of a lobster trap, the one from which there was no escape. Straight lines made him feel exposed; he was comfortable only with the camouflage of irregular angles. He learned what times of day the thoroughfares were crowded and when they emptied out.

No matter what, he took it for granted that he was under surveillance. Being an intelligence officer in Beijing meant never being sure, always feeling tingly without absolutely knowing why. It meant, in all probability, overestimating the effectiveness of the opposition. It meant better safe than sorry. The most conspicuous thing he could do was act invisible.

He never hurried directly to his destination, no matter how benign his purpose. If he walked straight to the grocery store on one occasion, but engaged in convoluted countersurveillance on another, he was tipping the watchers when he was up to something and they'd instantly up their guard. Always, he acted out the elaborate charade of shedding his elusive tail, lending an invigorating excitement to the most mundane of chores. He spent hours slipping in and out of public buildings, zigzagging erratically back and forth along main boulevards, suddenly cutting down near-deserted alleys. He stopped frequently and without warning, doing full, wonderstruck turns. Another stranger absorbing the marvels of the East. What he was really looking for was the slight stumble of the follower caught out of step, or the subtle hand-off from the person who walks by to the one who gingerly fills his tracks, or the barely perceptible head-wag of the cyclist signaling to another precisely where to find their man.

Feigning interest in drab window displays, he used glass storefronts as mirrors, keying in on subtle features of people's faces in the vain hope he might pick them out if he noticed them in different locations, hours apart. It took headache-inducing concentration, masked as utter nonchalance. Perfect surveillants have the doughy, pliable features that defy description. They are muscled men with the knack of rounding their shoulders until they appear soft. They are women who can bundle their hair such that you think it would cascade down their shoulders if released, while in fact it just brushes the nape of the neck. They have noses that elude one-word description. Their skin is contour-free, absent of telltale moles or freckles on which to anchor a sketch.

The ubiquitous uniform made Beijing claustrophobic. You could hardly look down any street at any time and not see a uniform. People's Armed Police. People's Liberation Army. Boxy Mao suits and slouchy peaked caps. Everything was uniform. Everything blended into background until it obfuscated the foreground, and one no longer saw the trees for the forest.

Complicating matters was that much of the surveillance employed was static. The old woman who sits morning-to-night on a stool at a busy inter-section and gratefully collects a few yuan to point out which way a certain person of interest to the state passed. Or the doorman at a hotel who maintains cordial relations with anyone in authority because he's grateful for his job and sees no reason to jeopardize it by being uncooperative. Or the police officer manning a watch box, whose duty it is to keep track of comings and goings and report any unseemly occurrences. Or cabdrivers who take notes on where foreigners boarded and alit throughout the day.

Or bus conductors who win praise at their work groups because they recall the stop where the Chinese in the American-cut jacket jumped off, and whether he appeared to pay attention to the man who stood beside him for the duration of the ride. Or the store clerk with the foolproof memory for who bought what and when.

Then there was the practice — which to an American was particularly intimidating — of open surveillance. It usually involved three or four obvious followers, most often young, thuggish men who would glue themselves to his back, even jostle him, smirking lewdly should he dare to make eye contact, leaving no doubt as to who owned these streets.

Plus the overt surveillance enveloping foreigners under the guise of security. Whenever he left the embassy or his residence in the legation district, the American came under the baleful watch of police, smug as prison warders. Small men in huge, round parade caps that added a good four inches in height and pea-green greatcoats with stiff, outsized epaulets giving them broad, stolid shoulders. Before he was even out of sight, the sergeant was speaking into his walkie-talkie.

In these early days of contact with the People's Republic, American agents were especially risk-averse. Getting caught was inexcusable. On the other hand, no reprimands would be forthcoming for overcaution.

Eventually it became clear to the Chinese that mere observation wasn't going to reveal insights into the American's activities. With a reliable indication that the American was intelligence, Public Security was eager to try to turn him. Ultimately, Yu had to make a direct approach. He was pressured by his superiors for results.

Unreasonably so, he felt, by one in particular: Miss Wong, the Bitch of Beijing, as he'd come to think of her. Only a portion of his animosity might be attributed to any professional disagreement; the preponderance, to her firm resistance against his persistent advances. He came across as a happy-go-lucky womanizer, but reacted spitefully when rejected. She was uninterested in being mistress to a subordinate. It was tawdry and dishonorable.

Yu moved cautiously, gradually becoming acquainted with the American on the cocktail circuit, that mainstay of diplomacy. With Beijing's rigid controls and limited nightlife, it provided welcome diversions, where bureaucrats domestic and foreign had the opportunity to mingle and take the measure of one another. As an intelligence officer, the American likely accepted every invitation, no matter how tedious. He attended each screening of the Albanian film festival, staggering out in wonder at how many movies could be made about heroic collective farmers tilling fields from dawn to dusk. He hardly grimaced during the Romanian wine-tasting soiree. He gulped down unidentifiable delicacies at the Mongolian reception for a newly arrived cultural envoy. He listened politely to the anecdotes of the Congolese defense attaché, laughing heartily in unison as the man reached the sadistic climax, though certain everything he said was literal.

Who among them were the spooks? The American couldn't always tell. They all had reports to submit, so the line between diplomat and spy could be fine. It was safe to assume every conversation ended up in a report some-where, so care was in order with each exchange. Remain noncommittal and nonjudgmental, neither contradict nor commit. Say nothing that could be misconstrued or taken out of context. Expressions of diplomatic nice-ties, good and peaceful intent. Avoid praise or criticism. Consider every comment a potential controversy and refrain from making it.

Given his rank, Yu would have been something of a regular, keeping up a greeting acquaintance with any of the diplomats in whom he might take an interest but staying aloof enough that few knew positively who he was. Whatever suspicions they harbored could only be based on a general assumption that any Chinese trusted enough to mix with foreigners was, at the very least, collaborating with the security services, if not a full-time serving agent. Surely he was whispered about. Yu did nothing to confirm or deny his role. To be both known and unknown was proper for his work. Too secret and you weren't in a position to gather any intelligence; too recognizable and your freedom to operate was compromised.

Over time, he maneuvered himself into proximity to the American. Trade a glance. Quickly avert eye contact. A sidelong stare. The hesitant nod. The shy introduction. The mundane small talk. The forthright exchange of opinions about the weather. Getting to what, in other circumstances, would be innocuous social details about each other. Married? Kids? Where did you go to school? What did you study? Questions posed with a disinclination to reciprocate answers. Vagaries given whenever specifics could be politely withheld. Every remark finding its way into a thickening file with tightly controlled circulation.

Casual banter could only carry on for so long, the pawns moved only so far up the board. The tension building in anticipation of the next move, sooner or later the rooks and bishops venture out, and the gambit is made for queens and kings.

Conventional counterespionage wisdom says you can no more induce treason than you can corrupt the man who is honest at heart. First and foremost, a person convinces himself to commit the act. The job of the intelligence officer is to recognize who is predisposed to cross the divide and to be available when he decides to do so. Forcing the issue on those who aren't emotionally ready can have the contrary effect of awakening them to the consequences of what they've been contemplating and driving them away from the brink.

The American willingly engaged with Yu. He would have been under instructions not to rebuff Yu, but to do nothing incriminating or provocative, always put him in the position of the initiator.

Eventually, at Yu's invitation, they would meet discreetly at restaurants and teahouses. The lounges of international hotels, where each noticed that the other took care to nurse his drinks. Yu arranged to be seated at a table by a wall in the back, apart from anyone who might overhear. Nonetheless, they spoke in low voices, an occupational habit.

Whether Yu's pitch, when it came, was deft or clumsy, he left no room for misunderstanding. He wanted the American to spy for China. His efforts would be compensated, he was assured.

Once treason had been proposed, each man suddenly became vulnerable to the other.

The American picked up on something halfhearted in Yu's tone or indecisive in his body language. Through the manner by which we speak to

others, we can unwittingly divulge things about ourselves. Listen closely
to the salesman selling a product beyond his means, and you'll often hear
about his own desires. Those features he insists should appeal to you are
really what appeal to him.

Instinct told the American that when Yu discussed compensation, he was
speaking about something for which he yearned. In the customary manner
of a Chinese recruitment, Yu would have stressed that he didn't mean for
the American to do harm to his homeland. In fact, by collaborating, he
could advance friendly relations between China and the United States,
thereby bringing benefits to both countries. China, he assured him, had
no hostile designs against America. Indeed, the Chinese wanted nothing
more than to gain a better understanding of Americans, a channel through
which they could deepen trust and nurture warmer relations.

Realizing that he could be falling into the horrible maw of a trap, the
American decided to take a huge gamble. My country shares your desire
for warmer relations, he agreed. And we, too, recognize the need to better
understand each other.

Bracing himself to be roughly arrested, he propositioned Yu. Perhaps
we could achieve these objectives if the channel ran in the other direction,
from China to the United States. That, too, would advance the cause of
friendship between our two countries. And we, too, would be prepared to
compensate such efforts.

Had Yu ever fantasized about the rewards that a chance to meet alone
with an American might present? Even to let on that he might contemplate the idea was compromising.

When his companion didn't reply with indignation or threats, the
American pressed on, allowing no time for second thoughts to dampen
impulse or for common sense to cool ardor. First, of course, he said, Yu
would have to confirm that he was in an important enough position to be
truly helpful. The American flattered, noting that he must be quite senior,
given that he was trusted to meet alone with a Western diplomat. But he
didn't even know his counterpart's rank.

This was how it began, Yu understood. So easy. A simple question. Just to find out if you'd tell. Something that cost nothing. Until they slipped in a question that cost just a little.

Resist, you're one person; surrender, you're another.

The American felt a sticky pool of sweat collecting in the hair of his armpits and in the cleft where his rib cage gave in to his stomach.

He whispered, We'll look out for you. His voice reverberated in Yu's head as if coming over a loudspeaker.

Now was the moment for Yu to name his price. In America was a life-style that fulfilled every fantasy, where no lust was so depraved that it couldn't be indulged.

Resettlement? Yu eyed him hopefully.

Antoine de Saint-Exupéry wrote, You are forever responsible for what you have tamed.[21] Resettlement meant committing the US government to a lifetime responsibility.

You have to earn it, the American admonished.

Obviously, Yu stood to reap considerable material benefits from defecting to the United States. All things considered, that, alone, isn't a convincing explanation for his actions. To uproot himself, to sever all his relationships, to disengage from everything familiar is a trauma of monumental proportions. But China was undergoing rapid change. And in a system where one's personal ties largely determined one's place, he had good reason to be anxious about who was in ascendance.

Yu took a deep breath and declared that he was chief of the Foreign Affairs Bureau of the Ministry of Public Security.

*Guanxi* refers to the network of relationships that are the indispensable currency of China. A man spends a lifetime stockpiling *guanxi*. Whenever he can, he helps relatives, friends, friends of friends. If he can perform a service on behalf of an acquaintance, he will do so, thus creating a new relationship. The unspoken promise is that favors will be reciprocated.

"*Guanxi* doesn't mean I love you," Magers stresses. "It just means I was obligated to help you and I did. It doesn't even mean I wanted to. It may mean that if I don't, I fear that I'll be in trouble."[22]

That PLANESMAN was even a member of the Ministry of Public Security was *guanxi* from Kang Sheng. Kang had helped him because of his relationship with Jiang Qing, who, in turn, owed her influence to being Mao's wife. After his patron died and with Jiang in disgrace, PLANESMAN felt increasingly vulnerable. Under a regime that wields power absolutely and punishes indiscriminately, friends are fleeting and enemies, stealthy. He recognized that his privileged status was on the wane. More than enough skeletons clattered in his closet for ambitious or vengeful colleagues to single him out whenever the next round of political purges came about.

Furthermore, he'd likely heard reliable rumors about Deng Xiaoping's plans to reorganize China's security apparatus. Ultimately, Public Security would be swallowed up by an expanded Ministry of State Security.[23] Since it was his ministry being dissolved, he couldn't expect to fare too well in the new structure; serving State Security members would move quickly to entrench their positions against the interlopers, leaving old Public Security officers in a subordinate position.

The American offered what had to look like a most attractive solution. Until a man feels desperate, complacency rules. PLANESMAN's decision was a measure of his desperation.

For the American to run a covert Chinese source in Beijing was extraordinarily perilous — for both men. However, this case had unique and unassailable cover. Sanctioned to meet with the American under the guise that he was betraying his country, Yu's official duty justified every contact.

Normally, the handler manages all operational logistics. In an unconventional — and unnerving — reversal of responsibility, the American had to hand over to Yu a considerable measure of control long before he had reason to trust him. The American left it for Yu to arrange for a safe house and to secure their meets. Under the circumstances, in Yu's bailiwick, it was an essential element of the deception.

The operation would have been tightly restricted at the embassy in Beijing, the CIA chief of station probably being the only local apprised. As such, the American had to be guarded around the rest of the staff. Though often resentful at the apparent lack of accountability of the spooks, State

Department personnel had no choice but to tolerate their dereliction of cover duties.

The American had to adroitly sidestep his CIA comrades. To all appearances, he had to be deceiving his own side in order to reinforce the facade he was building around Yu. He expected that Public Security surveillance would become even more intense as they worked to convince themselves that he was genuine.

The whole thing was dangerous in the extreme because it could still turn out to be a well-staged Chinese provocation, the purpose of which was to manipulate the American into a compromising position.

On those first visits to the safe houses, he felt the dizzy vertigo of being at his source's mercy. This wasn't Washington. He was the one far from home. One wrong move and he could find himself rousted out and frog-marched none too gently to the nearest police bureau. Sure, he'd be released soon enough. The Chinese wouldn't abuse his diplomatic immunity for too long, beyond saying he resisted arrest to justify delivering a few cautionary blows. Then there'd be publicity, photos, and exposure. He'd ride the rest of the way to his pension at Langley, unpostable, his operational career ended in failure.

Meetings with the American demanded elaborate preparation on Yu's part. He had to go through all the motions of safeguarding his source against detection by the United States. It couldn't appear as if the American was too available, because he was supposedly skulking off unbeknownst to the CIA. Prudence suggests that they probably met no more than monthly or so.

The moment the American slipped into the safe house and locked the door behind him, Yu was relieved to surrender control; the American was relieved to seize it. Before a word was exchanged, the American opened the tap to foil listening devices. Time wouldn't be a major obstacle, though PLANESMAN would have to return to his headquarters with enough to justify however long they took. Keeping up the charade that it was the American being cultivated, the agency would provide some minor feed material for Yu to bring back to his headquarters. Nothing too substantive, just enough to show he was making progress. His superiors were bound to be pleased by anything.

Each debriefing session would be carefully scripted at Langley. The first questions the American posed would be controls: questions that the CIA was certain PLANESMAN would be able to answer and for which they already had the correct response. Moreover, the nature of the questions, and the terse manner in which they were phrased, ensured that nothing about US interests or intelligence-gathering capabilities could be lost if he turned out to be a double. PLANESMAN was never sure whether he was confirming old information or breaking new ground. The American was under orders to cut off all contact the moment he discovered PLANESMAN was other than forthright.

It is expected that a source will do some withholding at the outset. With only so much capital, he has to trade it wisely. Give up everything on the first pass and you undersell. Withhold too much, however, and you risk getting undervalued and passed up. The unknown variable is whether you're in a buyer's or a seller's market.

Once PLANESMAN passed the controls, the American sought details about the organization of, and personalities within, the Ministry of Public Security. He'd want to know who among the locally engaged staff at the Beijing embassy was intelligence. Had any Americans, wittingly or not, been compromised? Were any involved in illicit behavior that had drawn China's attention? Was there anyone in particular in whom Yu's department had an interest? Were any Chinese nationals under suspicion of being American agents? PLANESMAN would be instructed to detail the cases he was running and provide the name of any sources he handled. The American would take down this information without comment and notify headquarters, where it would be meticulously analyzed. The same queries would be made with regard to other Western embassies, though because of source sensitivity the answers would not necessarily be shared. Instead, they would be held until a propitious time when they might be divulged to the advantage of the United States.

The process was slow. The reply to each series of questions had to be scrutinized by headquarters analysts before the next series could be posed. Contradictions — which are inevitable when delving into a person's perceptions and memories — needed to be addressed until they were convinced that PLANESMAN might be mistaken, but not purposely misinforming. Often, only with deeper probing and follow-up questions could this be achieved. Given the time to transmit messages back and forth and the intervals between meets, frustrating weeks passed before issues were effectively resolved.

All the while, PLANESMAN's confidence had to be nurtured. He was, after all, the one whose actions were punishable with a bullet to the back of the head. He exhibited great self-control, approaching each meet with a stiff posture and steady gait. No one noticed how he flinched at the cough heard from the outer reaches of earshot. Shadows he saw on the way home were just tricks of light against dark, he assured himself. Nothing was hidden; what he could not see really wasn't there.

As he exhausted his store of intelligence, PLANESMAN began pushing for resettlement, as had been promised. The American replied that his headquarters was reluctant to bring him out. They insisted on more, he said regretfully, in a variation on the classic good cop/bad cop routine. He played the sympathizer, PLANESMAN's defender against supercilious bureaucrats without the craft to appreciate his contribution. The best way to placate them and bring about the outcome they both desired was to find out about ongoing operations running against the United States. Let us know about Americans cooperating with China. Do this, he said, and they won't have any excuse not to honor their promise.

PLANESMAN responded to the American's prodding. He proved to be a risk taker to the point almost of foolhardiness. Some who knew him cringe when they recall how daring he was. Smith describes him as "a gregarious, animated individual who spoke in fractured English, but who seemed to have a very real zest for life. . . . I had the impression he would have paid the CIA to allow him to be their spy."[24] Given the deal he cut himself, and what he stood to gain, this latter remark is a bit of literary hyperbole, but it does get across the idea of one who took to the role with enthusiasm.

He became exceptionally, though not obviously, attentive to all that went on around him in the office. He took notice of papers spread on other officers' desks and heard snatches of conversation as he went about his business, absorbing all he could. When a superior went on vacation and PLANESMAN had to sit in on a meeting in his place, another opportunity to hear fragments about cases was presented. He passed each disjointed snippet to the American, who faithfully communicated them to the analysts, who, in turn, labored to deduce their hidden meanings.

"All the defenses are set up to keep the outsider from getting in," Moore explains. "Once you're inside, and have reached a certain level of trust, there's more wiggle room. Intelligence services are forever struggling with how to run the organization efficiently against running it securely."[25]

Intelligence services frantically twist and spin the Rubik's Cube in search of the perfect pattern of security-versus-efficiency and trust-versus-suspicion to maximize their effectiveness. Despite all the effort, the solution remains elusive.

The Ministry of Public Security was compartmentalized and formally adhered to need-to-know, like all intelligence services. If, in practice, no officers knew anything beyond the confines of their own cases and the very limited information they needed in order to perform their assigned functions, a single penetration would be in a position to give up relatively little. But, unlike workplaces where there are no sanctions against confiding in spouses or close friends, intelligence officers may only drop their guard around one another. From the outside looking in, they appear to be tightly shrouded, impenetrable institutions. However, from the inside looking out, they are safe havens — intimate and trusting — against the treachery and duplicity that flourish everywhere else. Sometimes officers discuss things that are supposed to remain unsaid. They express a frustration or boast of an achievement. An indiscretion can be accidental. A report that ought to be locked in a safe is left unattended and is overseen.

It is all that an intelligence officer comes to learn inadvertently — what he isn't supposed to know, what nobody believes him to know — that poses the greatest threat to his service and his country. So it was with PLANESMAN, who never had any direct contact with Larry Chin.

Ultimately, PLANESMAN revealed that his department had penetrated the US intelligence community.

The American contended that so serious a charge could not be left hanging, and became increasingly assertive in his questioning. He needed to identify the suspect. Each time they met, he pushed and pushed for more details, increasingly impatient about deflecting PLANESMAN's requests to be pulled out. No way his superiors would agree to extract him until he'd helped them resolve this matter.

PLANESMAN felt he was fortunate even to chance upon mention of a penetration. He should have known the American wouldn't be grateful — that he'd instead find himself trapped into learning more. Thus he had to be proactive . . . but cautiously. Miss Wong controlled the file.

Late one night, it must have been, he was the last one in the office. He noticed some papers strewn on her desk. Making sure to remember how they were placed so he could return them exactly as they were, he quickly read them. Nothing exciting. After checking down the hall to make sure nobody was around, he gently jiggled a drawer. She had neglected to lock it. Inside he found operational documents referring to the penetration agent, though, to his disappointment, only by a code number.

"You can control legitimate access. When you get a file or document, you initial that you've seen it. It's the indirect access, that's the killer right there." I.C. Smith shakes his head. "You can never fully get your arms around the indirect access."[26]

The next morning, he watched carefully as Miss Wong moved about her workstation and was relieved when she found nothing amiss.

Smith describes PLANESMAN as "exceptionally resourceful and apparently reckless beyond belief."[27] Such traits are both dream and waking nightmare for a handler. The American lurched between pressing for all the intelligence possible and cautioning PLANESMAN against being too aggressive. Running the operation was like living in what mountaineers refer to as the death zone — that altitude above twenty thousand feet where the heart beats at a chest-bruising tempo, breath comes in frantic gasps, and the skin prickles; where sleep is elusive, appetite evaporates, and judgment dissipates. You pass a critical point where descending intact becomes more critical than completing the ascent. You rely on instinct, depending on your nerve not to fail and your ambition not to blunt your sensitivity to the subtle indicators that the operation has reached its limits.

From that point on, whenever he had a legitimate excuse to work late, Yu bagged Miss Wong's desk. He found notes to the effect that the penetration agent was traveling to Hong Kong, Macao, or China on appointed dates, including the crucial trip that ended up being Larry's undoing. He identified the hotels where Larry stayed. He even served as a member of the security detail at the airport when Larry departed Beijing. PLANESMAN was able to ascertain that the handlers assigned to meet with him were Ou Qiming and Zhu Entao.

Each piece of the puzzle he succeeded in picking up, he passed to the American, whose disposition improved markedly. He was noticeably more receptive to discussing PLANESMAN's future. Strangely, as PLANESMAN became more comfortable going through the Bitch's desk, the American expressed increasing concern for his well-being. PLANESMAN neither talked up nor diminished the risk of his enterprise. He let the results speak for themselves.

He took morbid glee in blowing her case, getting his revenge for being rejected. If only she'd been nicer, he thought, I could have shielded her. Now I have no choice.

# — 3 —

# Larry Wu-Tai Chin

*Virginia, July 1, 1981*

He hesitated a moment before turning out of the driveway onto the high-way. Watching through his rearview mirror. The steel gate swung shut behind him. Never again would he be on the other side. Like a secret pilgrim at the end of a perilous journey, he had seen his mission through. He had gotten away with it.

He exhaled until he'd emptied his lungs of stale air and coughed softly. Then he breathed in deeply. The air was heavy with the moisture off the Potomac River. He took pleasure from its density, the way it slid into him like liquid. A thin layer of moisture sprang onto his forehead, and he felt sweat dampen his back where it stuck against the vinyl seat of the sturdy sedan.

His sense of relief couldn't entirely offset the melancholy. At fifty-nine, he reflected, much more of life had passed by than was to come. He was left to commemorate lasts in place of celebrating firsts. Nonetheless — and here was the disappointing irony — he was not absolved of worries for the future.

He turned out onto the interstate, heading home to Alexandria. His eyes swept the black horizon beyond the beam of his headlights, and he felt the solitude of the night closing in. There would be no coming back to this place. Tomorrow he'd be the same man he was today, but his membership in the club had terminated. Retirement cut him off from the casual intimacies of the office. Were he to run into a former colleague at the mall, he could express curiosity about the office, but their small talk would be circumspect. This worried him. He had more at stake than watercooler camaraderie.

He had to figure out how he was going to make up the shortfall between the pension he'd receive from now on and the income to which he'd been accustomed. Trouble was, he'd parlayed his only marketable assets — languages and secrets — into the career he was leaving.

True, his expenses had diminished. For one thing, there was no more medical school tuition to pay for the kids. Yet his appetite for the good life remained, and that was costly. He had invested in property in Baltimore and Las Vegas. But the income he derived was modest. He had used his spare time well, acquiring a real estate license. The market was hot, but, with so many agents and only so many properties to list, it was a hustle to make real money. He wasn't looking for workaday commissions.

He glanced down at the plaque on the seat beside him. The green glow of the dashboard lights just caught the inscription stamped onto the brass plate affixed below a relief of the Central Intelligence Agency crest. CAREER INTELLIGENCE MEDAL, it read, along with his name and the years of his service.

He'd stood up in front of the crowd of colleagues, friends, and those who attended any retirement function for the free flow of booze and plentiful finger foods. It was a proud moment, a rare occasion to bask in the acknowledgment of a life's work carried out in secret.

Deputy Director Bobby Inman was there to present his medal. It was one of the chores of management. If you played your cards right, you could be in and out in about half an hour. Arrive ten minutes prior to the formalities for a drink and some handshaking, deliver a few remarks, have an aide whisper in your ear, nod gravely, and make for the exit.

Occasionally the director would do the honors for long-serving employees. William Casey had taken over at Central Intelligence barely six months earlier, but he was preoccupied by far more pressing matters. The Cold War was burning up. Covert anti-Soviet action was under way in Afghanistan. Central America was in turmoil, with a Marxist government having taken control in Nicaragua and an active Communist insurgency in El Salvador. The release of American hostages hadn't alleviated tensions with Iran. Libya was interfering in neighboring Chad and threatening further destabilization across North Africa. The Middle East, as usual, was explosive.

Furthermore, Casey was already embattled by accusations that his hand-picked deputy director of operations, Max Hugal, had engaged in insider trading and that he himself had misled stock buyers on a transaction in 1968 from which he had profited handsomely.[1] Needless to say, he could hardly be bothered with the retirement of some Chinese translator from the Foreign Broadcast Information Service (FBIS). Besides which, Chin fell under Inman on the organigram. That's why a man had deputies, after all: to dump off the grunt work.

Larry did receive a letter signed by Casey that read, in part, "You leave with the knowledge that you have personally contributed to our success in carrying out our mission. Your faithful and loyal support has measured up to the high ideals and traditions of the Federal service."[2]

Inman would convey the director's regrets. Unavoidable, he'd insist on Casey's behalf.

A subordinate prepared briefing notes to remind Inman who Chin was and give him some cues to personalize the presentation. A few minutes ahead of time, he hurriedly reviewed them and found a nice running American-dream line he could count on to go over well with a civil service crowd. Chin had earned a ticket to a better life by diligently studying English in China. Immigrating to America, escaping a life of servitude under totalitarianism. Determined to give back, for more than three decades he had demonstrated devotion to the cause of America's freedom and national security, or something to that effect. A few plaudits, sorry to see you go, but retirement well deserved, he'd conclude.

Certainly Inman had no reservations when he shook Larry's hand and congratulated him for his life's work. Larry accepted the award from his superior, along with the best wishes of his colleagues, with outward humility and quiet elation that, as with so much else in his life, he confided to no one.

———————

Larry had given a lot of thought to how he might parlay all of his experience and contacts into a profitable retirement. He had a big scheme in mind, one demanding that he enjoy the freedom to associate with Chinese officials and travel to China at will — freedoms denied serving CIA employees.

Banks regularly borrow currency from one another. A middleman is frequently engaged as a conduit between the borrowing institution and the one who has the sought-after funds. His compensation is a small percentage, but with huge sums at stake in a typical deal, he stands to make a tremendous amount for very little effort. Larry planned to convince Bank of China officials that his Washington-insider status established him as a valuable intermediary for such transactions.[3] Favors would have to be called in. Larry had spent a lifetime building *guanxi*, and now was the time to capitalize on it.

On July 7, 1981, barely a week after being honored by the agency, Larry traveled to Hong Kong. It was an eventful trip, as he recorded in his diary. On August 5, he met a gentleman he identified as Ding, the manager of the Foreign Exchange and Funds Department of the Bank of China. Also present at this meeting, he noted, was Zhu, undoubtedly Zhu Entao of the Ministry of Public Security. Larry contacted Ding again on the ninth and marked in his diary, "Ding agrees to change address & add title on letter to me (will consider Swiss Franc loan)." Later that day, Larry caught a flight back to the States, optimistic enough to jot down, "B of C negotiation success."

During a visit to London, on November 9, Larry had dinner with Ding, Zhu, and another individual he identifies as Zhao. "B of C accepts terms," he wrote with satisfaction. To celebrate his expected success, he spent the following two evenings enjoying the erotic entertainment at the Eve and Horseshoe clubs. On the thirteenth, he met again with Ding, Zhu, and Zhao. It appears, however, that their negotiations took a negative turn. The last mention of the matter in Larry's diaries is for February 10, 1982, when he met with Ding and Zhu at the Qianmen Hotel in Beijing. They shared a duck dinner, but there is no further reference to any deal being struck.

To uphold his status with the Chinese, Larry kept the news of his retirement a secret. A few stray morsels of intelligence might still be about, enough to demonstrate he had access. Was still a man of rank.

He was acutely aware that information was not a renewable resource. Once revealed, its worth dissipates like the vivid color off a cut flower. A wise man is prudent with his shears. Timing is everything. Reveal nothing except when it is advantageous. For Larry, this was second nature.

As he steered into the Watergate at Landmark, the gated community on Yoakum Parkway where he lived, Larry waved at the security guard manning the front post. Whatever didn't belong within these walls was held at bay. The orderliness and gentility in such short supply out there reigned in here, where neighbors nodded and smiled but knew to mind their own business. Dog owners picked up their animals' shit. Stereos were off by ten at night and weren't played above a hum before nine in the morning.

Larry was at that stage of life when what's most desirable is the absence of disturbance and surprise.

## *Washington, DC, February 1983*

With a name put to the UNSUB, the FBI immediately launched an investigation against Larry with one goal in mind: to build a prosecutable case.

The CIA, for its part, was anything but keen on prosecuting. Retired, Chin was no longer in a position to compromise classified material, the agency reasoned. The source, however, remained vulnerable, and its responsibility was to guarantee his safety under very volatile conditions. Even later on, when this ceased to be an issue, it argued that a trial posed unpredictable threats to national security. Moreover, going forward in open court exposed the agency to public embarrassment. Indeed, some in the FBI remain staunchly convinced that the CIA never would have brought the allegation to its attention had it not been convinced that the penetration was elsewhere in the government.

The agency frantically launched into a comprehensive damage assessment, which is standard procedure under the circumstances. Every file that could conceivably have crossed Larry's desk was reviewed with an eye toward ascertaining what may have been compromised. CIA's only consolation was that Larry had been off the payroll for nearly two years by then. Small comfort, indeed, given the thirty years he'd been with them. The results of the assessment were never shared with the FBI.

Special Agent Tom Carson had to proceed with extreme caution. While anxious to move forward, he was also — like a fugitive being tracked through fresh snow — afraid to proceed in any direction lest he leave a trace that Larry could detect. So long as PLANESMAN remained in place — and the CIA wasn't yet ready to pull him out — he was prevented from taking any steps that risked tipping Larry he was under suspicion.

He was able to become acquainted with his target by reviewing Larry's personnel file. He established that Larry was born in Beijing on August 17, 1922. He lived with his second wife, Cathy, whom he'd married in Reno on August 5, 1963. His ex-wife, Doris, lived in Hong Kong. They had been married from April 1949 to March 1959. He had three children from that first marriage, Roberta, who was then thirty-three; Peter, then thirty-two; and Homer, twenty-eight.

In 1940, he enrolled at Yenching University in Beijing, where he studied English. He earned a bachelor's degree in journalism and economics in 1947. He took a hiatus from his studies in 1943, going to Fujian and serving as an interpreter with the British Military Mission. In 1944, he went to work as a secretary at the US Armed Forces East China Liaison Office in Fuzhou (also known as Foochow). The following year, he became the chief announcer for the Foochow Broadcasting Station.

After graduating, he joined the US consulate in Shanghai as a secretary in October 1948. He moved with the mission when it relocated to Hong Kong in May 1950 in the wake of the Communist victory in the civil war. He continued to work for the State Department, assisting with the interrogation of Chinese prisoners during the Korean War. In May 1952, he joined the FBIS as a linguist in Okinawa. Cathy was an employee of the US Army in Okinawa, so presumably they met while Larry resided at Kadena Air Base between May 1952 and December 1960.

In January 1961, he was transferred by the FBIS to its bureau in Santa Rosa, California. He became a naturalized American citizen in January 1965. Five years later, FBIS decided to close its West Coast branch. Faced with an uncertain future, Larry applied for a position as a translator with the United Nations in New York. He was ultimately rejected upon being diagnosed with diabetes, leaving him ineligible for the international organization's health coverage. This proved fortuitous, as he was offered a post at FBIS headquarters in Rosslyn, Virginia.

FBIS, according to its Web site, "collects and translates current political, economic, technical, and military information from the media worldwide for the U.S. government."[4] It monitors foreign radio and television broadcasts, newspapers and magazines (and, today, the Internet). The description is intentionally banal, as are most public issues from the intelligence community. Part of a misdirection play: Take no notice, nothing much going on here.

Truth is, Larry was far more than just a run-of-the-mill translator processing open source material. His duties in Rosslyn called for top-secret access. He was, therefore, subject to a routine full field investigation by the bureau. Security screening is a high-volume, labor-intensive occupation. Pause to consider that, as of 1984, 2.6 million people in the United States possessed some level of access to classified documents.[5] This is an indication of how widely government secrets are *purposely* disseminated. But keeping secrets doesn't come naturally to people. We are social — communicative — by nature. We trade in rumors, we gossip. We are egotistical. We brag about our importance by hinting at the things we know to those who are excluded. Nothing explicit, perhaps. Just a tantalizing clue.

Screening inquiries delve back ten years. However, records checks can normally be depended upon to cover most of an individual's adult life. In Larry's case, his first twenty-eight years, spent on the mainland, would remain impenetrable. Nonetheless, over the twenty years since he moved to Hong Kong that could be accounted for, nothing was uncovered to call into question his fitness for a top-secret clearance.

National agency checks came back with no criminal record or derogatory data. Larry had no record with the US Civil Service Commission or the House Committee on Un-American Activities. A check of local police records in California turned up nothing. His credit rating was satisfactory. The Seattle and New York Field Offices interviewed references — put forth by Larry — who had known him since their days together at Yenching. As expected, they offered unqualified recommendations.

The State Department was charged with checking records overseas in Okinawa and Hong Kong, where Doris and Homer continued to reside (Peter and Roberta lived with their father).

San Francisco Field looked into his time in Santa Rosa. Investigators performed the usual drudge work that satisfies screening requirements, going out to where Larry resided and knocking on neighbors' doors. Invariably, the respondents said either that they didn't know him or his family well enough to comment, or they had nothing negative to report and, to the extent that they could comment, had no reason to suggest he shouldn't be employed in a position of trust. Interviews with FBIS co-workers were unanimously positive. Nobody had cause to doubt his loyalty to the United States.

As well, existing sources "familiar with some phases of un-American activities" — a euphemism for informants inside local Communist organizations — were questioned. None had ever heard of him.[6]

In accordance with standard procedure, the CIA polygraphed Larry. The FBI was told that he passed with flying colors. Not content to take the agency's word for it, Carson requested the original test result for the bureau's own experts to analyze.

"We found it was inconclusive, at best," he says. "They even admitted, but only later on, that, yes, there were some problems."[7] Indeed, the bureau would eventually learn that one of the sensor needles had malfunctioned completely.

Mark Johnson, who transferred from the China squad to the polygraph unit following this investigation, explains that the polygraph is not an absolutely objective process. Different polygraphers will get different physiological measures — heart rate, blood pressure, skin palpitations — based on how they calibrate their machines. Also, how the control questions are structured can affect the outcome. And there is the analytic component: An examiner who senses deception on the part of the subject may push harder on the relevant issue than one who accepts his honesty.[8]

Larry would later concede that he might have had a tougher time passing the lie detector had the questions been posed in Mandarin, his mother tongue, as opposed to English.[9] Having to concentrate harder to ensure he fully understood the questions, translating them in his head, his responses were more controlled, less reflexive.

There is also a cultural element that leads people to react differently to the lie detector. Western, or Judeo-Christian, cultures are guilt-based. Eastern cultures are shame-based. It is perfectly reasonable that, where a Westerner might feel guilt, Larry didn't feel shame when questioned, and therefore didn't react in such a way as to cause the needles to skitter in alarm.

In any event, nothing adverse was recorded against Larry and, in 1970, he settled into a translator-analyst position at headquarters, cleared to top secret.

From the outset, he was highly regarded by his managers, and his annual fitness reports consistently reflect his outstanding job performance. For example, his 1972 appraisal lauded him as "one of the ablest Chinese linguists in the branch, and the entire division. His native competence in the language makes him the natural focal point for the esoteric linguistic problems that arise among other Chinese linguists on the staff."[10]

His service was "marked by the highest degree of professionalism and dedication. Mr. Chin consistently demonstrated maturity, and dependability and personal integrity serving in a variety of increasingly responsible posts both at home and abroad," according to the recommendation for the Career Intelligence Medal signed by the director of FBIS.[11]

Because of his proficiency, Larry was much sought after. Moore explains why he represented an important penetration: "Larry was very educated, an excellent wordsmith in Chinese. When handlers need to compose concise messages to communicate with their agents in Chinese, for example, he becomes the go-to guy. Now, Larry isn't going to know the agent's identity, but he'll know the contents of the message. When he passes that over, they're going to have some indicators. That information is put to use trying to identify the agent."[12]

Herein lies the significance of Larry's treason. If a CIA officer consulted Larry regarding communication with an agent in China, Larry would naturally inquire about the recipient's age, level of education, local dialect, whether the person was male or female. Because these factors would affect the nuances of the message, such details would be freely shared . . . the very details that would help Public Security discover who was in contact with American agents.

Larry would also be able to profile the officers he met, identifying who was active and offering up character assessments.

"I think the fact that Chin knew CIA officers working on the China target put a considerable dent in the effectiveness of those officers," Moore indicates. "It wasn't just that Chin gave away secret information; he also damaged our ability to collect information."[13]

In 1974, his fitness report specified, "His expertise is also recognized by other components of the Agency who frequently call upon him to perform ad hoc services." The following year, his competence with "reverse translation" — from English to Chinese — was highlighted.[14] Obviously, the sort of media monitoring that FBIS is mandated to do on behalf of the government wouldn't entail English-to-Chinese translation. Anything in this domain would have involved more sensitive case operations.

Says Van Magers, "When you have nuanced information you want to translate into Chinese or from the original Chinese, you don't want to rely on my Defense Language Institute Chinese or even a *lofan* who has spent four or five years studying. You want somebody who is a native speaker, someone with a classical education, whose calligraphy is good. He will be able to extract allusions that would otherwise go unnoticed. There were a lot of legitimate reasons why Chin saw material he shouldn't normally have access to. Remember, he'd been with us since the 1940s. How could you not trust him?"[15]

When Moore learned the identity of the Chinese penetration, he experienced a jaw-dropping moment. Larry Chin was a friend.

Georgetown-educated Paul Moore joined the FBI in 1975 when few employees had the kind of learned knowledge of China, its culture, and its language that lends depth and texture to analysis. He was completing his doctoral dissertation on Sung dynasty commentaries about Li Po, a poet of the Tang dynasty, whose collected works, along with contemporary appendices, were written on wooden blocks in an archaic, unpunctuated form nearly a thousand years old. Their complexity exceeded his fluency. Seeking the help of an expert linguist, he was referred to someone at the FBIS. That person was unavailable, but recommended Chin.

"I called him up and his first question was, 'How much?'" Moore recalls, offering a glimpse at what motivated Larry. "We worked out a deal where I paid him fifteen dollars an hour to meet me for two hours every second week. He was disappointed I couldn't afford more, but, I think, he actually got to where he enjoyed it. I brought him my translations and we'd go over them line by line. He was really very good and, in several instances, saved me from very embarrassing mistakes. We did this for well over a year. After that, we saw each other from time to time."

When he advised his superiors, Moore was ordered to compose a long memo explicitly detailing the nature of their relationship. There ensued a debate about whether he should solicit further contact or scrupulously avoid it. The latter, he was instructed. Furthermore, it was decided that he wouldn't be assigned the case. He did, however, consult — "within parameters," he stresses — the junior analyst.

Reevaluating his friend as a spy, Moore reflects, "Larry was doing a lot of unsavory things. It surprised me; stuff like that was not recognizable to me. He was a scholar and a tourist, going around sampling life."[16]

The analogy seems particularly apropos. Like a tourist, the spy is navigating through discomforting, occasionally dangerous, territory where commonplace language and customs are foreign, making him feel awkward and self-conscious. He is watchful, absorbing the scene around him, wanting nothing so much as to be inconspicuous, fearful that an ill-considered turn will lead him to a place best avoided.

That Larry was retired complicated the investigation. The normal procedure with someone who was still active would be to feed him controlled material that you know to be of interest to China and then monitor all his activities. Video cameras could be installed to cover his office. He could be placed under intensive surveillance without calling attention to a source because it would be easier to concoct an excuse for why an employee fell under suspicion than under the circumstances as they actually existed. Ideally, he'd be caught in the act of handing a document over to someone, or at least of illicitly copying it and taking it out of the secure work site.

The FBI tried to convince the CIA to offer Larry a contract position, arguing that this might afford them the opportunity to charge him with a current act of espionage, which a jury ought to find especially compelling, as compared with something a good defense attorney might be able to downplay as a past indiscretion. Moreover, if the bureau built its case by collecting physical evidence of a demonstrable act of espionage, the existence of a source in China need never even be insinuated.

Carson says with a shrug, "It would have been common sense to bring him back, catch him in the act, arrest him."[17]

Fearing the myriad ways by which such a scenario could backfire, the Office of Security was opposed. However, Magers reports that the FBIS did offer Larry a job at the FBI's behest. The bureau was going to use this opportunity to have him submit to an overdue polygraph test in order to reinstate his security clearance. Expecting him to fail, this would have been the excuse they needed to confront him without jeopardizing PLANESMAN.

Advised that the job was dependent on his taking a polygraph, Larry suddenly became far too involved in other matters.

"I'd love to, but I'm very busy with the affairs of the Yenching University Alumni Association. I just don't have the time," he regretted to say.

Larry's formative days at Yenching had changed his life. There, he mastered English. There, he made friends whose impact would resonate for the rest of his days. Yenching was the Chinese equivalent of the Ivy League, where the up-and-coming elite were trained to take their place in the pre-Communist civil service. It had been heavily funded by the American Rockefeller Foundation and several missionary agencies.

Larry claimed he was working to reestablish Yenching's American sponsorship, which had been severed after the Communists took power. Since reconciling with the United States, China was incurring great costs sending gifted students to study here. If, he argued, American institutions resumed sponsoring universities, sending teachers and equipment there, far greater numbers of Chinese students could benefit from a more advanced education.

"China would have the means to bring up a new generation of leaders, English speaking, Western-trained, democracy-oriented, and technologically able leaders who would continue the present trend to develop the Chinese economy and form relations," he would insist.[18] This was all part of his larger mission to reconcile China and the United States.

The media would report that Chin "continued to work as a consultant for the CIA until his arrest."[19] In fact, records reveal that, beginning on March 1, 1981, he was contracted to work for the US Joint Publications Research Service, a federal organization that employs linguists to translate unclassified foreign source material into English at the request of other government agencies. Though his contract was only officially terminated in 1986, he ceased getting assignments after submitting a letter in March 1984 complaining that its rates were not competitive. Scribbled in terse handwriting by a service official on the bottom of an exchange of correspondence is, "Do not use/rehire."[20]

On April 13, the Foreign Intelligence Surveillance Court (FISC) granted the FBI a warrant against Chin. Established by an act of Congress in 1978, FISC is a special tribunal, convened in camera, to review warrant applications for national security investigations. It ensures judicial oversight of the most invasive tools in the law enforcement arsenal, such as wiretaps, mail seizures, and the like.

Eagle Claw, as the case was code-named, was finally well and truly under way.

The warrant granted the powers to install telephone and microphone surveillance against Larry at his home address. To restrict knowledge of the case, the tapes were not transcribed by the regular pool of translators. These people are cleared to the highest levels, but are not special agents. Two fluent Chinese speakers — George Liu, whose mother tongue was Chinese, and Bruce Carlson, who could be mistaken for a native speaker over the phone, where one couldn't know that he was Caucasian — were assigned the task. For the next two years, they would spend much of their working lives listening in on Larry Chin. Also, mail covers were authorized. These don't permit mail to be opened — only for envelopes to be scrutinized for return addresses and postmarks for the purpose of identifying contacts.

Carson briefed a select team from the Special Surveillance Group, the unit of specially trained operatives who conduct intricate and sensitive surveillance. Nobody knew how adept Larry was at countersurveillance, so they were especially cautious. Though he was never witnessed to perform any of the usual measures — doubling back suddenly on his route, running red lights at the last moment, erratically pulling to the side of the road until all traffic in sight passed — group members were under strict orders to drop him at the slightest hunch they'd been burned. They employed random spot checks of Larry's residence and tailed him occasionally. Their reports depicted a normal retiree's routine. No elaborate clandestine escapades in wooded areas. No mysterious nods to strangers in secluded bars. No sleight of hand exchanging documents along crowded boulevards.

Establishing effective static surveillance at the Watergate with a reasonable assurance of going unnoticed was impossible. This is a complex of several high-rises connected by underground tunnels, set back behind gates staffed twenty-four hours a day by security guards.

"We were probably too careful," Carson allows, "but we would never want to be responsible for blowing a source."[21]

Every week, agency and bureau personnel met at Langley. The agency gave a synopsis of intelligence emanating from PLANESMAN, who continued to be debriefed overseas and was instructed to be alert to anything he could pick up about the penetration. The bureau shared its progress and submitted new questions. They invariably returned to Washington Field with a tickling sensation along their spines that their counterparts were withholding.

"The best thing is for a case agent to sit down with a source over several days in order to corroborate everything he says, to break it down. How did you learn this? Were you told that exactly, or are you assuming?" Carson explains. "Of course, logistically, that was impossible. You know, the bureaucracy of security complicated matters. It made the entire investigation more difficult. But theirs is a cruel society. A shot to the back of the head, the bill for the bullet to the family."[22]

All transcripts from the wiretaps were dropped on Carson's desk. He read and absorbed everything. Slowly an impression of the type of man he was chasing emerged.

"Larry had some character flaws," understates Magers. "Had the Chinese known about them, they might not have recruited him. They expressly prefer strong individuals over the weak link."[23] Particularly with respect to those with whom it expects to sustain a long-term association, Chinese intelligence is not generally enthusiastic about exploiting character weaknesses. It regards recruitment by coercion as unreliable and considers people of dubious repute untrustworthy.

Larry was altogether obsessed with sex. Or, to put it as it was put to me, he was a "lecherous old scumbag." *Sordid* and *amoral* are other words that came up.

He had reached that time in a man's life when smiling coyly at young women is ridiculous and obscene, as opposed to seductive. Except for the most crippling attacks of midlife crisis, the inevitable is accepted, albeit reluctantly. Morality and propriety impose limits.

Adolescent girls are off limits.

But not to the hedonist. Not to a man accustomed to making decisions based on self-gratification. A man who, long ago, decided to ignore taboos. Larry set his own boundaries.

And so, when he happened upon a teenage neighbor in the laundry room of his Duke Street apartment building on August 31, 1983, desire welled up. He knew her parents to exchange greetings in passing. He made a special point to say hello to the girl. She didn't think much of it. She was used to having men look at her. She didn't mind.

Waiting for the dryer to finish, Larry made small talk. Her pouty indifference made her all the more alluring.

When she got back to her apartment, she told her parents that Larry had touched her. The parents called Alexandria police, who found enough substance to the girl's allegation that, on September 7, a simple assault charge was laid.

The FBI was in a quandary. As much as it didn't want to see its efforts come to a screeching halt, it couldn't interfere with a criminal investigation. There was no alternative but to let things run their course. Ultimately, issues arose that called the girl's credibility into question, and the charge against Larry was dropped.

Perhaps it was no more than coincidence, but on November 1 he and Cathy moved to the Landmark complex. This forced the bureau to resubmit warrant applications — they aren't transportable. It was a technicality, but it turned off the taps for a time.

Had this been the only sexual episode that came to light, Larry might merit the benefit of the doubt. Another incident, however — for which no charges were laid — alleged that he grabbed at a young girl riding around the new apartment complex on a bicycle.

"I didn't doubt that it was so," allows Moore. "He seemed to kind of come apart once he retired. I mean, he could have always been like that, only now he had more time to indulge himself."[24]

The wiretap picked up countless escapades with several women. He frequently engaged in lustily explicit phone sex with young "nieces." One conversation in particular caught the listeners' attention. Speaking in Chinese, Larry was arranging a rendezvous with a lady from Chicago. He reminded her to bring an item, using a word that could be translated as "machine" or "device." Carson and the linguists puzzled over how this remark could relate to espionage. Was she his contact to Beijing? Was the device a transmitter or coding mechanism? A new camera or a copy machine? Soon enough, in the course of follow-up conversations, during which they built anticipation with titillating descriptions of how their time together would be spent, it became evident that the thing was a mechanical sex toy they were anxiously looking forward to trying.

During this period, it seems almost redundant to say, his marriage — long unhappy — was truly on the rocks. In her account of their life together, Cathy acknowledges that she was aware of his affairs. One time, fed up with his unexplained departures, she followed him from their apartment to the parking lot. She tried to prevent him from driving off, only to be knocked down as he sped away.[25] On another occasion, Cathy discovered Larry in bed with a mistress. She made a hysterical call to a friend asking what to do. Her friend recommended she douse the amorous pair with a pot of water.

Cathy had the friend wait on the line while she dutifully took her advice. The next thing to be heard was Cathy's frantic screaming, "He's killing me! He's killing me!" Larry, naked and soaking wet, was beating her with the pot.

Soon afterward, Larry moved out of the apartment they shared and took up full-time residence in a second apartment in the same building he'd been using as an office. This complicated matters for the bureau because, in accordance with the law, the warrant had been issued to tap the one specific apartment on the grounds that he resided there. Once it was learned that he lived elsewhere, the wiretaps had to be shut down and, once again, application submitted for a brand-new warrant. Authority was, of course, granted, but days of coverage were lost.

Carson took note of everybody with whom Larry was in contact and went about the tedious business of trying to positively identify each individual.

Whenever he got a full name — not usually stated between friends on the phone — or heard mention of a third person, or matched a return address off an envelope, he'd run records checks, sketching the indistinct outline they allowed. Had he or she ever held a clearance? Been charged with a crime? Come up in connection with an intelligence investigation? Been spotted at the Chinese embassy? He collated whatever he learned in meticulously cross-referenced files. However, nobody could be interviewed because it was impossible to ascertain who might let slip Carson's interest.

Telephone taps revealed that Larry was making a concerted effort to stay in regular touch with several former CIA colleagues. CIA personnel who could be identified were called in by the Office of Security for a chat on some pretext or other. Without explicating the precise nature of his interest, a skilled interviewer steered the conversation to where the subject would bring up Chin's name — or, by not doing so, persuade the agent that the contact was of no consequence. Nobody was found to be conspiring with him.

Larry was, nonetheless, exploiting old friendships and his legacy of trust as part of an ongoing effort to be of use to China. While he no longer had a constant flow of secret material crossing his desk, he could casually call up former colleagues to catch up on office gossip and create the illusion that nothing had changed. Those in the know say that he tried to identify the whereabouts of CIA operatives.

"After his retirement, the only substantive information he could provide on current agents was who was overseas under diplomatic cover, who was traveling, who had been promoted," says Ken Schiffer, who had been a special agent on the Washington China squad almost since its inception, and replaced Smith as supervisor in November 1984. "We did pick up a pattern where he was trying to track agency operatives who would be of interest to the Chinese. But it sounded to us like he was forcing it. The agency is pretty good, they're reluctant to talk. Once you're out, you're out."[26]

All the same, there were old friends who saw no harm engaging in office chitchat as they had for years. A few felt compassion toward Larry for the loss of kinship shared within the intelligence fraternity, for how estranged he must feel adjusting to life in the open.

"Remember me?" Larry joked when calling someone up.

He spoke glowingly about retired life. Certainly he had plenty to do, what with his business ventures, freelance translation work, travel, and family. It was a terrific time of his life. How about you?

You still posted to the same unit? No? Where are you assigned now? Oh, interesting. Lots of cases, very active? What is so-and-so up to? he'd inquire. Did this-or-that guy get the promotion he was up for? An innocent question as to whether someone bought that new house elicits clues as to the finances of the purchaser. Asking after an agent's wife could unearth an indiscreet reference to marital strife or an illicit affair. In any other context, the conversation would be as innocent as it sounded. Between a former and serving member of an intelligence service, it took on an entirely different twist, the way the soundtrack to a film can turn the perception of a character from sympathetic to menacing.

For example, in his diary for April 15, 1982, Larry recorded: "Bob Yang went to HK PCS [Hong Kong Permanent Change of Station]."[27] If one is looking for irony, it could have been that the American who ended up recruiting PLANESMAN was originally identified to the Ministry of Public Security as a CIA agent by Larry. China reportedly treated an identification from him with the utmost seriousness.

One specific instance of Larry pointing out a fellow FBIS employee who might be susceptible to an approach did come to light.

He had been paying attention to Victoria Lowe for a considerable time. She once told Larry that she had a brother on the mainland from whom she and her mother had been estranged for thirty years. Perhaps she'd said it wistfully, one émigré to another, when Larry mentioned that his two brothers had stayed behind when he'd left for the West, but had since followed him to America.

On February 15, 1979, he noted in his diary, "Vicky tells prospective DDO assign [sic]." On August 24, he wrote that she had, indeed, transferred to DDO, the Directorate of Operations, the CIA branch responsible for running covert operations. There, she could be invaluable to his Public Security friends.

While meeting Ou Qiming, his handler, in Hong Kong in September 1983, Larry proposed that it could prove worthwhile to find Victoria's brother.

"I asked Mr. Ou's assistance to try to locate him," Chin admitted, explaining, "Mrs. Lowe's mother was really worried. I was doing her a favor."[28]

Ou succeeded in locating the brother and Larry passed the good news on to Lowe, deceiving her regarding the source. An overseas Chinese association was responsible, he said, not the dreaded organ of state security.

By doing this unwitting woman a favor, Ou was establishing *guanxi*. The brother could be approached and offered the opportunity to visit his family in the West. In return, perhaps he wouldn't mind introducing his sister to the friend who had been instrumental in making the reunion possible. That friend would proceed to pitch the sister in a very low-key fashion. No crude threats; the reminder of a service rendered, and the appeal of common blood.

As it happened, Ou didn't pursue the matter further and Lowe wasn't put in the difficult position of choosing between family and country. For his part, Larry suffered no bouts of conscience over maneuvering this innocent woman into a compromising situation.

"You can imagine the kind of person who would try to get them to recruit someone who had no idea." Carson shakes his head. "There's honor among spies to a certain extent. This just proved he had none."[29]

In the fall of 1982, *The Puzzle Palace* was a publishing sensation. Investigative journalist James Bamford succeeded in researching the first — and to this day, definitive — account of the history and workings of the ultra-secret National Security Agency.

Founded in 1952 and housed at Fort Meade, Maryland, NSA was initially protected by legislated anonymity that forbade any mention of its existence. Those who had heard of it joked that *NSA* stood for "No Such Agency." Thirty years later, Bamford remarked incredulously, "Its name is no longer classified information, but virtually all other details concerning the agency continue to be."[30] Only through prodigious use of the Freedom of Information Act did he gain access to the heretofore secret documents enabling him to write the book.

NSA is America's principal signals intelligence organization. Its mission is to intercept radio and telephone communications, computer and fax transmissions, as well as the telemetry emitted by radar and missile guidance systems. Its Central Security Service division is charged with encrypting all sensitive American communications and cracking the codes employed by foreign nations. Bamford refers to it as "the largest single espionage factory the free world had ever known or could ever imagine."[31]

Drawn by the buzz dancing around the DC Beltway like neutrons inside a reactor, Larry eagerly went to a local bookshop and bought a copy. A book purporting to reveal previously unknown details about America's most secret agency could certainly be put to some use. As his eyes raced across the pages, he was astonished by the little touches of detail that made him feel as if he had snuck past the high-voltage electric fencing and eluded the platoon of armed security officers with their pack of hypersensitive dogs, penetrating into the very buildings where the secrets of other countries were delicately teased out from the bulky tangle of numbers and letters and distracting static that eclipsed them; where America's secrets were encased in layer upon concentric layer of codes to prevent the corresponding efforts of those same other states. There was the nicely detailed description of the physical layout and security infrastructure, along with an account of the procedures necessary for entering the facility, including such tidbits as where armed guards are stationed and the color coding of the magnetized passes employees wear to indicate the offices and corridors they are permitted to enter.[32]

Every filmmaker knows that authenticity is a matter of detail; insert a stock shot of the Eiffel Tower at sunset and viewers are fooled into believing they're watching a romantic story unfold in Paris, despite the fact that the intimate tête-à-tête between lovers at the café was performed inside a soundstage in California. Larry employed a variation on this trick on his handler. He informed Ou that he'd taken a contract position with NSA giving him access to new information that would be of great importance. Given the agency's need for linguists, it was a perfectly plausible deception. He then proceeded to translate portions of the book into Chinese and pass them over to his old friend.

From the pages of the book, he gleaned that warning bells sound and red lights flash if someone tries to enter a wing of the facility without the proper access pass. He specified that employees' desks were gray, the chalkboards green, and that it took 180 people to staff the twenty-four-hour-a-day cafeteria.

What did Public Security gain by bloating its files with such trivia? Not much, practically speaking. It may have been enough to start analysts fantasizing about other intelligence he'd come up with. Remember, the Chinese mentality is to encourage sources with sensitive access to pass over what, in their best judgment, they could without unduly jeopardizing themselves. Give us what you can.

Chin would have extracted the agency's organigram, complete with the names and biodata of directors and deputy directors from its inception to the date of publication, as well as the names of many of the unit chiefs. The Chinese would have learned that within the Office of Signals Intelligence Operations, B Group was responsible for monitoring its communications and its chief was Milton Zaslow, a China expert.[33] Bamford gave some tips on how and whom NSA recruits, as well as insight into training at the National Cryptologic School.[34] In the event the Chinese sought to prepare an asset to penetrate NSA, such advance knowledge could prove helpful.

When dealing with SIGINT, clues regarding cryptographic technologies are most coveted. Being a linguist, Larry wouldn't be expected to have in-depth access to such intelligence. Bamford did allow him to confide the tantalizing trivia that in 1977 a rhyolite satellite was launched into geosynchronous orbit over Borneo to intercept Chinese and Soviet military communications and radar signals, which were transmitted to a listening station at Pine Gap, Australia. Another Australian post, code-named

Casino at Nurrungar, processed photographic reconnaissance conducted by satellites overflying China.[35] Each of these items is good to know, if not obviously actionable. They represent the start of building a dossier on NSA.

According to Larry, Ou was "very pleased" with his new batch of secrets.[36]

However, PLANESMAN contradicted this claim. According to him, the Ministry of Public Security was aware of Bamford's book — any Chinese official posted in the West, let alone a covert operative, could buy a copy and ship it to Beijing — and was disappointed with their agent's attempted deception.

"But still, it represented a continuum,"[37] Moore rationalizes.

With respect to this continuum, Magers allows that the Chinese never let on to Larry that they knew he was simply plagiarizing a public source and using it as the foundation for a lie. He explains it in the context of *guanxi:* "Can you go to the store and get me a pound of apples? If you come back with half a pound of oranges, you still fulfilled your obligation, even though I didn't get what I asked for."[38]

The analogy is a little tortured, but the principle is clear. Without being directly tasked, Larry was still taking the initiative to gather information he truly believed to be of value. To Ou's mind, this wasn't to be dismissed. Nor was the relationship to be put at risk by chastising him for the manner in which it was presented.

Continuity is important to the Chinese. Furthermore, it was reasonable to make allowances for an old friend. In a dishonest racket, you concede a certain level of larceny, accepting its place in the character of a spy because it's a trait you exploited in the first place. As Larry's longtime handler, Ou would be his defender in absentia before his superiors. Recounting past heroics, he would excuse the old man this, well, let's call it falsehood. Respect — for age, for long service — Larry had earned. Furthermore, Ou had his own interests at stake. A spy reflects on his handler the way a child reflects on his parents. Running a source inside the CIA conferred upon Ou a status equaled by few.

This incident is especially revealing. Even if one forgives Larry a degree of desperation to sustain his usefulness, it's difficult to ignore the contempt he demonstrated toward China with this fraud. Misrepresenting Bamford's book as secret information emanating from the dark, inaccessible interior of NSA, Chin showed himself perfectly content to deceive the Chinese for money.

To understand a traitor, one must define the bounds he won't cross. At the outer limits is where true insight into character lies. If Larry could be found serving a cause, whether or not we agree with it, his principles would bear some resemblance to our own. Lacking that cause, all we have is a mercenary. And it is always wise to look askance at the mercenary, for his stock in trade is to choose sides for purposes governed exclusively by his avarice, his longevity dependent on nimble entries and exits, his actions ungoverned by sincere loyalty. Larry betrayed the United States. He lied to China.

Later he justified the lie: "If I give him as a book it would be from open source. The Chinese are skeptical, skeptical about open source information. They are dubious, and also they wouldn't pay so much attention to open source materials. If it is stolen, then they will scrutinize it with great interest."[39] He would never be called upon to justify why he believed it important that China be apprised of NSA's functions.

To this point in the investigation, the FBI hadn't ascertained how Larry passed information to Public Security officers. It was commonly understood that Chinese intelligence preferred meeting agents outside their country of operation. Prior to becoming an American citizen, Larry was eligible for annual home leave at the CIA's expense. Because the mainland was off limits, he took this leave in Hong Kong. Analysts surmised that he met his handler on these occasions. Therefore, as they monitored his activities, they were especially attentive to any proposed travel.

The first time the bureau got advance notice that Larry was preparing a trip to Hong Kong and Macao was in June 1983. They couldn't be positive he was going to meet his handlers, but what other logical reason might there be? Perhaps he was transporting something incriminating.

Because the FBI was prohibited from conducting proactive operations on foreign soil, agents couldn't send surveillance on his tail. They
implored the CIA to cover him, but it declined. Once again, the sensitivity
of the source was invoked. Once again, the bureau had no alternative but
to defer.

Loath to allow Larry to depart completely unimpeded, the FBI settled
for searching his outbound luggage, and secured authority to do so through
a Foreign Intelligence Surveillance Court order. Executing the operation
was delicate. Surveillance was put on to take him from the Watergate to
Dulles International Airport, west of the capital, and walk him discreetly
into the terminal. Agents kept him in sight as he joined the line at the
counter to present his ticket and check his bag. Other agents were standing by at the end of the chute down which luggage was conveyed for transfer to the aircraft. Those agents were radioed by the surveillants as soon
as Larry's bag was placed on the belt. They grabbed if off the line and
brought it into a private room.

Arrangements were made to delay the flight in order that the search be
executed and the bag placed aboard prior to departure. Under no circumstance was the plane to leave without it. In the world of espionage, where
every coincidence is stripped bare as a bleached carcass under the desert
sun, the disappearance of his bag would immediately raise red flags.

The suitcase was laid on a table and opened with care not to disturb any
of his belongings. Polaroids were shot of the contents, layer by layer, as
they were removed. This procedure enabled the agents to replace each
item precisely as Larry had packed it once they were done examining it.
They proceeded slowly and methodically. When someone questioned the
crease in the sleeve of a shirt, the Polaroid was studied until all were satisfied that nothing looked amiss.

As the agents worked, the pilot was advised that he was being held back
at the gate. He announced to the passengers that heavy traffic had backed
up the taxiway and that they would depart as soon as possible. Delays
are a routine inconvenience of air travel. Larry had no reason to suspect
anything untoward.

The agents found all the expected clothing and toiletries one would bring on a trip. They discovered only one unusual item: a key stamped with the number 533 and some Chinese characters. It was like a clue dropped nonchalantly into a Sherlock Holmes mystery without any portent to suggest it would prove pivotal to the denouement. It was photographed along with everything else. Carson made a note to himself to show it to a translator.

A spy's fate twists on such details. He will be caught if a diligent investigator pays attention to each one, no matter how seemingly trivial . . . in case. That key was a crucial find for Carson; a devastating oversight for Larry.

# — 4 —

# Bernard Boursicot

Sometime around early 1983, a Chinese intelligence officer defected to the British Secret Intelligence Service (BSIS, also known as MI6). He has never been publicly identified, but by all indications he was fairly low-level, definitely of lesser rank than PLANESMAN. Based on the coincidence of events, it appears that this incident presented the CIA with an unusual opportunity to test PLANESMAN's reliability, which it seized.

While it was premature to go after Larry, PLANESMAN had identified another penetration, one of far less significance, who had ceased to be active. The facts of his espionage stretched the limits of credulity. Indeed, the story was so preposterous that, if it could be verified, whatever else PLANESMAN said would gain substantial credibility.

In February 1964, France reopened its Beijing embassy, which had been closed since the Korean War. Bernard Boursicot, only twenty years old, was posted as the mission's accountant.

Shi Pei Pu was a star of the renowned Beijing Opera who also gave language courses to foreigners. He met Bernard at a diplomatic reception. Shi's presence alone telegraphs that he had somehow earned the confidence of the authorities.

Bernard was a naive youth on an adventure, a boy from rural Brittany feigning worldliness out of desperation to fit in. No matter what he did, the snooty diplomats treated him condescendingly because his suits were ill fitting and not à la mode, and his hair wasn't styled au courant. He lacked a degree from the proper school and failed to adopt the mannerisms that he, in turn, disparaged as Parisian affectations.

He was also wrestling with the demon of sexual confusion. Bernard had yet to be with a woman. He had, however, dabbled in homosexuality. He tended to dismiss these episodes as innocent, even exuberant, experimentation, rather than expressions of any definitive orientation. A man who embraces life to the fullest samples everything, he reasoned, without exception, without reservation. He had once ventured to Algeria to visit a friend, whose father was the assistant consul general. Indiscretions had a way of coming to the attention of the Algerian security services, with whom the Chinese enjoyed friendly relations.

Bernard initiated a conversation with Shi; Shi was merely the opportunist, welcoming his advances. Bernard was anxious to disengage from the confinement of the diplomatic circuit, with its malicious innuendoes and compulsive rumormongering. Shi agreed to escort him around Beijing, showing him secluded corners, taking interest in him, providing scintillating companionship. Shi offered him a completely authentic experience of China.

Shi paid Bernard the great honor of bringing him to the home he shared with his widowed mother, located in a *hutong,* one of the laneways and courtyards that snarled confusingly through Beijing like loosely tied silk ribbons. Bernard slipped along them like a shadow, living out his every fantasy of the exotic and the forbidden. All the while, he was reassured that the diplomatic passport he carried in his pocket shielded him from serious harm. If, on the other hand, the regime found out Shi was consorting privately with a foreigner, his punishment would be severe. He faced forcible relocation from Beijing to the countryside, if not imprisonment. If you judge the quality of a friendship by the risks it entails, Shi was the truest friend Bernard had ever known.

The only protection he could offer Shi from the Chinese was to keep faith with their secret. He was proud to have a private life all to himself. Let his colleagues think what they wished of him. For all their suave manners and courtly etiquette, it was lowly Bernard the clerk who had actually cultivated a Chinese relationship. He was delving into the Beijing that the authorities went to such great lengths to fence off from foreign view. He was having free-flowing jazz-riff conversations, while theirs were orchestrated by faultlessly rehearsed mandarins in harmony with party dictums.

Everybody has one dramatic secret that makes them feel vulnerable to the outer world's harsh judgment. They clutch it like the ripcord on a parachute until they decide to break their free fall by pulling it open and trusting the one person they decide will be their soul mate. Shi seemed to do that with Bernard, revealing the greatest secret of his life. Shi confided that he was not the man he appeared to be. He was, in fact, a woman forced to live in disguise. Shi was raised a boy in order to protect her mother, who feared being cast off by her father's family if she failed to bear a son.

Bernard was overwhelmed. On the one hand, at this show of confidence; on the other, because it legitimized the strong sexual desire he felt for the effeminate Pei Pu. A desire that shamed him, for it reinforced his fear that he would have to admit, once and for all, if only to himself, that he was a homosexual. Shi's revelation presented an opportunity to act upon his arousal.

Shi responded to his advances, not without trepidation. When she finally allowed him into her bed, she insisted that the room be kept in darkness. Bernard assumed this was Asian shyness and let it excite him all the more. When they commenced, Shi took charge, guiding him, restricting his explorations. It was this way every time they made love. For all the years they made love. Thus could Shi sustain one of the unlikeliest of all possible charades. Bernard even observed the bloody rags that indicated menstruation. The deception was total.

Bernard was not surprised when Shi told him that she was pregnant. Fearing the consequences of having a child with a foreigner, Shi soon claimed to have self-aborted, messily and excruciatingly. Bernard rushed to see her. Extremely sick upon first glance, Shi underwent a miraculous recovery before a doctor could be summoned.

In December 1965, when Bernard told Pei Pu that he had been transferred, Shi informed him that she was, again, pregnant. This time, Bernard was adamant: There was to be no abortion. Nonetheless, he had no choice but to return to Paris, leaving behind his paramour and his unborn son.

His concern over the fate of Shi and the child he never met turned to fear in the succeeding years as he followed the hysteria of the Cultural Revolution in the French press. Report Chang and Halliday, "Bloody house raids swept across China. . . . Many of those raided were tortured to death in their own homes. Some were carted off to makeshift torture chambers in what had been cinemas, theatres and sports stadiums. Red Guards tramping down the street, the bonfires of destruction, and the screams of victims being set upon — these were the sights and sounds of the summer nights of 1966."[1]

Shi was at risk under nearly every dictum of the Cultural Revolution: as a recognized opera star, a French speaker, and one who openly fraternized with foreigners, not to mention the confusion surrounding her gender. It was almost unfathomable that she could escape harm.

Bernard became increasingly impatient to return to China, but there were no openings. In desperation, he approached the Chinese embassy in Paris offering his services, if only they would find a place for him in Beijing. They rejected him, but not without taking note.

In the meantime, he was posted by the foreign office to Saudi Arabia. Two years passed without any word from Pei Pu. Worry did not curb his social life. He freely indulged himself with both women and men over the period.

When an archivist position opened at the embassy in Beijing in September 1969, Bernard enthusiastically accepted the job. He was cleared to defense-secret level. Upon his arrival, he wasted no time searching out Pei Pu. He found her living in a *siheyuan* or "courtyard house," one of a group of four homes around a central courtyard, which are the most prized residences in Beijing.

In the midst of blatant hostility against foreigners and all things foreign, Shi told Bernard that she had been granted permission by the Writers' Association of Beijing to meet him twice a week to study the thoughts of Chairman Mao. In short order, two men, calling themselves

Kang and Zhao, became his teachers, replacing Shi. Bernard's story is that their instruction brought him to an understanding of the objectives, and acceptance of the excesses, of the Cultural Revolution. He told his new teachers that he was prepared to advise them about news coming through the French embassy. They supposedly thanked him, but declined the offer.[2] Undeterred, Bernard brought Kang documents on his own initiative.

Magers reconstructs it differently: "Where he says he volunteered, he was offered two choices: We can PNG [the term for declaring foreign nationals persona non grata and formally expelling them from the country] you or you can continue your relationship. But if we PNG you, we're going to arrest your inamorata and you'll never see him again. Or, if you continue, all will be status quo, so long as you cooperate. Even with that, in typical Chinese fashion, they never pushed him for really tough information."[3]

Eerily foreshadowing Larry, Boursicot would later explain, "I was not betraying my country; I was helping China. Even the Chinese told me, 'We do not want to know the secrets of your country. France is a friendly country; we do not want to know about France, but about Russia.'"[4] As the Americans would learn to have been the case with Larry, Bernard was cautioned against stealing anything marked TOP SECRET, on the assumption that controls over such material were too stringent to warrant the risk of getting caught.

There was a particular matter about which Kang did express interest. Without explaining why, he asked for any information regarding US policy toward China that might be passed to the embassy. China was embarking on secret talks with the United States about the possibility of a visit by President Richard Nixon. Henry Kissinger, his national security adviser, made a clandestine visit to Beijing as a preliminary step to what would be a very public and radical shift in America's foreign policy. Nixon had discussed his plan to open the door to China with French president Charles de Gaulle, who had passed the information along to his ambassador in Beijing, Etienne Manac'h.[5]

The moniker *Kang* was most definitely an alias, and probably chosen as a symbolic bow to Kang Sheng. Faligot and Kauffer suggest that the man calling himself Kang was none other than Yu Zhensan.[6]

Meanwhile, Shi explained to Bernard that their son had been sent to live outside Beijing because she could hardly explain how *he* suddenly came to have a child. In May 1972, Bernard was rotated back to Paris without ever having met his son. He had been cooperating with the Chinese for nearly three years. He parted with his handlers on good terms. Without any specific promise, there was always the prospect they might connect with their agent again.

In November 1973, Bernard traveled to Hong Kong, for which he didn't need special permission from the ministry. From there, unbeknownst to France, he submitted a visa application to the mainland. Of course, his friends made all the necessary arrangements, and he was finally able to meet his son. It was a joyous encounter, Bernard relishing the chance to play the affectionate parent. The boy, Du Du, was clearly of mixed race and, Bernard fancied, looked much like his father.

Bernard was also reunited with Shi, though he had long ceased to love her. Nevertheless, their bond and the secrets between them were not easily forsaken. Sex had become routinized. Bernard never troubled Shi to make love like other women (or men) he'd known. The hurried struggle to climax held no more wonder for him. They did it without exuberance, quickly, in the dark. He no longer sought the intimate touching Shi never permitted. When happy couples have sex, it fulfills a promise for the future. For Bernard, sex with Shi was merely acknowledgment of the past.

Come 1977, Bernard was given a position in Ulan Bator, a three-person mission widely considered the most miserable outpost in the French foreign service. He was assigned as general factotum, typist, archivist, accountant, and courier. Working out of rooms in the Ulan Bator Hotel, security was practically nonexistent. Nor, given the nature of most of the material they handled, was it much needed.

Bernard reestablished contact with Kang, who was pleased to hear from his old agent. The Soviets were the resident power in Mongolia, and the Chinese were curious to learn whatever they could regarding their Communist nemesis. Every six weeks or so, Bernard made a courier run to Beijing. He brought Kang anything he could get his hands on. However, the take proved largely useless, a mass of Mongolian agriculture statistics. During a meet in the summer of 1978, Kang actually advised him not to bother anymore.[7]

Moore is rather ambivalent in evaluating Boursicot's value: "Hard to say how important he was. He was pretty good because he was giving whatever passed through his hands for a while. He provided something like 150 classified documents, all told. It wasn't a huge take. But he would have been well regarded because he was so much better than no information."[8]

Recounting this story to the American, PLANESMAN had another surprise. Shi was not a woman, but, as he had first appeared, a man. Furthermore, he had never broken cover.

That the Ministry of Public Security kept up this charade over eighteen years is fantastic enough. What's truly inconceivable is that agents scripted it from the start. It is too outrageous to imagine an officer proposing to entrap Bernard by these means.

"Anyone who's ever tried to get a pencil sharpener through the system realizes what goes on," Moore says, chuckling. "But someone got this done, and that really took our breath away when we learned of it. The Chinese still laugh over how ridiculous this case was."[9]

Blackmail is thought to be an uncommon tactic for Chinese intelligence. Their overall attitude toward sex is prudish, but there is one publicly known case wherein they employed a classic honey-trap — running a female agent against a man in an implicit, if not explicit, attempt to take advantage of a sexual situation. Xu Meihong, a military intelligence officer, was assigned to the Center of Chinese and American Studies, a joint venture between Nanjing and Johns Hopkins Universities, in 1988. She was tasked by the Ministry of State Security to become friendly with, and report upon, Larry Engelmann, a visiting American scholar. Though her handler contended Engelmann was a secret agent, Xu insisted he was exactly as he appeared to be: a curious, if rather naive, academic.

The operation went sour when letters written by Engelmann to friends and family in the United States suggested China was losing control over their personal relationship. Intercepted and read by State Security agents, these missives convinced the authorities that Xu was collaborating with Engelmann's supposed covert activities. Unable to convince them otherwise, Xu was arrested, discharged from the army, and ordered to her home village. Eventually, Engelmann married her and, ultimately, secured her exit.[10]

It is a matter of conjecture when Shi's relationship with Bernard became a controlled intelligence operation. What the Xu Meihong case demonstrates is that Chinese security is not above directing an intimate relationship for intelligence purposes.

More than likely, Shi was a Public Security co-optee when Bernard met him. This accounts for his being permitted to attend diplomatic functions and give language lessons to foreigners. For the most part, his reporting would be limited to character assessments, gossip, insights into who demonstrated the sort of flaws that intelligence services are constantly looking to exploit. His own homosexuality, a crime in the Communist state, was enough incentive to cooperate with the security forces.

Bernard's seduction was probably pure improvisation on the part of Pei Pu. I suspect that he decided to pose as a woman upon sensing Bernard's repugnance toward homosexuality, despite how irresistible he found it. Shi often assumed women's roles in traditional opera and, using his distinct flair for the dramatic, staged the ultimate tragic romance, one for Bernard to interpret as a uniquely Asian love story. When lust and vanity reach critical mass, you often discover a spy.

Once Shi pulled it off — undoubtedly to the delighted surprise of Kang/Yu — the introduction of a child to the plot offered a more stable hold on Bernard than the vicissitudes of a love affair. When Bernard fell for the ruse, Kang/Yu knew that he was well and truly hooked.

An intelligence lead sputters and sparks like a lit fuse. Unless anyone bothers to attach one end to a detonator, it has no impact. The Boursicot affair was of little use to the Americans, but intelligence pertinent to another nation's interests can be traded off against future concessions. Indebted friends are the best of friends. And in a business where friends are received with little more confidence than enemies, creating indebtedness is most desirable.

The key to a successful strike is firing off missiles in such tight sequence that the radar detects only a single blip. A Chinese officer goes over to the British, the French pick up Boursicot. Cause and effect. Nobody wastes another thought on a second infiltration. And the Americans move closer to confirming PLANESMAN's reliability.

The potential for France to pursue a case was obvious. Based on the information at hand, there appeared to be no issue about revealing state secrets in open court: Statistics on how much yak shit covered the Mongolian countryside were the most recent haul from Bernard's exploits. But France could charge him simply for meeting with an agent of a foreign government. Clandestinely passing documents, regardless of content, constituted a crime.

Meanwhile, Shi had come to Paris in October 1982 at the invitation of the Maison des sciences de l'homme to give lectures and performances, and to teach classical Chinese opera. He was accompanied by his teenage son. Shi could be charged as a secret agent of a foreign power.

### *Paris, June 30, 1983*

Bernard Boursicot was strolling along the Avenue Bosquet on a sunny afternoon. He could have looked dreamily over his shoulder and seen the Eiffel Tower looming above the city, though no self-respecting Parisian took notice of it, spurning it as a monstrosity to woo the unsophisticated, chattering tourists.

He was gazing cheerfully in the shop windows, paying no attention to those maneuvering around him. Suddenly he was accosted by two men and dragged toward a dark Renault sedan that had pulled up alongside.

Bernard resisted. Two other men scrambled out of the car to join the fray. One of them flashed a badge. Bernard sagged, the fight gone. They clamped cuffs around his wrists and shoved him into the backseat.[11]

The car tore north, across the Seine, and turned into the tiny Rue d'Argenson, pulling up at the headquarters of the Direction de la surveillance du territoire (DST), France's internal security service. Bernard knew fully well why he was there. What he didn't know was how much *they* knew. He used the time between being arrested and being seated in the interrogation room to compose himself as best he could.

The DST indicated that "within the normal surveillance of the activities of the Chinese representation in Paris" during the winter of 1982, it became aware of a relationship between Boursicot and "a Chinese national living in Paris, later identified as Shi Pei Pu."[12] Shi was seen in contact with China's embassy in Paris.[13] A DST report dated July 2, 1983, said, "The Service suspected a cooperation between Bernard Boursicot and the Chinese intelligence services through the intermediary of Shi Pei Pu."[14]

They confronted Bernard with candid photos in which he was easily recognizable, if slightly off focus from the distance and size of the telephoto lens. They knew about his overseas postings — but then they would. One ministry tells another, no mystery. They told him — didn't ask — he'd visited the Chinese embassy back in February 1967 and April 1968 to meet the cultural consul. Normal surveillance of the property, okay, no surprise. Careless of him, but that was so long ago.

In April 1971, the People's Republic provided him a plane ticket to Beijing, the DST agent stated. That was a noose dropped roughly over his head: proof they knew more than could be gleaned from routine observation of the Chinese establishment in Paris. Whatever they'd been told, whoever had told them, would have cast him as a villain.

If he could change their perception of him, Bernard felt they would understand his plight, perhaps even sympathize with his motives. He wasn't a venal man. He was a romantic. This wasn't a sordid scandal of greed, but the stuff of great art, of poetry and opera.

You see, gentlemen — he took a deep dramatic pause — to let them fully appreciate the magnitude of what he was to say — Pei Pu is a woman. Her son is my son. That's why . . .

Forty-eight hours after his arrest, the DST had a fifteen-page confession. Fearing for his lover and their son when China became engulfed in the Cultural Revolution, he paid out secrets, the only currency with which he could barter their safety. He was desperate, without any other means to protect his family. It seemed little enough in return for their lives.

Shi was then picked up and charged. The DST was confused. Shi, they had a doctor confirm, was — as he appeared to be — a normal man.

Confined to a cell awaiting trial, Bernard was facing serious charges and trying to come to terms with the enormity of learning how Pei Pu had made such a fool of him. He was overwhelmed. Alone, in a closed space, Bernard had nothing to do but face the awful truth about himself. He wasn't the tragic hero of an epic romance. He was just pathetic and weak and ridiculous. An absolute sexual naïf so enslaved by his libido that he couldn't distinguish a woman from a man.

With nobody to contradict the mockery screaming within, he pried the blade off the plastic head of a disposable razor and dug the sharp side into the flesh of his neck. Blood spurted out, but the metal strip was too narrow to penetrate to the artery. He sawed away until the blade became too slippery to grip and he passed out.

Whether the suicide attempt was legitimate or a halfhearted effort to win sympathy, perhaps even Bernard couldn't tell. It left a bloody mess but inflicted only minor damage.

On May 5, 1986, the two old lovers went on trial together at the Palais de justice, charged with "conspiring with agents of a foreign power, in such a manner as to bring harm to the diplomatic situation of France." Specifically, for supplying thirty-five government documents to China between 1977 and 1979, while Bernard was posted to Mongolia. France's statute of limitations had run out for any harm done earlier. By this time, Bernard had been imprisoned for three years. Shi had served less than eight months before being released due to poor health.

A jury of magistrates found both guilty and returned a sentence of six years incarceration. In 1987, China privately importuned for Shi's release. On April 6, apparently seeing no advantage to keeping him in jail, President François Mitterrand granted a presidential pardon. And because it was patently nonsensical to hold one but not the other of the pair, Bernard, too, was pardoned. Without a foreign power to lobby on his behalf, however, he remained incarcerated until August 3.

The French explanation that Bernard was detected on the basis of less than a year's surveillance of his contacts in Paris is preposterous, especially in light of the fact that his acts of espionage occurred years before and overseas. Only a well-placed source could have furnished enough information to warrant his arrest. Since we know that PLANESMAN was active and in a position to know about Boursicot — even more, that he was likely his handler — it is logical to conclude that he was responsible.

Protocol dictated that the DST not take action without the CIA's approval, in deference to its source. Thus it is certain that the Americans were forewarned about Bernard's arrest, and sanctioned it.

When word flashed in to Public Security headquarters that Shi and Boursicot had been arrested, Yu's intestines must have roiled inside him like a storm-churned sea, blending the remains of his breakfast into a fine spume of vomit. Those first days following disclosure of the arrest, all his energy was concentrated on exhibiting natural concern for the fate of a source and righteous outrage for the betrayal, all so as to conceal the hellish anticipation of any intimation that he was considered responsible.

When it became clear that the British jumper was being blamed, PLANESMAN's relief was almost as hard to conceal as had been his fear. Nonetheless, he padded lightly around the bureau, taking care not to gaze upon any desk but his own. He was able to continue meeting the American because he was ostensibly the handler. It is to be expected, however, that he did so warily and without enthusiasm. He had every right to feel jumpy in the wake of Boursicot's arrest. Some time would pass before he acted with the boldness he'd displayed in rifling Miss Wong's desk. Eventually, he adjudged the situation normal enough to resume his efforts. After all, he had yet to achieve his objective. Unless he continued, all he'd done thus far would go for naught.

## *Beijing, Fall 1985*

The source–handler relationship is pure narcissism. Neither gives anything without believing he is getting something of greater value in return. It is a conspiracy carried out between competitors trapped by mutual dependence. A variation on the classic kidnapper's dilemma: How are hostage and ransom exchanged without either side being vulnerable to the other for even an instant? In this case, we're talking about information and compensation. Each depends on the honor of the other: the handler that the information is true, the source that the compensation is forthcoming as promised.

Pulling a source out early is permissible, even prudent. Failure to safely extract an in-place carries far-reaching repercussions. If his discovery can be kept under wraps, the source can be used as a conduit for disinformation that might be cleverly manipulated to call into question the authentic intelligence provided to that point. Ultimately, the source quite probably ends up with a death sentence or lengthy prison term. Once his fate becomes known, other sources will question their handler's heartfelt promises to protect them no matter what.

PLANESMAN's in-place life span was finite from the outset. The end of the American's tour in Beijing was the natural finish. Because PLANESMAN was supposed to be handling the American, introducing a new handler was impossible. When the American departed, the operation would be terminated.

How and when PLANESMAN could leave still posed a significant challenge. Where state control is omnipresent; where an individual's movements are restricted and comings and goings, within and without, are monitored; where borders are razor wire and blinding spotlights and armed sentries — exfiltration is an exceptionally delicate enterprise.

Spying is timing. Timing is everything.

The American promised PLANESMAN a warm welcome on the other side. Until then, he'd have to sweat the cold passage all alone. They would have opted for simplicity over elaborate arrangements that, the American assured, would only risk making him more conspicuous.

He had some vacation coming and, he explained when submitting his application for leave, relatives in Hong Kong he hadn't seen in a long time. As a trusted member of the regime, deserving of a reward for recruiting and running as valuable a source as the American, his superiors approved his request. He went about obtaining a passport and having it stamped with the mandatory visas for departure and reentry.

He must have talked through the final days before parting with the American. Not rehearsed. The American didn't want him thinking in terms of a prepared script. Just go about your business naturally, the American instructed, put it in your mind that you're going on holiday for a couple of weeks.

Doubt and excitement clashed like volatile air masses, setting off thunderbolts in his chest. He'd never been abroad before. He only had a vague concept of what the United States was, derived from a potpourri of virulent propaganda he'd been fed his whole life and utopian wishes for an Eden where every comfort and consumer good was to be had at the snap of a finger.

As time drew near, I imagine that he visited all his favorite spots in Beijing, ate at all his favorite restaurants. He'd never experienced homesickness, but he had a premonition it would be intense. Spying was an irrevocable decision. He had to leave and never return. He walked familiar streets slowly, taking care to notice everything. Like Monet, rendering his beloved garden and haystacks in exquisite detail in all different seasons and every permutation of light, PLANESMAN noted how the sun made streaks along the boulevard outside his window; how moonbeams took their place when darkness fell. He breathed deeply as he walked, storing up memories of fragrances he couldn't identify by name. The smells that permeated Beijing reminded him that he was home no matter where in the city he roamed.

He called on friends for tea and spoke excitedly of his imminent vacation. So excitedly that, in his agitation, he might have feared he went on too enthusiastically for an absence of only a couple of weeks. But nobody seemed to notice. Permission to go to the British colony was exciting. He graciously accepted lists of goods they asked him to bring back. He froze their faces in snapshots with his eyes. Happy expressions that would bring him sadness in the future. He silently wished them well, hoping they'd remember him fondly even after they discovered what he'd done.

The night before, he painstakingly sorted through his belongings. Pack only what you'd bring on vacation, the American instructed. Even with all your papers in order, you might be searched at the border. He couldn't use his ministry identity card to circumvent scrutiny because he was expressly forbidden from carrying it in Hong Kong. Clothing and toiletries enough for the length of his vacation, even though these were the most replaceable of his possessions.

The mementos of his life, however, would have to be discarded. He read over letters and postcards he'd saved, smiling at remembrances of special times. As he finished each, he methodically tore it into tiny pieces, tossing the fragments into the coal stove, sifting the embers to consume them into fine ash. He sorted through his photo albums, selecting a portrait of his parents and sliding it into a thin compartment of his valise. He separated the photos into two piles: living and dead. He burned those of anyone living. His actions wouldn't offer much protection. At least when his former comrades rampaged through his apartment, they wouldn't find any proof of his relationships. All his immediate family was listed in his personnel file. Under interrogation, they'd reveal the names of his closest friends. He wouldn't be able to do anything for them. They'd simply have to denounce him and deny any foreknowledge of his intentions, which was the truth.

Would they understand? Would they probe honestly into their own hearts, stare into the depths of their desires, and recognize why he'd done it? Would they forgive him?

The night before his departure was sleepless, spent pacing the apartment he'd never see again, regarding his possessions and trying to disassociate from them. Mere objects. In America he'd have a color television and an expensive sound system.

And a new American identity. A dream come true for how many men?

A new name in a new country, with a new language and a new culture. No longer a traitor, but a hero. A new person. A better person, he vowed.

That morning, PLANESMAN boarded a train destined for the Guangzhou frontier. He took the chance of paying for a first-class ticket. It was an indulgence, but he wasn't coming back to have his finances scrutinized and he no longer needed his meager savings. He took a window seat and affected to be fascinated by the scene outside so as to discourage conversation from his compartment mates.

He watched the grandeur of the city's core where the political elite lived in their isolated splendor give way to the ugly industrial suburbs where so many were submerged in the sodden filth of monotony, their dreams long ago suffocated, and on to the farmlands where, so recently, fertile soil had yielded only famine thanks to political lunacy.

He thought about death. About being returned to the earth. He was going far away to die. He would rest in strange soil. He grieved for his peace. The adrenaline of spying, the glee of settling the score with Miss Wong had kept his emotions at bay. How is it that remorse comes — when it comes — never in advance, only in retrospect?

A study of people who survive a suicide attempt shows that their last conscious thought after jumping, or swallowing the pills, or slicing with the knife, or pulling the trigger, was regret. And in that split second of clarity, none of the problems that had brought them to such despair seemed so extreme. Asked what they would do differently, most said they wouldn't try to end their lives.

Was there anything PLANESMAN would do differently as he chugged toward no-turning-back? Memory plays an odd trick of preserving an improved version of the past. The searing pain and fear are smothered in the murk of hindsight because dread over the outcome is no longer a factor. However scarred, you've emerged. He'd never have to surreptitiously read another document or slip into a safe house again. The worst part of the ordeal — the only part that remained uncertain — was what remained ahead. Stay in Guangzhou, take my vacation, then go home. The next step is still mine to take. The American isn't going to follow me back to Beijing to rescue me. Truth be told, he'd be relieved not to bother with a defector who'd long since served his purpose.

Deceiving himself with the illusion that his choices weren't irrevocable, he fell into a fitful sleep where the truth lurked in wait.

The air was far warmer in the south of China than it had been when he'd left Beijing. As PLANESMAN unbuttoned his jacket, he realized how threadbare it was. The cheap fiber stuffing protruded where the lining had worn to threads. The cuffs and collar were frayed from the years of daily wear. He heaved a sigh. I'll get a new one in America. That's what I did it for, after all, he thought bitterly.

The crowds at the frontier station were his best cover. He knew it would take hours to pass through. The Chinese border police cared nothing for convenience. Because of the officers' discretion to arbitrarily deny exit, nobody dared to complain or even shuffle their feet impatiently. When he reached the wicket, PLANESMAN was greeted with the same scowl as each person who'd preceded him. He had used the time in line to closely study the procedure. He wasn't alarmed when his papers were scrutinized line by line, smudge by smudge for authenticity. They weren't interested in detaining illegals so much as finding some excuse to extract a bribe. Nothing to be found on PLANESMAN's documents, the blunt *thwack* of the stamp was delivered like a hatchet through shackles.

He had to hold himself to a casual walk those few yards across the no-man's-land to the Hong Kong border post. His shoulders were tensed. He willed his knees not to buckle, bringing him to the ground to accept the bullet he deserved for being a traitor.

He was perspiring heavily, a combination of nerves and the too-heavy clothes he wore. With each step he felt himself pushing against a rising torrent of water. Men, women, children were rushing past him until the crowd backed up to meet him and he could only inch forward.

The Hong Kong police were coolly efficient. A couple of questions:

Length of stay? Fourteen days.

Purpose of visit? Seeing family.

Stamp. He was in.

He boarded the ferry to cross the Hong Kong Strait. He stood by the railing and breathed in the salty humidity. As the ferry pulled from the dock, the thrum of the engine, the belch of the diesel fumes, and the stench of putrefying fish made him vomit over the side in a cathartic heave. He felt momentarily better, as if a bilge tank had been blown before rupturing at the rusted seams. Then the corrosive acids began sloshing and burning his stomach anew. And he retched drily.

Hong Kong wasn't home free, he knew. The small island swarmed with Chinese intelligence agents and informants. And while the Royal Hong Kong Police – Special Branch was a highly professional and diligent force, it was inundated. The agency wouldn't have enlisted its assistance to protect him. Too much risk they'd be penetrated. Far safer to rely on the two weeks' time his vacation bought to hold his comrades at bay. He wouldn't be in Hong Kong nearly long enough to be missed.

The American had provided detailed instructions on what to do upon his arrival. He was told which unassuming guest house to check into that night. He was told which restaurant around the corner he should eat at. Presumably, his presence would signal that he was safe. He was given a specific taxi company to enlist at a precise time the following morning out to Kai Tak Airport. There he would present himself at a designated check-in counter, where he was handed an envelope and directed to a departure gate.

Time was purposely cut tight. He made his way across the concourse at a quick march, clutching his ticket and a new US passport. He passed through security without incident.

PLANESMAN should have allowed himself the luxury of relief when he felt the aircraft begin taxiing toward the runway. Instead, fear being the great incubator for the imagination, he worried up squadrons of Chinese jet fighters scrambled to shoot the plane from the sky. He sat white-knuckled for hours, releasing the armrest only to gulp the whiskeys he repeatedly ordered. When the alcohol was dense enough in his system to float his courage, and he was sure the plane was out over international water — only then — he sighed. *I'm out.*

Not really free. There'd be hour upon hour of debriefing. Followed by months, if not years, of adjustment. Practicing with a new name until the spirits haunting his dreams called him by it. Recalling a life he hadn't really lived as his past.

Spying leaves you hollowed out, like an autopsy. Then punishes you farther by forcing the remains to go on living.

# — 5 —

# Eagle Claw

*Washington Field Office, November 1984*
When Ken Schiffer took over the China squad, Eagle Claw was moribund.

"The case had been open for more than two years. Either it is or it isn't; if it isn't, let's close it. Let's do something with it," he insists. "You have a good investigator trying to do his job. As a manager, my job is to help him do it."[1]

Schiffer is the kind of manager who is first off the bench to back up his men in a fight. He grew up on a ranch in Wyoming and is an accomplished rodeo rider. Before joining the FBI, he'd been a teacher. He possesses the combination of intellectual curiosity and physical courage every lawman should have. As a rookie agent in 1970, he fell afoul of J. Edgar Hoover himself when he wrecked a bureau car. His punishment was assignment to Counter-Intelligence — China. He spent the next twenty-one years there, becoming one of the mainstays of the section. Today the letter of reprimand that defined his career, hand-signed by Hoover, is framed and prominently displayed in his study.

Special Agent Tom Carson continued about his routine as he had since Larry was positively identified and the warrants went into effect. He pored over transcripts, noted down names of contacts, ran indices checks, and built voluminous files. Unaware of Tom's watchfulness, Larry became his unwitting confidant, revealing those nasty disgraces indulged when he was certain nobody could see or hear.

"I can't think of any other case I was involved with where we knew the subject quite as well as we did Chin," claims Schiffer,[2] who met Carson at the end of every day to go over the take. It didn't feel like progress, but, in fact, this familiarity would prove providential.

Nineteen eighty-five is recalled as the Year of the Spy for the unprecedented number of cases that broke. American secrets were being bled out by a thousand cuts, inflicted on the CIA, FBI, NSA, State Department, Naval Intelligence Service, and private contractors. Security was breached from as far afield as Russia, Israel, Ghana, and China. Feeling besieged, the American government needed to reinforce how seriously it viewed the crime of espionage.

Without doubt, the most significant of the American traitors was John Walker, who began spying for the Soviet Union in the late 1960s. When he retired from the navy in 1976, he recruited his son Michael and friend Jerry Whitworth, both of whom were on active duty, to continue supplying him with the highly sensitive cryptological data for which he was so well paid by Moscow. His brother, Arthur, who was employed with a defense contractor, also funneled him classified information. Further, he made an effort to recruit his daughter, Laura, even encouraging her to have an abortion rather than leave the army when she became pregnant in the hope that she would eventually move into a position that would support his espionage.

The Walker ring passed over the keys to the navy's secret castle: the information necessary to crack the cipher system by which all its communications were encrypted, along with the daily key lists to unscramble the military's coded communications. Simply put, it enabled the Soviets to read all the top-secret transmissions between America's battle fleet and command posts. As well, he furnished data relating to submarine operations and technical data on how the United States silenced its most advanced subs.

Oleg Kalugin, a former KGB general who served at the residency in Washington for a dozen years, calls Walker the most damaging of America's traitors. "We could read all correspondence between U.S. naval headquarters and your subs across the world. We could have delivered a pre-emptive strike" in the event conflict had erupted, he claims.[3] In an affidavit submitted for the prosecution of Whitworth, Bill Studeman, director of naval intelligence, asserted that the Walker ring "might have had 'powerful war-winning implications for the Soviet side.'"[4]

In the end, it wasn't good intelligence work that led to Walker's undoing, but a drunken phone call to the FBI in 1984 from his ex-wife, Barbara, who had been aware of John's activities for sixteen years. He was arrested in May 1985. In October, under a plea bargain, he accepted a sentence of life imprisonment and promised to testify against Whitworth in exchange for relative leniency for Michael, then only twenty-three years old, who received twenty-five years with the possibility of parole in eight. Whitworth was sentenced to 365 years in prison, with no possibility of parole in less than 60, pretty well assuring that the then forty-six-year-old would die behind bars.

Another navy breach ran concurrent to the Chin investigation. The case of Jonathan Jay Pollard, a civilian intelligence analyst with the Naval Investigative Service, had a novel twist in that he was giving secrets to a close American ally, Israel. This, he continues to argue loudly from his prison cell, is a mitigating factor that should win him clemency.

Besides the timing, other striking parallels with Chin would emerge. As did Larry, Pollard claimed to have exercised discretion in his betrayal. Pollard "did not adopt the blind attitude that what was good for Israel was good for the United States," his lawyers claimed; "he would not divulge information concerning U.S. military or intelligence capabilities, or take any other actions deemed to damage the U.S. national security."[5] He said he only betrayed documents concerning the capabilities and intentions of Middle Eastern countries that were demonstrably hostile to Israel and technical data of Soviet weapons systems that were being delivered to those countries. However, the truth of the matter was that "the most important single document"[6] he supplied was a US handbook on communications intelligence, which could have compromised future American SIGINT capabilities and had nothing to do with his stated interests. This document was specifically requested by his handler.

Pollard was paid but, like Larry, was adamant that the money was merely incidental to the fulfillment of his mission. He only accepted it at his handler's behest. "I never considered myself to be a mercenary, no matter how corrosive the payments were on my sense of personal integrity," he said later.[7] Nonetheless, he and his wife seemed to enjoy the lavish dinners that an extra twenty-five hundred dollars a month afforded, as well as the luxury trips to Europe and Israel. Following his arrest, Israel continued to pay five thousand dollars a month into a Swiss bank account to compensate his sacrifices to the state and ensure a nest egg in the event of his release.

To the horror of American Jews, Pollard's arrest raised questions about whether the community harbored latent dual loyalties that made them fundamentally untrustworthy. On this basis, the loyalty of any ethnic minority with cultural ties abroad could be called into doubt. Certainly, overseas Chinese have also long had to deal with this stigma. The ties that bind can be an intricate cat's cradle, difficult to disentangle. Pollard expressed guilt "about the propriety of living safely in the materialistically affluent West while the Israelis were sacrificing their hard-won economic gains on the altar of Mars."[8]

His plea bargain stipulated that the prosecution wouldn't pursue a life sentence, leaving it to the judge to be as lenient as he saw fit. Unmollified that Pollard was aiding an ally as opposed to an enemy, and dubious of the pure altruism of his motives, the court nonetheless did condemn him to life imprisonment. Following his arrest, Pollard eerily foreshadowed Larry with his self-rationalization.

"I'll be the first to admit that I broke the law," he told reporter Wolf Blitzer. "But give the kid a little empathy. I thought I was helping Israel and the United States."[9]

Arguing that Israel was a staunch ally, his two years of espionage, he insisted, caused no damage to America, "I could admit to its blatant dishonesty, but never its disloyalty."[10]

Meanwhile, there was the baffling defection of KGB colonel Vitaly Yurchenko. A onetime security officer at the Washington embassy, he went on to become deputy chief of the First Department of the First

Chief Directorate, which supervised Soviet residencies across North America and coordinated international operations against the United States. The CIA ranked him fifth in the KGB hierarchy. In August, while on assignment in Rome, he jumped to the Americans and was flown to the United States for intense debriefings. He left behind his family, hoping to rekindle an affair with the wife of a diplomat who was then posted at the Soviet embassy in Ottawa. To his dismay, she rebuffed him. By November, depressed and regretting the choices he'd made, he walked out of a Georgetown restaurant where he was having dinner with a CIA minder. He turned up at the Soviet compound and was paraded at a press conference where he demanded to be repatriated, claiming the CIA had held him against his will.

Accepted wisdom is that Yurchenko was a legitimate defector. Of course, there lingers suspicion that he could have been under Soviet control the entire time, tasked to spread disinformation and distract American investigators with dross that was, in fact, spun to protect an even more sensitive spy than those who were rolled up on the basis of information he betrayed. This theory gained credence in 1994 when Aldrich Ames, a long-serving CIA officer to whom Yurchenko never alluded, was arrested. However, the consensus is that what Yurchenko divulged was too sensitive to have been discarded on the KGB's initiative.

Nineteen eighty-five was also the year Oleg Gordievsky was exfiltrated from Moscow in a daring mission by MI6. The highest-ranking KGB officer ever recruited by Britain, Gordievsky divulged top-quality intelligence for eleven years. He was acting resident — that is, head of the KGB establishment — at the London embassy when he was suddenly recalled and subjected to intensive interrogation. Unbeknownst at the time, he had been betrayed by Ames. And, in one of those many strange convolutions that characterize spy stories, the lifesaving tip that he was in trouble came from Yurchenko.[11]

Working directly under the nose of the KGB on its home turf, MI6 flawlessly executed the emergency plan that had been devised for just this eventuality. Gordievsky shook his surveillants and made his way out of Moscow.

He was picked up by British agents and smuggled over the Finnish border in a car outfitted with a hidden compartment. Though it marked the termination of a highly successful operation, the nature of his escape was, itself, a major coup and a huge embarrassment to Soviet authorities.

Details Yurchenko supplied were instrumental in exposing Ronald Pelton. Bankrupt and desperate, the fourteen-year veteran of the NSA walked into the Soviet embassy in 1980. Though Yurchenko didn't know Pelton by name, he was able to provide a physical description of him. He also revealed that this spy had exposed an extremely sensitive joint navy–NSA undertaking. Code-named Ivy Bells, it was a daring and ingenious electronic intrusion against a Soviet military communications cable on the bottom of the Sea of Okhotsk. An American submarine had attached a pod that tapped into the cable and recorded all traffic onto a tape. The tape was picked up twice a year for downloading and analysis. The pod was designed to break away if the cable was ever raised — for instance, for maintenance. Because it was attached externally, it left no trace on the cable itself. In 1981, satellite photos showed the Soviet navy converging on the spot where the pod was located. When next the Americans went to recover the tape, the pod had disappeared.

Only with Yurchenko's intelligence was the FBI able to narrow down the possible suspects based on a short list of people who knew about this project. In the fall of 1985, they arrested Pelton. Bob Woodward called him "one of the biggest spies the Russians ever had. He had given away crown-jewel intelligence-gathering operations, not just Ivy Bells. His job in the NSA placed him at the crossroads of information on all communications intelligence operations aimed at the Soviets."[12]

Investigating Pelton was extremely high priority at the Washington Field Office. Personnel were drafted from other squads for the labor-intensive task of manning surveillance teams kept on the suspect twenty-four hours a day. Few agents were working on anything of comparable magnitude, and so they happily put their normal duties on hold. Not so the China squad assigned to Chin. But to avoid tongue-wagging as to why they were exempt from the overtime, they had no choice but to take their shifts. As if it weren't enough to bear the stress of chasing their own spy, they had to maintain the cover that they weren't up to anything special.

Without hard evidence to implicate him, just imprecise allegations from a defector whose every word was called into question when he repudiated his defection, two FBI agents confronted Pelton. Encouraged that he might avoid being charged if he could persuade them of his value as a double agent, Pelton admitted his espionage and was arrested in November. He was tried in Baltimore in June 1986 and received three concurrent life sentences.

A host of lesser spies were also coming to light. Sharon Scranage, a CIA clerk posted in Ghana, was caught giving information to her lover, an agent of the host government. Sentenced to a five-year prison term, she served eighteen months. Samuel Loring Morison, a former navy intelligence analyst, sold sensitive spy satellite photographs to the British publication *Jane's Defence Weekly*. Charged with unauthorized disclosure of military documents, he was given a two-year sentence. A former Northrop engineer, Thomas Patrick Cavanaugh, was sentenced to life in March 1985 after he offered to sell plans for the stealth bomber to FBI agents posing as Soviet spies. In early 1986, Richard Miller, assigned to the Los Angeles area, became the first FBI agent convicted of espionage. He passed classified documents to the KGB in exchange for sex and money. Originally condemned to two consecutive life terms plus fifty years, his sentence was eventually reduced to thirteen years, and he was released in 1994.

But it was another investigation, instigated by Yurchenko, going awry halfway across the country that would most influence the Chin operation.

## Santa Fe, New Mexico, September 23, 1985

Edward Lee Howard joined the CIA in 1980. For his first posting, he was slated to go undercover at the US embassy in Moscow. It wasn't unusual to send novice recruits to Moscow, as the agency was desperate to post

people they were certain hadn't been identified by the KGB. In preparation, he was briefed on the sources and methods at play in the Soviet capital. Among the assets he was to take over was Adolf Tolkachev, a missile
and aviation expert who had been recruited in the late 1970s.

A routine polygraph examination administered in advance of Howard's
departure in 1983 revealed deception around his use of illegal drugs.
Follow-up exams uncovered an incident of theft as well as alcohol abuse,
and he was summarily fired. He ended up getting a job as an economic
analyst with the New Mexico legislature and settled in a suburb outside
Santa Fe.

Yurchenko informed his handlers about a former CIA agent, code-named
Robert, who was expected in Moscow but had suddenly been dismissed.
Robert had met with senior KGB officers in Vienna in September 1984.
Though Yurchenko knew the source only by his code name, Howard
alone fit the profile. He was familiar with the tradecraft employed by the
CIA in the Soviet Union and was able to provide intelligence that identi-
fied undercover officers and agents. Tolkachev's handler was arrested in
Moscow on the way to a meet in June 1985 and was expelled from the
Soviet Union. Tolkachev himself was later picked up, and his execution
would be made public in the fall of 1986.

While he was active, Tolkachev provided decisive information about next-
generation Soviet fighter aircraft and radar systems that was exploited by
American designers to effectively counter their capabilities. He claimed to
be motivated by a deep hatred of the Soviet regime. Initially, he wouldn't
accept any payment. Later, he decided that "he wanted the CIA to pay
him so he could be certain that the agency took him seriously and that
the Americans valued his information." He was uncomfortable with the
hundreds of thousands of rubles he received, anxious not to draw attention to himself. He did purchase a small dacha and an automobile, but
eventually asked the CIA to give some of the money he was earning to the
families of jailed Soviet dissidents.[13]

Though Howard proclaims his innocence in his self-serving autobiog-
raphy, Tolkachev's capture was due to Howard's treason.[14] While refer-

ring to Tolkachev contemptuously as the "[f]ascist scientist," he insists that Ames, who was much higher placed than he, was really responsible.[15] Ames, recruited in 1985 and not arrested until 1994, was unknown during the Howard investigation. However, even sources that postdate the Ames case continue to attribute Tolkachev's demise to Howard.[16]

In September 1985, the FBI placed Howard under surveillance. Keeping up a covert tail in the sparsely populated development where he lived was extremely difficult. Unfamiliar cars were quickly noted by residents, and there were no public spaces, such as shops or cafés, in the vicinity where a stranger could loiter unobtrusively.

It was decided that the most sensible approach was to confront him directly. On Thursday, September 19, Howard accepted an invitation to meet special agents at a Santa Fe hotel. He was uncooperative but agreed to a second meeting the following day; at that point he said he needed to consult a lawyer, which he couldn't do before Monday. The agents gave him the weekend. Surveillance was maintained, but the agents from the Albuquerque Field Office had little, if any, experience tailing a subject who was trained to counter surveillance under the most hostile conditions.

Saturday night, Howard and his wife, Mary, left the house to go for dinner on Canyon Road, a popular stretch of restaurants and art galleries. The watcher in control of Howard's residence failed to see him leave. Hence, on this fateful night, nobody was covering them.

Though the Howards had grown accustomed to being followed and were pretty confident they could pick up the tails, of course they could never be absolutely certain. So despite detecting no watchers upon leaving the restaurant, they implemented their plan. From Canyon Road, Mary behind the wheel, they turned onto Acequia Madre, then south along Garcia Street. After a sharp turn onto Camino Corrales, around a bend that put them momentarily out of view from any pursuing vehicle, Mary slowed up and Ed rolled out of the car into the brush by the side of the road. In his place popped a jack-in-the-box, a crudely fashioned dummy, to mask his exit.

Mary continued back home. Ed, meanwhile, brushed himself off and made his way to a nearby hotel, where he caught a shuttle to the

Albuquerque Sunport. He grabbed the first flight out, to Tucson. From there, he purchased a ticket to Copenhagen via New York and London.

Having missed his departure, the watchers were shocked to see the Howards' car pull into their garage. But the dummy in the passenger seat convinced them that their error had done no harm. By the time Edward was missed, an arrest warrant issued, and all exit points notified to be on the lookout for the fugitive, he was long gone.

From Copenhagen, he proceeded to Helsinki, where he entered the Soviet consulate and sought protection. He resurfaced behind the Iron Curtain in Hungary.

"When Howard flees, you're suddenly worried: What if Chin realizes we're on to him?" explains Magers. "Will he disappear? We had this one problem losing a guy; having a second is just a real disaster."[17]

Fear of failure is the leading excuse for inaction. Fear of repeating a highly publicized failure will jolt-start you right into action.

*Washington, DC, October 1985*

Eagle Claw was beginning to look like one of those cases — there are lots of them — that go unsolved forever. They're worked, increasingly sporadically, over the years until filed away as dormant. Not a failure . . . officially. Only in the minds of those haunted by the translucent sight of the spy's face, drifting away higher like a kite that's slipped its string, the disembodied sound of his voice, the certainty of his crimes, growing ever fainter.

When it comes to espionage, the things you know don't necessarily equate with what you can prove. And vice versa. Truth could be cover. Information could be disinformation. Agents might be doubles. Doubles triples. Measures could be counters. Reality is a distorted muddle, clarity rendered opaque by reflections. Investigators shuffle the paradoxes in search of a vague consistency around which to build a coherent narrative. They know that when grasping at air, their hands appear empty, but are actually full of molecules.

Senior management at headquarters wasn't prepared to give up, but was uncertain about making a definitive move. Benign monitoring was a safe enough strategy. In the opinion of the field agents who'd been doing nothing but for months, it wouldn't result in any new revelations.

In the wake of the Howard debacle, headquarters' ambivalent command was the paradoxical "Don't lose him and don't get made." Somewhere along the line, if you carry on observing a target long enough, you'll end up in a position where that very choice is unavoidable. Either lock-step him or drop off. It's a stalemate, like teetering halfway across a crumbling swing-bridge over a deadly drop. Do you dash ahead or slowly retreat?

Run down the checklist of conventional means for trapping a spy, and it becomes evident that none applied vis-à-vis Larry. You'd like to catch him red-handed in possession of a classified document or, even better, in the act of handing it over to a Chinese officer. Well, he didn't have the opportunity to get his hands on classified documents anymore. You'd like to witness a covert meeting, but you couldn't hope for that without ensuring infallible round-the-clock surveillance, for which the necessary resources couldn't be applied indefinitely. Besides which, he's now a private citizen, free to travel wherever, so any such meets are probably happening in China where he's beyond reach. More than two years of wiretapping hadn't provided any substantive indication of espionage, nor had it led to the identification of a contact who might be recruited to run against him. You could do a forensic accounting of his finances. This becomes increasingly complex as time passes, however; even if you can ascertain a discrepancy between an individual's declared income and assets, it would be next to impossible to trace the origin of that discrepancy to an act of espionage. The best you could hope might be to propose a connection between espionage and money. *Propose*, which is not to say *prove*.

There remained just one gambit for catching Larry Chin: to confront him directly and coax out a confession.

As PLANESMAN's exfiltration opened a window of opportunity, the FBI feared another force rushing headlong to slam it shut: the possibility that Larry would be warned about the defection.

Now, this isn't *necessarily* going to happen. In the first place, there's the couple of weeks during which PLANESMAN is absent on leave. Nothing is amiss until he fails to show up to work. In the second, PLANESMAN had no authorized knowledge of Larry. Nevertheless, being that he was a member of the section running him, a conservative damage assessment argues in favor of assuming the widest possible breach. Taken to the extreme, Public Security would be compelled to warn all human sources run out of this directorate.

"If you assume a defection, they're going to tell Larry to get out of Dodge," insists Moore, careful as ever to qualify any suggestion of a human source. "If we're going to do something, it has to be before Larry leaves the country for good. Suddenly, it's expedient to consider arresting Larry Chin. Only, you can't arrest Chin until you have a provable case against him."[18]

### New York, October 1985

The method by which an agent communicates with his handler need not be terribly sophisticated so long as it is sufficiently inconspicuous and reliable. It was believed that Larry's communications with China ran one way, initiated by him. When he had something to pass over, he posted an innocuous letter to an accommodation address in Hong Kong. A predetermined line — something that wouldn't cause alarm in the event the letter was intercepted, like, "My wife has recovered from the flu and is feeling better" — would signal that he wanted a meet, which would then occur as previously arranged. Because he had to allow several days before the letter was delivered, this method was suitable only for routine exchanges.

Should Larry have something critical to deliver, he had a phone number to call in Toronto. A similarly innocent exchange of greetings could trigger a meet with minimal delay.

What neither of these avenues allowed for was an urgent message from Beijing to reach him. In all the time that the bureau had mail covers in effect, no incoming letters originating from the overseas accommodation address were observed. Nor did the wiretaps catch a hint of double entendres coming in.

PLANESMAN identified a Public Security sleeper who was established in
New York City for the purpose of being available to Larry in the event of
an emergency. A sleeper is a deep cover agent who is assigned to take up
residence and establish a normal life in a target country, discreetly awaiting activation. A sleeper is given a very specific, often onetime, assignment. While the sleeper is usually self-supporting, the time and effort
devoted to training and preparing him represent a significant investment,
indicative of the high priority of that exclusive mission. The Chinese are
big believers in preparing for problems before they arise. Better to have
a hundred resources in place and never call upon them than to need one
and realize it's nonexistent.

Mark Cheung spent at least a decade building his legend as a Roman
Catholic priest at parishes in Hong Kong and around the South Pacific
before settling at the Church of the Transfiguration on Mott Street in the
heart of Chinatown. Larry could access him anytime by appearing at the
confessional. An enduring mystery is whether Cheung also had the means
to get urgent communiqués to him.

In terms of moving forward with the plan to interview Larry, of course,
the assumption had to be that China could signal him if it believed he was
in imminent danger.

Once he was identified, Cheung was placed under surveillance. Soon
after the defection of the low-ranking Public Security officer to the
British, Cheung up and left New York for Hong Kong. This proved to
be a coincidence, as it subsequently became clear that Cheung had simply
completed his tour. This fact alone indicates that Chin had a succession
of contacts; moreover, it is logical to assume that Cheung was replaced
by someone who has gone undetected. Otherwise, one must consider the
ironic possibility that Chin was without an emergency outlet on the one
occasion it may have served him.

Two New York special agents were dispatched to Hong Kong to interview Cheung. Though he was uncooperative, Cheung did meet with them on three separate occasions, the first time on the morning after Chin was arrested. He likely felt he had no alternative and hoped to stall for time. After the third meeting, despite being on a Special Branch watch list, he managed to slip across the strait and onto the mainland, from whence he has never reappeared. Rumor has it that his impersonation of a priest was a total fraud and that he has settled down with his wife and children in Shanghai.[19]

### Langley, Virginia, Fall 1985

Were it not for the armed guards, the high razor-wire fencing, and the isolation of the surrounding wooded area, CIA headquarters at Langley, just across the Potomac from the District, could pass for a sprawling university campus. But, because of those unmistakable features, it carries the hushed whisper of something important and sinister going on.

Here — and only here — were things ordered as the CIA would have the world. Here, everybody was presumed to share common cause. Gray midweight suits, white shirts, and muted ties were the uniform. All that was missing from an earlier generation were the fedoras. And while you could no longer take it for granted that a woman was a secretary, the back-slapping bonhomie of an Ivy League fraternity prevailed. Still, if you observed closely, you noticed the frightened shiftiness of people under siege. People who were confused because the rest of the world wouldn't conform and who resented how that recalcitrance forced them to behave cruelly.

Tom Carson dreaded the regular meetings at Langley. Anticipating the frustration tied him up in knots before he even left his home on those mornings. He took exception to the way the sentries examined his badge and looked him over disdainfully.

For two years now, Carson had been consumed by a case that threatened grave consequences for national security, yet he'd gotten practically nowhere. The euphoria of pinpointing the penetration had been sadistically punctured by the dull blade of the bureaucracy. His energy and desire were being sapped by the constant struggle just to get anything done.

The Langley confabs were rancorous, resembling tripartite arms control summits among hostile and wary adversaries more than discussions between separate organs in the same government. Tripartite instead of bilateral — in the minds of the field participants, at any rate — because the bureau's headquarters contingent sometimes acted like delegates representing a separate interest.

The junior man in the room, Carson was held in check by his rank. He was invited for his knowledge of the details. He was also the one with the most personal investment. His workmanlike style was deceptive, making him appear more tentative than assertive. In truth, it was just that he was methodical and, unlike some lesser agents, more patient at assembling and assimilating details. This didn't make him any less eager about going after Larry.

The agency spooks had a way of hustling into a conference room in formation, carrying thick accordion files that they never opened, sitting down as one, and tapping their fingers on the desk as if beating out the seconds before they could dash out to attend to far more urgent affairs. They looked at you with their eyes half rolled upward to let you know that, if only you understood what they knew but could never tell, you'd come on side.

Carson resented the agency's reluctance to share openly. He didn't appreciate the condescension or the implication that he was untrustworthy. Especially given that the spy they were discussing was a full-bore penetration of their service, not his.

"I personally doubted that the CIA was giving us everything. To this day, I have never seen all the details of their internal investigation," he recalls.[20]

Speaking from a headquarters perspective, Magers suggests, "Ultimately, I think the agency gave us everything they had. In the initial stages, I wasn't as confident. Some of the stuff did come out piecemeal. In the end, it was a pretty good working relationship."[21]

The most sensitive people in the room were the liaison officers from both sides. Charged with nurturing relations between the agencies, they were referees responsible for assuring sportsmanlike conduct. They viewed themselves as big-picture guys, surveying the totality of the relationship from the high ground, assuring case officers in the valley below that no single skirmish superseded the amalgam of all the cooperative endeavors occurring on other fronts. They cringed whenever decorum was breached.

Some of the worst acrimony surfaced once the bureau was informed that PLANESMAN had safely reached the United States. Schiffer reasoned that the agency had no further excuses for resisting efforts to pursue the investigation and, ultimately, to prosecute Chin. However, it continued to vehemently object to the prospect of bringing a case to court.

The CIA argued that, since Larry had given up his clearance four years ago, the problem of the penetration had, in effect, been solved. Prosecuting him for his crimes might bring fleeting satisfaction — like the short-lived joy of a spoiled child with too many Christmas presents to open — but, long view, it would end up doing more harm than good.

The agency's reasoning was twofold. First, it was concerned that the judge might require that the defense — and hence the accused — be granted access to classified information in order to prepare its case. The defense would have the opportunity to ask all kinds of unpredictable and, who could tell, embarrassing questions of government personnel. It could press hard for disclosure of the source, putting witnesses over whom the agency had no control — that is to say, FBI agents — in an awkward position. Never underestimate the capacity of an honest person to say the wrong thing under oath.

Which speaks to the second argument: that completing a thorough damage assessment was far more urgent than securing a conviction. Punishing Larry, it argued, was a little like locking the barn door after the horse had escaped. The CIA still had no idea what he had compromised. Better to use the threat of prosecution to induce him to cooperate and, perhaps, reverse some of the harm he'd done.

The bureau countered that the two were not mutually exclusive. Once convicted, a number of incentives could be employed to elicit his cooperation — lenience in sentencing, being housed in a lower-security facility with more privileges, or even the prospect of early parole.

The FBI conceded that PLANESMAN was to be shielded from testifying. Unable to refute the agency's contention that his life was in grave peril, it simply capitulated on this point. A survey of China hands reveals but a single instance when China dispatched an agent to perform wet ops, as assassination plots are dubbed. However, none was able to attribute any actual overseas execution to China's security service. Regardless, in an instance where the consequences involved life and death, all parties were agreed to err on the side of caution.

Besides, Schiffer argues, "There's a good chance getting PLANESMAN on the stand wouldn't help anyway, because all he'd be able to do was validate the circumstantial information we'd already gathered."[22]

The strategy the FBI proposed — interviewing Larry — would safeguard any reference to a human source. Beyond that, it simply wasn't buying into the CIA's objections against going to trial under any circumstances.

Moore explains it along personal lines: "Larry Chin penetrated US intelligence. He wasn't a file clerk. This was someone you invited in and gave special access, who has betrayed you. The counterintelligence people take this very seriously and will go to the ends of the earth to get you. They voiced great opposition to the notion he could just walk away."[23]

## Washington, DC, October 1985

Those working the Chin case were advised when PLANESMAN's exfiltration was imminent. Afraid this might trigger Larry's flight, time pressures immediately dialed up to intense and preparations for an interview were begun.

Carson's worst fears about outside interference were coming horribly true. He had been tenacious in uncovering the identity of the spy and meticulous in assimilating every ensuing detail that was accumulated. Now that the climax was at hand, theories on how best to proceed were heaped onto his growing weight of insecurity, adding to the pressure he'd borne these past two years.

There's a particular pride law enforcement officers take in being the individual who stands between the bad guy and escape. Out of the bureaucratic tangle that ensnares any major investigation, with countless approvals preceding any initiative, they dream of that moment when they will emerge like Gary Cooper at *High Noon* to right the wrong and enforce justice. It wasn't just the federal government or the FBI that caught you, Mr. Chin, it was me, Special Agent Tom Carson.

Those on the criminal side experienced this tall-in-the-saddle feeling with some regularity. In counterintelligence, it was a real rarity. Many work an entire career without catching *their* spy. Even those responsible for running effective cases and recruiting worthwhile sources often never investigate, let alone arrest, a genuine spy. Now Carson had his arms extended, his fingertips just grazing the back of Larry's collar. He anticipated the satisfaction of confronting Chin, of clawing his way out from under this case. Of confirming what he'd known for so long — that Larry was a Chinese agent — and of learning the full extent of his treachery. To hear it straight from Larry himself. Of being able to sleep easy again without troubled thoughts about Larry Chin and the debilitating doubts about whether this journey he'd undertaken with such trepidation would end in triumph or disaster.

It goes without saying that the case agent is responsible for interviewing the subject of his investigation when the time comes. Logic argues that the officer most deeply immersed in the facts is best equipped to engage the subject in dialogue, pick apart lies, and challenge inconsistencies. To Carson's surprise, his suitability to conduct the interview was called into question.

An enemy is an enemy, and you pretty much concede his intent to do you harm. It's the wounds inflicted by your own side that are the most searing. It was with medieval cruelty that Carson, in particular, fell under the scalding oil of internal politics.

Tom had never busted a spy, it was whispered in some circles at headquarters. Larry was a hardened operator. Day after day after day, he'd looked the very pros he'd been betraying straight in the eye without a twitch or a blush. He'd beaten the poly. Was Tom up to that, they wondered aloud. The stakes were too high to take any chances.

How many spies had they caught? Carson countered.

Agents at Washington Field would tolerate no interference in tactical decisions. Their case, their interview, their decision on who was best qualified to perform the interview. Schiffer would fight this one to the death.

Within intelligence services, there are two distinct sensibilities — the bureaucratic and the operational — that square off toe-to-toe in an unsteady logroll. Each side eyeballs the other with contempt and fear. Contempt brought on by a sense of superiority; fear due to the sneaking suspicion of slipping into an inferior position. The field agents see themselves as the vigorous blood and guts being unnecessarily obstructed by the bureaucrats, spongy, yellow lipids that sludge the entire system.

Yet the headquarters types could argue with just cause that their world was the more ruthless. The bureaucrats were gougers and biters. Their jobs had little connection with *the* job. Their profession was their career, and they scrambled from position to position for advantage, like rock climbers feeling for the securest grip to the summit. They would short-rope a colleague for strategic advantage, cutting loose whoever threatened to pull them back. And never, never look down.

Carson reacted with hurt. After all he'd put into pursuing Larry, to have colleagues, people he knew and whom he trusted knew him, question his ability. Then he got angry. Then he began to sweat with uncertainty. Did they see him in ways he'd managed to conceal from himself?

He was a lifelong street agent. He'd been down and back the rough blocks. Who had anything on him?

He had spent about as much time on the China squad as anybody else. And nobody knew Larry better than he did. Nobody had the multitude of cross-referenced facts at their disposal. He knew where Larry'd been and when. He knew his contacts. His predilections and peccadilloes.

Moreover, he'd earned it. He hadn't wanted the case in the first place. But he'd taken it. He'd fevered over it. Lived it when others would have dropped it. Countless times, Larry could have gotten away from him — gotten away with it — but Carson caught every muffled echo hinting at espionage like a shark picking up the faint electric currents of a distant fish's death throes.

Objectively, selecting the best interviewers was crucial to the success of the interview strategy. Those who didn't think Carson was the right man for the job argued that the facts could be mastered by anyone. More critical was the less tangible factor of creating a psychological dovetail between Larry and the interviewer.

One of the resources assigned to the case was an analyst from the Behavioral Science Unit (BSU) based at the FBI training academy at Quantico. The practice of building psychological profiles of criminals began in the late 1970s and quickly became popular, especially for investigations of serial murderers and rapists, where behavioral quirks and patterns identifiable at the crime scene could reveal key indicators about the offender's makeup. The unit's work was popularized in *The Silence of the Lambs* and a series of books by John Douglas, the agent who headed it up and was largely responsible for refining its methodology and applying it to catch some of America's most notorious offenders.

There were those, however, who thought the *BS* in *BSU* was less an unfortunate quirk of acronym than an accurate description of its contributions (Douglas admitted that it was rechristened the Investigative Support Unit to remove the offending initials). Not surprisingly, Carson was scornful of the behaviorist's input, suggesting that he was just somebody the field office tolerated to humor headquarters. "He didn't tell us a single thing we didn't already know."[24]

The profiler reviewed all the material that related to Larry's character in order to flesh out a sketch that would help determine the composition of the ideal interview team. In his first book, *Mindhunter*, Douglas addressed the importance of "casting" interrogators: "My preference is usually for someone a little older and more authoritative than the subject, a sharp dresser with a commanding appearance, someone who can be friendly and outgoing and make the subject relax, but become absolutely serious and directed as soon as circumstances call for it."[25]

With the strategy decided, tactics became the subject of a heated debate between headquarters and the field.

"We went into the interview confident we had the right guy, but knowing that unless we get a confession, we haven't got a case," Schiffer says, defining the dilemma. "According to PLANESMAN, the asset had passed over secret information, but what the Chinese take to be secret could have been lifted from the newspapers. We didn't have identifiable secret material for prosecutorial purposes."[26]

"With a successful interview, we expected to have a successful prosecution," says Magers. "Without, we may not have a prosecution at all. Everything depended on a good interview."[27]

Opinions differed on how best to achieve this, creating a huge rift between the field and headquarters. The former advocated going in for a onetime confrontation — more interrogation than interview, truth be told — while the latter argued for the slower process of establishing *guanxi*, building rapport with Larry over the course of several sessions lasting days. Their proposal was to appeal for Larry's cooperation as a friend, rather than browbeating him as an adversary.

The idea was to appropriate the Chinese approach for the Americans' purposes.

"China's intelligence is much more dominated by its social behavior system than by tradecraft," Moore explains. "The way they look at it, it isn't an intelligence relationship per se, but a social relationship with an intelligence dimension."[28]

Those in the field office strongly opposed this strategy. In the first instance, they contended, *guanxi* was no more liable to succeed than the direct-confrontation approach. Moreover, any attempt at developing a relationship was likely to drag on for so long — and it *would* drag on, since any sign of impatience threatened to make Larry suspicious — there was at least a possibility that news of PLANESMAN's defection would reach Larry in the interim and he'd suddenly disappear, whether via the Cheung channel or some as-yet-undiscovered escape route.

Remember Edward Lee Howard, they chided.

Confident they had a guilty man in their sights, they were sure the best chance for arresting Chin was to surprise him with the information at hand. Under most circumstances, a guilty man will dig himself deeper in before he'll pull himself out.

"*Guanxi* is effective in recruiting a source," allows Carson, "but for confronting a suspect it would have been a disaster. Chin was too smart, he'd have ripped those people to pieces."

Headquarters countered that you couldn't approach Larry with the same attitude as a Westerner, who is culturally predisposed to defend his innocence when slapped with an accusation. Chinese culture demands that he uphold his face or dignity, which is quite a different response.

Carson scoffs, "I'm not a psychologist, I'm not a Sinophile. I think most all of us are the same. Now, there are some cultural specifics on the fringe you might use. Bruce Carlson and George Liu alerted us to the dos and don'ts. In my opinion, that's secondary to knowing him as a person."[29]

Mark Johnson is more direct. "I thought headquarters didn't have a clue."[30]

In my discussions with Moore, he never raised this conflict directly. He did, however, allude to a distinct disadvantage to confronting Larry: "It's all psychological, it's all a bluff. Because if he doesn't confess to espionage, there's no fallback position."[31]

Each side's preferred approach is arguable on merit. It is also important to keep in mind that, notwithstanding ego and ambition, all those involved shared a common goal and were championing what they sincerely believed was the best method to achieve it.

But Carson is uncompromising. "You'd have had a riot at Washington Field over that. We weren't going to do it. Most everyone would have quit the squad, transferred someplace else."

The friction between headquarters and the field was sending fiery sparks dangerously close to a powder keg.

"We were like Fort Apache surrounded by people who didn't know the lay of the land," he goes on.[32]

Carson, Schiffer, and Johnson took to jogging together daily. Schiffer broke out in hives. Carson wasn't sleeping.

None of this had anything to do with the consequences of China's penetration of American intelligence. The spy had become disconnected from the spying. The imperative to catch the spy hovered aloft within its own bubble.

Finally, it was decided that those in the field were going to do it their way. Had Schiffer expected a gracious *Give it your best shot, we'll back you up no matter what* out of headquarters, he was sorely disappointed. He hadn't. He and his men were experienced and understood that any victory over bureaucratic rivals bred resentment. The consolation prize won by those who'd opposed the direct interview was to be shielded from blame should things go sour.

*You'd better not screw up* was the concession of defeat issued by ranking headquarters officers.

In preparation, very realistic mock interviews were staged employing different combinations of interviewers. Bruce Carlson and George Liu, the translators most familiar with Larry's thinking, attitudes, and ways of turning a phrase, alternated in his role. They were isolated from the preparations undertaken by the prospective interviewers. The only guideline they were given was to respond exactly as they believed Larry would react under the circumstances. Since each man had a slightly different interpretation of Larry's character, using two different people in the role gave the interviewers more variation on what they should expect and provided them the opportunity to devise more permutations on their follow-ups.

These role-playing sessions were extremely successful at simulating the stress of the real situation. Enclosed in the confines of a Spartan interview room, the hum of the fluorescent lights just audible enough to scratch everyone's nerves, the prospective interrogators matched wits against the imitation Chins. The advantage in a pretend scenario clearly went to Carlson and Liu, who could play Larry as quick-witted and audacious, slippery and glib, malevolently uncooperative, or deliberately aggressive.

Besides demonstrating how Larry might behave, they elicited realistic performances from the interviewers. The sessions were observed by other members of the squad and mercilessly critiqued. This was not the time to spare feelings, but to candidly evaluate whether the interview team could be expected to bring off a successful outcome.

"There's nothing more embarrassing or demeaning than having to perform in front of your peers," allows Schiffer, who was among the constant observers.[33]

Preparation enhances performance; it does not eliminate improvisation. However well Liu and Carlson got to know Larry, they had only ever made his acquaintance from a distance. However convincingly each pretended to be Larry, the best they could do was suppose his reactions to different scenarios.

For weeks, that's what they did. To the point at which, according to Johnson, "The real interview felt very comfortable thanks to the role-playing. It seemed very natural, as if I'd done it before."[34]

Customarily, interviews are conducted by two officers. While the lead interrogator is engaging the subject, posing questions, the other can concentrate on taking accurate notes. It also ensures the subject is outnumbered, but not so overwhelmed as to be unduly intimidated. In the event of a dispute in court over what was said, the officers can reinforce each other's testimony, giving added weight to their version.

It was up to Schiffer to select the interview team. His first choice was Rudy Guerin. He was acknowledged to be the best interviewer on the squad (an opinion, by the way, that is voiced independently by Carson as well[35]). A nine-year veteran at the time, Guerin had earned a reputation as a "door opener." Outgoing and personable, he had the salesman's enthusiastic handshake and interest in starting conversations. Accompanying the smile was a firmness in the jaw that offset his friendliness with impassivity. He favored carefully tailored suits and wore his hair just a bit shorter than average, hinting at authority without the fanaticism implied by a buzz cut. If he had any handicap it was that his hair was a bright red and made him appear to be about twenty-two. Despite the look of exaggerated youthfulness, he had established a solid reputation in China operations. He eventually rose through the ranks, recently retiring as chief, East Asia Section, Counter-Intelligence Division, at headquarters.

Guerin had an appreciation for Chinese culture and how to appeal most effectively to Chinese subjects. He was a successful source recruiter, which in itself is a strong indicator of an agent's interpersonal skills. Relying on bluster to move Chin to talk could backfire and, instead, lead him to shut down, when their only hope was to persuade him to open up. Guerin had the skills to finesse the conversation to the end they desired.

To his detriment, he hadn't participated in the investigation, and so lacked the intimate grasp of the details that would be advantageous in a lead interrogator. Asked whom he preferred to be teamed with, Guerin took for granted he should go with Carson.

Over the course of several mock interviews, however, Schiffer became convinced that Carson wouldn't work out. He was stiff, nervous. Imagining himself facing the man he'd been obsessed with for so long, he was so anxious to extract the truth that he squirmed with discomfort. The discomfort, in turn, made him more awkward because the feeling was so abnormal. Confronting suspects was nothing new to him. The more uncomfortable he felt, the more he concentrated on that, the less he focused on the interview. The more attention he was compelled to pay himself, the less he spent on Chin.

Schiffer, who, as noted above, is highly complimentary toward Carson, concedes, "It became apparent that he was not the right individual for the interview. He knew the case so well, he couldn't step back and be the interrogator. He simply wasn't going to do well in that role."[36]

If Carson was to be replaced, Rudy wanted to team with his regular partner, Terry Roth, with whom he had built an effective rhythm.

Despite having barely two years on the China squad, Roth was the most seasoned of all the agents, with more than fifteen years' service, most of it spent on the criminal side in several offices around Alabama. His hair already turning to gray, Roth looked like the most senior man, which would prove to be to the team's advantage. It was expected that Larry would naturally defer to him, assuming he held the highest rank.

Roth has a relaxed bearing, but with blue steel in his eyes that announces he should not be underestimated. He comes across forthrightly, but with the proviso that he expects the same in return. Schiffer liked it that Roth was familiar, from his extensive experience on the criminal side, with the requirements to meet stringent evidentiary standards. He would recognize when they had enough to make an arrest stick in court.

"Bottom line, you pick who you think is going to conduct the best interview. That's Rudy, along with Terry, both of whom had tremendous backgrounds on the street," Schiffer says. "When it became obvious that mastering all the details of the case was so burdensome that it was going to distract from the conversation, we decided that we needed to have a third in the room — that was Mark Johnson, who was most in command of the facts."[37]

Johnson, Carson's handpicked partner, was a hard charger who'd swoop in on a case like a caped avenger. Tall and lean, with a mop of sandy brown hair and the trim mustache favored by many policemen, Johnson had a tendency to lean toward you when speaking in a way that might suggest either intimacy or intimidation. He could be brazen to the point of disrespectful. His disgust for anyone who'd dare commit treason against his country precluded him from displaying the deference that might appeal to an older Chinese man like Larry.

Mark wasn't there to participate in some cultural sensitivity pageant. He was there to capture a criminal. He barreled straight ahead, oblivious to promising detours. His professional view was uncluttered by abstraction. He lacked sympathy with adversaries, preferring to keep the lines clean. He didn't empathize with their transgressions, nor would he pretend to.

Instead, he drove at them with an unrelenting antagonism that might defeat them, but not win them over.

"Mark's the kind of guy who can piss you off within about sixty seconds of meeting," says one.

Johnson, Schiffer was convinced, couldn't create the essential rapport with Larry. Indeed, some feared that his impetuousness might not only alienate Chin but also cause Mark himself to blurt out the wrong thing. Whether he ought to participate was the subject of considerable debate among case supervisors. His knowledge of the case, however, was indispensable. There wasn't time enough to get anyone else up to his speed on the file. Rudy would be the guy to win Larry's confidence, reinforced by Terry, with Mark able to call up the facts that would (hopefully) make him feel helpless.

Admitting it was unorthodox, Schiffer saw how having three agents present solved more problems than it posed. Guerin and Johnson would lead the questioning. Roth would stay in contact with the Justice Department officials and senior managers who would be nearby in a command post while the interview was in progress. He could excuse himself to the telephone without ever causing a situation in which one agent would be alone with Chin. Although Schiffer never said it aloud, he also liked the idea of a third man balancing off Johnson.

The wisdom of his decision was called into question. Could it prove detrimental at trial? In fact, the defense would claim that it was an intimidation tactic.

In truth it wasn't.


One final preparatory step was to obtain a search warrant for Larry's apartment. The bureau intended to carry out the search regardless of Chin's response when the agents went knocking. If he refused to speak to them, they would slap him with the warrant and give the residence a thorough going-over. If he spoke to them but was less than forthcoming, the warrant would be brandished as a tool to induce his cooperation. And if he cooperated, the search would be conducted in order to seize any evidence that confirmed the FBI's contentions.

This is the point at which the Department of Justice was brought into the case. The Internal Security Section was responsible for handling the prosecution of all espionage suspects. The government's lawyers agreed there was substance to the allegation. Although it isn't Justice's role to counsel the FBI on tactics, once apprised of where the case stood, it supported proceeding with an interview.

Justice advised Joseph Aronica, chief of the Criminal Division in the US Attorney's Office for the Eastern District of Virginia, which was the jurisdiction covering Alexandria, Larry's place of residence and where the interview would be conducted. With the promise of a high-profile, and potentially controversial, trial, Aronica elected to handle it himself.

Because Chin was to be interviewed in his home, it was defined as a noncustodial interview. That is to say, Chin was explicitly *not* under arrest. That fact was to be made very clear to him. Accordingly, the agents were not obliged to formally advise him of his rights. These conditions were enunciated to establish a suitable legal framework in order to forestall defense efforts to suppress whatever might be elicited from Larry. A confession obtained from an individual in custody who has not been properly advised of his rights is inadmissible in court. However, a suspect need not be advised of his rights until such time as he is being placed under arrest.

The legalities were critical.

Says Aronica, "A person can have the feeling of being in custody without actually being placed under arrest. He was at home, he could have said he didn't want to talk."[38]

Advice of rights is a rather delicate procedure in that it sets a confrontational tone. Once you tell a suspect that he has the right to an attorney, he begins to think that maybe he needs one. Once you tell him he has the right to remain silent and that whatever he says can be used against him, he doubts the wisdom of speaking. It immediately puts the subject on guard and discourages efforts at building trust. Intelligence officers, more accustomed to recruiting sources than arresting criminals, prefer conversing without the threat of arrest whenever a subject will consent.

The decision to answer questions was entirely Larry's. If at any time he wanted the agents to leave, they were to comply. If at any time he insisted on having an attorney present, the interview was to be terminated.

To further reinforce that the agents did not have Larry in custody during the interview, Aronica expressly forbade them from placing him under arrest prior to consulting with him. Thus, by absolving them of the decision to arrest and reserving the power for himself, Aronica put the agents at a further remove from taking Chin into custody.

# — 6 —

# A Very Long Story

*Alexandria, Virginia, November 22, 1985*
Washington is a jumble of one-way streets converging on intricate traffic circles, all enclosed in a single ring road connecting to routes through the Virginia and Maryland suburbs. Since a majority of the civil servants who make up the bulk of the District's workforce live in the suburbs and devise their schedules around beating traffic, *rush hour* becomes a euphemism for "all-day congestion." A major inconvenience to those with places to go.

The Plymouth, which looked so much like an unmarked police car it might as well have been outfitted with roof lights and decals, shook slightly to the skipped beats of its mistimed engine. Piece of shit, thought the three men inside. It was just past three thirty and they were inching west toward the freeway from the Washington Field Office on 4th Street, Southeast.

Like commuters in a hurry, Special Agents Guerin, Roth, and Johnson were swiveling their heads, craning to find that phantom lane where the cars glide along unimpeded. Guerin rode the brake while his passengers squeezed their toes down on imaginary gas pedals.

Surveillance set up at the Watergate had confirmed Larry was currently inside Building 1, Apartment 1719, the condominium that was intended to be his office, but in which he had been living since his latest marital crisis.

He was probably in for the night, the agents surmised. But what if this was the odd occasion when he took it into his head to catch a movie? They had to get there. Guerin stomped the gas, jerking the car up a few inches into the exhaust of the car ahead, quickly flattening the brake.

They hardly spoke. Each man had turned inward, concentrated on taming the snarling rat of tension that scratched and clawed through the maze of his intestines. During the weeks of rehearsing, they'd devised a plausible rejoinder for every contingency they or their many colleagues who'd had a hand in the preparation could conceive. Now they had to divert their thoughts from last-minute second-guessing or conjuring up some oddball chance they'd overlooked.

More than two years of investigative efforts were going to climax this evening. One way or another.

Eyes from up high were on them. They felt the sun-hot laser boring into the backs of their necks.

Make the case, they'd been instructed. Lurking beneath this active command was the more threatening, if passive, proviso: Don't fuck up.

Supervisors, senior officers, Justice Department officials, and lawyers were on standby to scrutinize the work being done by the agents in almost real time. This is our guy. Make the case.

Fucking office boys. What did Kurtz call them in *Apocalypse Now?* Grocery clerks. Grocery clerks with authority.

Traffic thinned out once the agents turned south onto I-395 into Virginia.

Alexandria is a genteel community to which government workers have fled the decay and crime that encircles them in their office sanctuaries in the District. It's a neat refuge, a place where you can stroll aimlessly at night with little fear of making a wrong turn into the middle of a housing project. Menacing panhandlers don't crowd the streets of the city center, a stretch of restaurants and boutiques that has preserved the distinct charm of the small-town South. You'd let your kids walk home alone from school if you lived somewhere like this.

Guerin turned off Yoakum into the main driveway to the Watergate. Residents are shielded from unexpected visitors by a guard post. All callers must identify themselves and whom they are coming to see. The guard then calls ahead for authorization to admit them and issues a numbered visitor pass. A quick flash of the badge and the agents dispensed with these formalities.

Each building is further protected by an intercom entry system, so that the visitor must be buzzed in at the front door. Because the bureau had secured access to another apartment in the building for use as a temporary command post, the agents had a card-key, which would allow them to enter the premises unannounced. Seemingly by preordination, every finely honed plan has some unforeseeable glitch built in. After swiping the card-key through the slot, there was no reassuring click of the latch releasing. The three men uttered a collective curse and tried again. The lock held securely.

A couple of women, dressed in the modest head scarves of pious Muslims, were sitting in the lobby with their young children. Johnson tapped on the glass, and a smiling little five-year-old boy bounded over and let the men in without a second thought.

Johnson chuckles, "An unknown hero of American intelligence."[1]

At 4:25 PM, Chin answered an unexpected knock at his door.


*Foggy Bottom, November 22, 1985*

The State Department is located at the opposite end of DC from Washington Field, just off the western edge of the National Mall, nearby the Lincoln Memorial, barely blocks from the White House.

The makers of foreign policy and practitioners of diplomacy may espouse a realpolitik outlook, but they nonetheless inhabit a world of careful civility, strict protocol, and ornate facades. Preferring their tea served in delicate china cups, they bear little esteem for the intelligence bulls rampaging through their shop.

There persists a vestige of the quaint notion that gentlemen don't read one another's mail, that they do more harm than good when they conspire to steal one another's secrets. They prefer to debate. They agree to disagree when they must, and they negotiate to mutual advantage when they can. Above all else, though you may be called upon to upbraid in private, you do not humiliate in public. If you are backed into a corner and forced to mete out punishment for some transgression you absolutely cannot ignore, you do so without fanfare.

America's foreign relations are a subtle and dense, frequently unpalatable stew of carrots and sticks, incentives and deterrents, assurance and intimidation, trade and embargo, checks and balances. Every action is linked — and not always with evident reason — to a reaction.

Relations with China were especially delicate. When Mao Zedong's Communists emerged victorious over Chiang Kai-shek's Nationalist government, the United States stood staunchly against the new regime and steadfastly recognized Chiang as the legitimate leader of all China, reduced though he was to ruling from the outpost on Taiwan where he'd taken refuge. Thus was the fiction that Taiwan represented the Chinese of the mainland perpetuated and the legitimacy of the People's Republic denied. Thus did Taiwan occupy the permanent China seat on the United Nations Security Council for more than two decades. Thus was the Communist regime enraged, insisting that Taiwan was but a province of China and the Guomindang nothing but a rebellious faction staging what amounted to an illegal occupation. Any state that supported Taiwan was interfering in its internal affairs. Only America's pledge to intervene should China take military action to seize the island kept Mao at bay.

In 1970, the United States initiated the first tentative — and secret — steps toward recognizing the existence of the People's Republic and acknowledging its de facto status as the sovereign authority over China, excluding Taiwan. The effort turned out to be a triumph for President Nixon and for Chairman Mao. For the Chinese, relations meant access to long-sought Western technology; for the Americans, access to a gargantuan market. To both, it promised a formidable counterweight to the menacing Soviet Union. Still mired in Vietnam, Nixon was anxious to engage China as a partner in its search for an honorable exit strategy. He also hoped they could influence the North Koreans to ease tensions on the peninsula where American and Chinese armed forces had engaged in brutal combat less than two decades before and where troops remained on constant high alert. By 1979, formal diplomatic missions were exchanged and the US withdrew its opposition to the People's Republic taking the

China seat as a permanent member of the UN Security Council and its rightful place at the table with the most powerful states on earth.

Years of shrewd high-stakes diplomacy could be undone by some ill-timed spy buffoonery. The State Department was brokering trade in the billions of dollars, nurturing alliances, and neutralizing foes. What good comes of a spy scandal?

Though its mystique often has the effect of exaggerating its importance in the popular imagination, intelligence is usually jousted off to the periphery by higher priorities, be they economic or diplomatic. A pending trade agreement trumps a prospective intelligence scandal every time. The ephemeral promise that concessions may be forthcoming on human rights is sufficient excuse to mute all critical bluster.

China could certainly be told in no uncertain terms that its behavior was unacceptable and that it would be held accountable. Perhaps a diplomat could be quietly asked to leave. By keeping matters behind closed doors, the Chinese wouldn't be put in the position of feeling compelled to retaliate in order to save face.

Call attention to China's spying and they'd be bound to one-up by demonstrating that the United States was spying. This leads to reciprocal expulsions. And if the Chinese cannot identify a genuine spy, they'll sully a regular diplomat's career with banishment. Or worse, they'll feign indignation and retaliate in a separate domain by, for example, canceling a trade agreement or calling into dispute some issue that had been otherwise resolved.

Magers quips that China–US relations "are always in one of two stages: either they're good and we shouldn't do anything to mess them up, or they're bad and we shouldn't do anything to make them worse. Which means, basically, we shouldn't do anything."[2]

As required, the FBI informed State officials that they were investigating an individual who might be arrested and that the case involved China. State's first concern was whether a Chinese diplomat was implicated. It was assured that the person under investigation was an American citizen. As such, the matter was outside its jurisdiction except, it would argue, insofar as it would impact relations with the Chinese.

Those at State could conceivably contact the attorney general and try to thwart the arrest by invoking *sensitive geopolitical issues that we can't specify, which will be negatively affected should this go forward*. However, since they weren't apprised of the specifics underlying the investigation, it would be difficult for them to sustain their opposition.

Moore was standing by the phones at headquarters the night of the interview in the event State called over in an attempt to intervene, in which case he was, as he phrases it, "to put them off until we saw whether this thing went okay."[3]

### *Alexandria, Virginia, November 22, 1985*[4]

No sign comes to forewarn on the day your life gives way and avalanches uncontrollably bottom-over-top down a steep precipice.

Larry Chin didn't seem alarmed when the three men knocking on his door identified themselves as FBI agents. Men who introduce themselves with badges invariably bring ominous news.

"We're investigating a leak of classified information to the Chinese intelligence service and we were wondering if you could help us out by answering a few questions," Guerin opened informally.

"Certainly." Larry stood aside, inviting them in. He was under no obligation to do so.

Getting past the door, the agents had cleared the first — and arguably most difficult — hurdle.

Schiffer wasn't surprised. "Our assessment was that his ego would convince him he was smart enough, adept enough, to handle anything, and curious enough to want to find out why we're there."[5]

Larry led them through the living room to the dining room table, where he bade them sit. Tall and thin, rather frail in bearing, he walked with a slightly forward-leaning shuffle that gave the impression he was trying to get along faster than his legs were capable of propelling him. His head was covered with a thick mane of combed-back black hair. His wide, round face caved in at a shriveled chin, giving him a somewhat effeminate countenance.

A large picture window looked out toward the center of Alexandria. The apartment was neat and comfortably furnished. Past the dining room was the kitchen. From the living room, closer to the entrance, a short corridor led off to the bedroom and a study, and the bathroom.

Despite being at leisure, Larry kept up the habit of dressing professionally. He was wearing a white shirt, subdued tie, dark slacks, and stiff black shoes. He diffidently waited until the three agents were seated — Guerin to his left, Johnson closest to him on his right, Roth beside Johnson — before he took the chair at the head of the table. (Interestingly, Chin would testify in court, "I was directed to sit at the center of one side of the table.")

Guerin's most vivid memory is of how hot it was.

"It was like a hundred degrees and we're all wearing wool suits because it's November," he recalls with a slight grimace. "I mean, as soon as we sat down, it was just like a furnace."[6]

The agents reached into their breast pockets and pulled out their notepads, which they set on the table. Johnson removed a thick file folder from his briefcase and placed it ostentatiously in front of himself.

Larry watched patiently, waiting for them to commence.

The outcome of the interrogation hinged on how good the agents were at high-stakes poker. Their cards in hand were weak. But uncovered in the proper order and with sufficient bravado, they might bluff an impression of omniscience. They'd have to proceed methodically, snapping each card like a shot, creating the illusion of an endless supply, an infinite wealth of information. Larry would have to be made to believe they knew more than they were willing to admit. To do so, however, they'd actually be telling him just about everything they had.

Guerin began by repeating that the FBI was investigating a leak involving the Chinese intelligence service and hoped that Chin might be able to help them.

Of course he would help them. It only made perfect sense that they would approach him for his expertise, Chin gloated, proud to still be held in such high regard for his understanding of Chinese affairs.

He seemed at ease, unaware of any ulterior motive the agents may have. If he felt relief at not being immediately accused, he showed none of it, though it's difficult to believe that it didn't occur to him.

"He was very self-possessed," Guerin recalls. "I think he asked us in because he was playing a little game, trying to find out what we knew. He expected to learn more from what we'd say than he'd give away."[7]

Painting broad strokes, Guerin told him the leaks he was investigating had occurred in the 1970s and early 1980s, confining himself to the period for which Chin held a top-secret clearance.

"Oh, that's when I was active in CIA." Larry grinned, pleased that he could, indeed, be of assistance.

"That's correct," Guerin said, leaning toward him and locking onto his eyes like a heat-seeking missile.

"You see, Mr. Chin, you're the person we're investigating," he added, dropping his affected affability.

"Oh really." Punctuated with a nervous little giggle.

"That's right, we believe you committed espionage," Guerin stated.

Larry steadied his grin. How does an innocent man react to a dreadful accusation? Does he convey the same shock as a guilty man who never imagined getting caught?

"Why me? What do you think I did?" he asked calmly, more curious than concerned.

He returned Guerin's steady gaze. He kept his cool, which, in a literal sense, was more than the agents were able to do in the roasting apartment.

Roth asked Chin whether he might remove his coat.

Larry nodded his assent.

As Roth slipped his jacket off and hung it across the back of his chair, and Johnson followed, Larry noticed that they both had guns clipped to their belts. He remarked on it.

"We're law enforcement officers," Guerin explained. "We carry weapons to protect ourselves and the lives of others."

Larry seemed satisfied, not showing any sign that he was at all intimidated.

Guerin refrained from removing his jacket. The formality of the suit, especially while the others were in shirtsleeves, he felt, strengthened his position as the authority figure. He could feel the sweat streaming down his back and puddling at his armpits and sternum, but he held fast.

"Have you ever had contact with members of the Chinese intelligence service?"

"No."

Guerin looked over at Johnson, who opened the file folder. He pulled out a photograph and slid it along the table until it rested right in front of Chin.

"Have you ever met this person, Zhu Entao?" Guerin inquired.

Zhu was a vice minister in the Ministry of Public Security, who became well known in international police circles as China's representative on Interpol's National Central Bureau, the organization's vice president for Asia, and a member of its executive committee. In this capacity, he frequently attended conferences around the world. In 1989, he would apply for a visa to attend an Interpol General Assembly in Washington. China made some back-channel inquiries as to whether he would face any consequences as a result of the Chin case. He was informed that the FBI intended to question him "extensively" about his knowledge of espionage activities should he ever set foot in the United States. Thus, it was understood that he'd be better off if he was denied entry. It presented a good opportunity for the American government to signal how seriously it regarded Chin's activities. As a result, the General Assembly was hastily moved to Lyons.

Larry inspected the photo closely. The man pictured had a long neck and a narrow chin flaring up like a water spout to broad cheekbones under a wide forehead, topped by a thick shock of black hair. His eyes were slightly obscured by the flash reflecting off his large, black-framed glasses. Larry took his time, maintaining his calm by breathing steadily, holding himself in check against the impulse to react too quickly.

"No, I don't recognize him," he said, but continued staring hard at the face. In his mind, he would have been shuffling his own deck, worrying through his options. Perhaps he'd do well to disclose some benign recognition. "I think this is, maybe, a Bank of China official I met on my last trip to China."

"Are you aware that Mr. Zhu is an intelligence officer with the Ministry of Public Security?" Guerin asked.

Because the transliteration of Chinese characters to English is artificial (for instance, a common name such as *Wong* or *Wang* might be represented by one of several distinct characters) and the intonations of the language are nearly impossible for non–Chinese speakers to imitate, Johnson passed over an index card with ZHU ENTAO and MINISTRY OF PUBLIC SECURITY (Gong Anbu) written in English and Chinese characters so as to dispel any confusion.

"No," Larry said adamantly.

Guerin again signaled Johnson, who consulted his file. He didn't have to read off the paper; he knew the details by heart.

Johnson eyed him with a mix of disappointment and contempt. "You traveled to Beijing on February 6, 1982, returning to the United States on the twenty-seventh aboard CAAC Flight 983. While you were there, a banquet was held in your honor. You were presented with an award."

Because PLANESMAN was never going to testify, it was critical to get the information he'd provided on record by presenting it to Larry and seeking his confirmation. By this technique, they'd be able to put it into their report without reference beyond this conversation.

"How did you get that information?" Larry inquired.

Guerin gave him a little smirk. "Now, Mr. Chin, I'm not going to reveal my sources. Are you denying the information?"

"I am not denying anything."

"You worked for the US government, American intelligence. Why was China giving you an award?"

"Because I'm their friend," he conceded cryptically. Did he mean this to assuage the agents' doubts, or was he confessing?

"Did you meet Mr. Zhu during this trip?"

Larry sort of grimaced in response.

"Can you recall now whether Mr. Zhu was an intelligence officer?"

"I never knew he was an intelligence officer."

As Roth assesses it, "He was trying to calculate how much he could tell us and still walk away from this thing."[8]

"Do you know this man?" Another picture was put in front of Chin.

"I don't think so."

"He is Li Wenchong, and he is the vice minister of Chinese intelligence."

Larry stared dumbfounded. Li had presented his medal. He realized the American authorities had some solid information; they weren't merely fishing. Just how much information they had, however, was a mystery he needed to solve on the spot.

"We know that you met with intelligence officers and that you are working for Chinese intelligence," Guerin continued.

"Are you serious?"

"Mr. Chin, I am very serious."

On cue, Johnson jumped back in. "Mr. Chin, we are aware of your illegal activities. We know of your meets in Toronto. We know you traveled to China again on June 1, 1983. You were checked in to the Qianmen Hotel, Room 533."

An interrogator will often do better by sticking to the minutiae than resorting to sweeping accusations. That he knows the smallest details can cause the suspect to assume the bigger issues are self-evident. When Johnson was able to recite the exact number of the hotel room Chin had occupied — thanks to finding that key when his luggage was searched at Dulles — he was sent reeling. Pressure's tentacles swelled in around reason, like a tumor taking root in healthy tissue.

I was spied on. I was followed. They have everything.

No, hotel clerks are known to be informants. Somehow they saw the register. How would the Americans have access to a Beijing hotel clerk? Only someone in authority in China could have informed on me.

At this point, Larry had no idea what to think. That they knew his actual room number made his tormentors seem right on top of him. His mind began to race with the blind intensity of a rabbit feeling the hot breath of a fox on his back legs. He envisioned these very interrogators glowering over him while he slept in his warm bed in Beijing, untroubled by dreams of danger.

"Well, tell me what concrete evidence you have?"

"We aren't going to do it that way, Mr. Chin. We've given you an idea of the evidence we have."

"How do I know you aren't bluffing?"

The interview was at a pivotal juncture. Unbeknownst to Larry, the agents had slapped him with most of what they had. If he could withstand one final onslaught, he'd have exhausted their ammunition.

Johnson moved in for the kill. "In September 1983, you traveled to Hong Kong, where you met with Ou Qiming, an officer of the Ministry of Public Security. He was your handler. You informed him about a fellow FBIS employee that you knew. You told Mr. Ou that he had an opportunity — a rare opportunity — to recruit this individual. You even proposed a scenario for how this could be accomplished. You suggested they could use one of the employee's siblings, who still lived in China, against her. You also informed Mr. Ou that you were having marital difficulties and requested that he give you $150,000 so you could pay off your wife and get divorced."

Larry was floored. Ou Qiming was the only one who knew about all this.

Johnson showed him an index card with OU QIMING printed in English and Chinese. "Do you know this gentleman?"

Yes, Larry Chin knew the gentleman extremely well.

He had the presence of mind at this point to state aloud that perhaps he ought to consult with a lawyer before proceeding.

"I'm not a lawyer." Larry hesitated, coming to terms with the gravity of the situation. "And I'm not sure I know all my legal rights."

"Well, Mr. Chin, I am an attorney," piped up Johnson.

Guerin and Roth felt their jaws drop in unison. In neither man's years of confronting suspects had they heard much more blatant a blunder. Either one could have reached over and grabbed Johnson by the balls to choke him off from speaking further.

Instead, Guerin jumped into the exchange to get Chin's attention back on him. "Go right ahead. Anytime you want to call an attorney, that's your right. You don't have to talk to us. You want us to leave, we leave. But when we leave, we're going straight to the Department of Justice and present our case without the benefit of your side."

"Why should I talk to you?"

"Good question," Johnson retorted. "There are two possibilities of what we can do tonight. One is, you decide you don't want to talk, and we go to Justice. Or you do talk, and we take your reasons and explanations along with our case when we present it. Just imagine you are the Department of Justice, Mr. Chin. I come to you as an FBI special agent with a clear-cut case. And I give you this case and tell you I went to interview the subject and he slammed the door in my face. But what if I come to you, Mr. Chin, as the Department of Justice, with the identical case, same set of facts, and I tell you we interviewed the subject and he said he was really sorry for what he did, and he gave us names, dates, places, he even gave us tradecraft that was used. Now, who would you, as the Department of Justice, have more sympathy for?"

It's the standard cop's gambit. More than anything, you want your suspect to talk. About anything. You'll listen. When one excuses an action, he is, first and foremost, admitting it. An interrogator has no fundamental interest in why you did what you did. He just wants to hear you say you did it. Got an explanation? Save it for court.

Chin mulled that over a moment. "What would an attorney say if I called him?"

"An attorney will tell you not to talk with us," Guerin interjected. "But we're offering you an opportunity . . ."

Of course counsel would instruct him not to talk. A guilty man's best hope never rests in the sympathy of law officers; always in the chance that the evidence against him isn't sufficient to dispel reasonable doubt at trial. The justice system is adversarial by design. Nothing in the outward friendliness or compassion of the police ought to disabuse the suspect of their intent to do him no good. And when a cop tells you openly that an attorney working on your behalf would advise you against talking, what on earth could possess you to continue the conversation?

Whether conscious of Johnson's blunder or not, Larry asked him directly, "Since you're an attorney, could you provide me some legal advice? Could you represent me?"

Desperate to derail this train before it gained steam and ran away from him, Rudy reclaimed control. "Mr. Chin. Mr. Chin, look at me. I am not an attorney. Agent Johnson is, but he's an FBI agent. He is not going to represent you and he is not going to offer you legal advice. You said you think you need to consult an attorney. If you want an attorney, the phone is right there. You pick up that phone and call an attorney anytime you want during this interview. Anytime. In fact, if you call an attorney, I guarantee what that attorney will tell you."

"What?" Chin directed his attention back to Guerin.

"He will tell you to tell us to get the hell out of here. And, Mr. Chin, we will. I will leave this room right now and you will never see me again. But what goes out the room with me is your chance to cooperate in this investigation."

Guerin paused here for effect. "This is an ongoing investigation, Mr. Chin. And it does not end here just because you tell us to leave. And that means I'm going to have to go and interview everybody who knows you that I believe might have relevant information. That includes ex-co-workers, business associates, your wife, your girlfriend."

"Go ahead, tell my wife," he leered. "She knows about the girlfriend."

"And your kids." For the first time since they'd first leveled an accusation at Larry, he betrayed real emotion: dread. Guerin saw instantly that he'd hit a nerve from the way Chin's mouth slackened, the tiny grin disappeared, and his eyes glazed with the mist of uncertainty.

Guerin pressed on. "Right now, I have agents waiting outside your son's house, outside your daughter's house. When I leave this room, I make a call and those agents are knocking on their doors and asking them questions about your illegal activities."

"Why would you do that?" Softly, a voice asking for mercy.

"Because I have a job to do, I have an investigation to conduct."

"They don't know anything." He shook his head slowly.

"I'm sorry, Mr. Chin, I don't know that, and I'm certainly not gonna take your word for it. What I am gonna do is go out and talk with whoever I think I have to. You read the paper. You know about the Walker case; there was a whole family of spies. How do I know this isn't the same thing?"

Guerin admits he had no reason whatsoever to suspect that Larry's children were involved. Furthermore, he was bluffing: There were no agents poised to pound on their doors.

"With any suspect, you do your homework in advance, you find that soft spot where they don't want to go," he explains. "You hope they have something that they love more than they fear prison and that they'll fall on the sword to protect that thing, that last thing they hold dear. For Chin, his kids were the sword."[9]

"Believe me, they know nothing," Larry implored.

"I'm sorry, Mr. Chin, but I don't believe you."

"What if I talk to you? What would happen? Would you leave my kids alone?"

"You have to tell me what's going on. If the kids aren't involved, maybe we won't have to interview them."

There followed a long silence. Inside his head, Guerin invoked a mute prayer. God, don't say anything. Mark, don't say anything. Please, just don't say anything. The silence taunted each man to fill it, to make some sound to break the twinging of the trip-wire tension.

"What concrete evidence do you have?" Chin asked his interrogators assertively.

"We're certainly not going to present the entire extent of our evidence to you," he was told.

"Why don't you come back tomorrow and we can discuss it then," he suggested, desperate to buy time to ponder his options. Or to effect an escape.

"I'm afraid, Mr. Chin, this is a onetime deal. If I walk out that door,

I'm not coming back tomorrow. I'm going to the Department of Justice tonight."

Larry took in a long breath of air, soothing himself, stiffening his resolve. Making the fateful decision that would determine how the rest of the evening would play out. How the rest of his life would play. Calculating the repercussions of decisions made in a different time and place, under different circumstances. Perhaps when he was a different person.

If the FBI had Ou, they had everything. They had him.

"He has to think on his feet and he's not really prepared to do this," Paul Moore says, assessing the situation as it stood that night. "He's in a poker game, but he's not a great player. He's a gambler, but he's lost a lot. Because of the suppositions he makes, he begins to lose his nerve."[10]

Larry could demand that lawyer now. But could he afford to have the FBI go to Justice with everything Ou told them without a rebuttal? He couldn't just say nothing.

Larry picked up the index card marked OU QIMING.

As if talking to himself, he reflected, "I only knew him as Mr. Ou."

The fox had sunk its teeth into his meaty thigh.

For decades, Larry had depended on Ou. He was the person with whom he relaxed his guard, upon whom he depended for his safety, with whom his deepest secret was out in the open. The person to whom he relieved himself of whatever classified material he'd collected, along with the doubts, fears, and shame that accumulate on the spy until he begins to sag under the burden, the way the aged slacken under the accumulated weight of years.

Nobody ought to be more mindful of the potential for betrayal than the betrayer. Nobody ought to be less prone to shock upon learning that someone isn't who they appear. Larry was always at the mercy of his handler should Ou ever be seduced by those same forces — money, ego, conflicted loyalties — that caused him to double over to the other side.

Larry looked at the FBI agents around the table. "The character is wrong." He covered over the last part of the Chinese pictogram. "That's the character for Mr. Ou."

It was just a gesture, but the kind of gesture that has interrogators struggling to conceal their excitement. With this concession, Chin put discussion of his rights aside and signaled a willingness to engage in dialogue, fully aware that they presumed him guilty.

"I don't understand where you got this information." He felt light-headed, almost levitating out of his body. He watched himself be decapitated with a single stroke, surprised at how little resistance the flesh and sinew and bone gave. His head rolled a little distance from his torso, coming to rest upright, an odd grin of resignation on his lips. They know, he marveled. They know everything. "Only Mr. Ou knew about my wife."

He voiced his worst nightmare. "Mr. Ou must have defected to you."

Convinced that Ou had betrayed him, Larry was convinced he was doomed. It was a fatal error.

"Perhaps you could tell me your evidence and I will either confirm or deny the information," he said, trying to compromise.

Guerin would have none of it. "Mr. Chin, that isn't the way we're going to run this interview."

"If I tell you everything, it's going to take a very long time." Larry sighed.

"We'll spend as much time as you need to tell your whole story."

"I need to think about this. You could come back tomorrow and I will tell you if I will talk to you or not."

The interview was at a critical juncture, the agents knew. Control of the situation still eluded them, but they could taste it. They had successfully leveraged what little hard information they had to where he was leaning from seeking legal advice to confessing. The momentum was moving in the agents' direction, and they weren't about to allow it to shift.

"No, sir," Johnson insisted, "this is a onetime deal. We walk out that door and we're not coming back tomorrow, we're going straight to the Justice Department to present our case."

Whatever pressure the agents were under to finesse the situation to their advantage was nothing compared with the forces detonating inside Larry's head. His whole life, he realized, had come down to this one chance to make the right decision.

One thing for sure: He didn't want the agents going to Justice with the wrong impression. Mr. Ou, he assumed, would have painted him in the worst possible light in order to assure the best deal for himself. Furthermore, since the FBI already had the details, it was left for him to seize this opportunity to demonstrate that the simple fact of his sharing information with China was subject to different interpretations. Truth is to be teased from the nuances.

"It will take a long time," he repeated. "It's late. If you come back tomorrow, you could listen to what my entire story is; that would be fine. But we should meet elsewhere, maybe a hotel room."

Chin was thinking ahead, trying to enlist them as co-conspirators. "If I talk to you, we can work out a deal. You could use me? I could go back to China for you, see my contacts and report to you what they say."

"Mr. Chin, I can't promise anything until you tell me exactly what happened. The US government can only make a decision about that once we know your whole story," Guerin said, encouraging him to read some implied assurance in his tone.

Larry faced a conundrum. If he hoped to convince the agents of his value, he'd have to accentuate his importance. The alternative was to maintain his innocence and run the risk of learning too late that the case against him was incontrovertible. There seemed no in-between option. The former was particularly attractive because, Magers explains, "Traditionally, the agency had let doubles turn and then retire quietly, sometimes with their pensions intact. The United States had a very poor record for prosecuting spies."[11]

But in this case, the authorities were determined to prosecute. "Our perception was that we had made a significant espionage case, and we didn't believe we'd get anything out of him we didn't already have," asserts Aronica.[12]

"Well, it's a very long story." Chin sighed. He looked Roth right in the eye as he said this.

Roth, who had been mostly silent to this point, preoccupied with taking notes of the proceedings so that the flow of the interview would be accurately preserved for the use of the US attorney, looked directly back at him.

Softly, he said, "Mr. Chin, we've got all night."

Recalling that moment, Johnson speaks a little more gently than usual. "Larry was looking to the senior person in the room for acknowledgment that it was okay."[13]

He expressed the need to go to the bathroom. The agents consented.

Roth went to the telephone to advise Schiffer, who was in the observation post with Carson, of the progress they'd made. He spoke in a hushed tone so as not to be overheard.

Chin was going to talk, he said.

When Larry returned, he offered the agents a beverage. They declined.

"I wish to fix myself some tea." He excused himself. The agents allowed him to go to the kitchen by himself. They sat in silence, nerves scraped raw by anticipation.

He resumed his seat, setting his mug down on the table. Despite the heat in the apartment, he warmed his fingertips delicately in the rising steam. He took a contemplative sip, moistening his lips and tongue.

"In 1948 . . ."

The agents were dumbfounded.

*Beijing, 1948*

Yenching University was founded by American missionaries out of a merger between four existing colleges that was completed in 1920. It was funded largely by US-based philanthropies. English was the dominant language of instruction, in response to increasing demand for fluency within government and business. The campus was spread over an idyllic sixty acres at the Jin Wang Garden, one of many that had been the private preserve of Manchu royalty. Midway between the fetid city and the fragrant Western Hills, it reflected the Westerner's dream of what all of China should look like: pagodas crowned with intricate glazed tiles, moon gates opening onto quiet courtyards, and tranquil streams meandering by lovely shade trees.

The university's motto was noble: *Freedom Through Truth for Service.* The students' concerns, however, ran to the pragmatic: "How was service to be rendered? The question plunged to the heart of career preparation and employment upon graduation."[14] It certainly preoccupied Larry.

His father was among the last of the old-time Qing dynasty officials, a product of the strict examination system that trained Mandarins in the classics, language, calligraphy, literature, and Confucianism. He had his children homeschooled by tutors in the same tradition.

"The idea was to educate in order to turn out educated people, with the ability to recite good poetry, who would manage the bureaucracy," Moore explains. "Along comes the Republic in 1911, and you still have the residue of these officials running things because somebody has to. But there's no need for another generation of people trained in this manner."[15]

Larry was a good student. He spoke little English when he arrived at Yenching. He discovered an aptitude for it, however, and worked hard, quickly becoming fluent.

Much though language skills were valued, China was sweeping past the other archaic arts in which Larry was proficient. Craving modernization, China needed scientists and engineers, a skilled industrial workforce. The last thing it needed — or had the capacity to employ — was more antiquated scholars. Furthermore, in the midst of the simultaneous war against Japan and civil war, the government was in too much disorder to promise much in the way of a career. The expectations with which Larry was raised were disintegrating around him. He was being educated to follow in his father's footsteps, except those footsteps were kicked over in the stampede of forces rushing to take control over the Middle Kingdom. And young men like Larry faced life-defining choices.

Larry enjoyed university life, with its lively intellectual debate and agitation (in 1946–1947, there were at least six different student strikes lasting
two or more days[16]). He shared the student's conceit that philosophies
and ideas have relevance and immediacy. Less than one in ten thousand
Chinese attended college or university; those studying in Beijing were an
elite within an elite, and he delighted in belonging.

Still, he was never too far removed from anxiety over his future.
Undoubtedly, his education vastly improved his prospects. He was qualified for a civil service position, but that didn't guarantee him a posting. Merit was never the first consideration of the bureaucracy, anyway.
Coming from a family with modest influence, he would find positions to
which he'd hoped to be appointed going to sons of higher officials, who'd
purchased them with bribes of money or favors. Having done everything
within his means to succeed, he was discouraged to find his ambitions
undermined from the very outset.

Even the university administration recognized the problem, as the 1939
Report of the Presbyterian North China Mission at Yenching reflected:
"Are we training builders of the New China, or a lost generation who will
have no real place in the future?"[17]

As far back as the mid-1920s, Yenching became known as a hotbed of
Communism. By the mid-1940s, anti-Americanism had become a popular
outlet for the pent-up frustrations generations of Chinese had felt toward
the West. Communism was the promise of renewal and assertiveness,
while the ruling Nationalists embodied a return to familiar corruption
and obsequiousness. The liberal Christianity propagated by the faculty
felt outdated to students restless for bold action. The majority anticipated
the Communists' success in the civil war enthusiastically.[18]

Count Larry among them. And why not? If only because it foretold
unpredictable outcomes, drastic change was irresistible — as it has been
to young student radicals the world over throughout history. Larry was
a student, in a more inclusive sense than what is implied by a purely
academic definition. In his abiding inquisitiveness about the world around
him; in his longing to penetrate surface effects to hidden causes. He

was open-minded, listening without prejudice to whatever he was told. Accumulating information, measuring intentions. Calculating reward.

He spent long hours in conversation with his roommate, Wang. Wang did a lot of the talking, impressing Larry with two qualities a young man is most apt to admire in another: passion and certainty. In Larry, Wang recognized two qualities to which he was ever alert: ambition and intelligence.

Larry sometimes felt as though he wasn't quite getting the point of what Wang was telling him with such earnestness, but something in his tone, the careful way he had of enunciating each word to lend it gravity, kept him listening. He enjoyed their all-night discussions, sharing in the illusion that a couple of intellectuals sipping steaming tea and smoking harsh cigarettes in this protected enclave could remake China, and slightly intoxicated by the risk of radical political discourse. Unlike his professors, who came directly from the past, he sensed that Wang was preparing him for the future. And the more Larry feared the prospects for his future, the less interested he was in the past.

"Now is a time of dangerous opportunity," Wang said, using the word *weiji* — *wei*, meaning "danger," and *ji*, "opportunity" — which an English-speaker would translate as "crisis." "Our country has always turned on such moments. Here's to a turn down the left path."

They clinked cups in a toast.

Wang would utter cryptic remarks full of portent: "Being seen for who you really are is to set yourself up for failure."

Sounding much like Sun Tzu, the author of *The Art of War*, the classic treatise on intelligence, he added, "If you want to know the enemy, you must be able to walk with him."

Larry had every reason to listen. Perhaps his next move would be inspired by the things Wang had to tell him.

"The world has changed and China must take a place in it," he said. "For generations, the foreigners have come here, exploiting the masses, enriching a few. Their power has been a function of their expansion. That's the whole nature of imperialism — the Europeans increase their power exponentially by swallowing up distant lands, weak lands, but wealthy in those commodities valued in the West.

"Imagine if China were to extend itself. Not for the purpose of exploitation, but in the spirit of proletarian solidarity; not to take advantage of local populations, but to bring advantages. Would we not be embraced as the Westerners are resisted? If we reach out gently, hand outstretched in friendship, not clenched in a fist, we can find our destiny."

Where could his place be in this new China? Larry wondered.

Wang chuckled. "The world will not learn to speak Chinese."

One way or another, China's insularity was going to be cast off; whether dictated by the Chinese or foreign interlopers, as had for so long been the case.

Foreigners had coveted the Chinese market since the days of Marco Polo. Christian missionaries worked diligently to win over Chinese souls. Rare indeed was the foreigner who encountered China with the desire to learn from its culture, rather than subjugate with theirs. Gottfried Wilhelm Leibniz, the seventeenth-century court librarian in Hanover, made the extraordinary claim "that we need missionaries from the Chinese."[19]

Each contact between foreign states involves friction between arrogance and modesty, superiority and insecurity. This is surely the case for China, which is absolutely convinced of its preeminence over other nations, and therefore confused by how humiliatingly it has been dominated by intruders.

Larry had thought about leaving China, but only in the way people consider improbable things all the time. He had no destination picked out. The United States, of course. How?

"Language will be our most valuable asset," Wang assured him. "We will need to speak with our friends, and our enemies. In our mind the distinction is always clear. But in theirs . . . enemies are won over by friends. Submission is an imperialist strategy; persuasion is ours. Communication over combat.

"Why do the imperialists only believe they benefit if it is at another's expense? That's not the view of the world we project. Our motives are in the people's interest."

Wang paused to sip tea and puff on his cigarette. Larry didn't feel compelled to speak during these interludes. Wang's discourses had the quality of lectures, and Larry was content to listen and absorb.

"Christian doctrine promises wonderful kindness, but also threatens horrible cruelty. Which appeals to you?" Wang asked.

"The kindness," Larry agreed, though, to himself, he acknowledged the strong impression left by the priests' graphic descriptions of how God punishes transgressions.

"We will be kind," Wang assured him.

Larry knew Chinese history. As with Christian theology, the cruelty trailed not far behind.

Did Wang ever come out and announce to Larry whether he was a Communist cadre? Maybe not.

He never encouraged — indeed, if the conversation ever arose, he likely discouraged — Larry to join the Chinese Communist Party. No open declaration of fidelity was necessary.

Wang didn't go out on the street to celebrate the triumphant arrival of the Red soldiers in Beijing.

When Larry invited him along to witness the historic moment, he smiled enigmatically. "Not everyone in the streets is genuinely happy. Not everyone who stays inside is dismayed."

He looked penetratingly at Larry. "Truth isn't revealed in the smile on a man's lips or the tears from his eyes. In his heart. When he silently whispers in absolute solitude. Only then does he never lie. That's where you want to get: at the place he works hardest to protect."

"As with countries," he added, an afterthought Larry barely caught.

He did that, Larry noticed. Remarks tossed off with the least emphasis carried the most meaning. As if he was testing Larry's attentiveness.

"It stands to reason, a country doesn't invest millions to secure its lies. Those it gives freely. The truth." He smiled longingly off into the distance. "It's getting late, if you want to participate in the welcome of the troops."

Larry detected the clear note of disapproval in his voice.

"No," he replied, "I think I'll remain here and study."

Wang nodded and reached over to the end table and picked up a book himself.

"Let's take a walk," Wang proposed a few days later.

The streets of Beijing were calm. Whether that reflected the mood of the citizens or a prudent reaction to the People's Liberation Army soldiers, who were out in force, Larry couldn't say. He and Wang wandered aimlessly.

"This is the new reality," Larry muttered, looking around as if seeing Beijing for the first time.

"You shouldn't be displeased."

"Oh, I'm not," he replied quickly. "It's a lot to comprehend, to appreciate."

"On the surface, change is dislocation, but underneath it's an opportunity," Wang proposed, using the term *jihui* for "opportunity," as distinct from *weiji*. "We will need everybody to contribute for it to take hold, for all our benefits."

A comforting idea, but Larry felt unbalanced. He hadn't yet found solid footing.

"We need you," Wang said casually while looking away from Larry at a soldier who had stooped down to pick up a piece of paper lying in the gutter. "I hear you practicing. Your English is very proficient."

Larry was surprised. He'd had no idea Wang was paying attention or that he could understand.

"I want to introduce you to a friend," Wang said. "He might offer you important work."

By not refusing, Larry acquiesced.

The man to whom Wang introduced him was a Communist security officer. His responsibility was monitoring American officials. He allowed how he could always use another set of eyes and ears to help him out.

The meeting occurred in what Larry took to be some kind of a safe house, though he knew little about such things at the time. It was deep within an inconspicuous *hutong* in a teeming section of Beijing, where they easily melted into the throng of working people.

Wang beat a quick exit once the formalities were complete.

Larry was terrified. With the carnage of Japanese occupation over, Chiang's Guomindang government and Mao's Communists were fighting for control of the vast and devastated country. Neither side was tolerant toward the other's followers. When authoritarian rivals square off, margins of error are minute. To participate in a clandestine rendezvous with either was decidedly perilous. Taking the wrong side could prove deadly.

Impressed by Larry's language skills and his previous experience working with the British and Americans, the official suggested a career opportunity.

Larry could go to Shanghai where, he knew, the American consulate was in need of translators. His expenses would be taken care of, and he'd be provided a place to stay until he got settled.

I will see to everything, he assured, and look in on you from time to time.

What am I to do?

Just apply for the job. If you get it, stay alert. Watch what goes on, and if you see anything you guess might interest me, tell me when we meet.

Larry had no other prospects looming. Here was the promise of a good job and solidifying a friendship with an influential official.

How conscious was he to the undercurrent of the course he was setting upon?

He was a neophyte to the machinations commonplace to spies. But he understood *guanxi*. He knew favors granted obliged favors returned. And while he may have been intimidated against rejecting such a request from a security officer, he also considered the benefits of having one indebted to him. He had far more to gain than lose.

In the most peaceable times, Shanghai tilted precariously toward hysteria. With Communist forces less than a year from seizing control, times were anything but peaceable. Shanghai was even more overcrowded than usual as people, whose home villages and hamlets had been churned to bloody mud under the relentless movement of armies in retreat chased by those in advance, sought refuge in the illusory safety of the city. Larry, who had been relatively sheltered from the war, must have been awed by the homeless children, the helpless cripples, and, everywhere, the hopeless men without means to provide for their families, all scrambling ceaselessly for a day's food and a night's shelter. Today's success wouldn't avert tomorrow's failure. The treadmill went nowhere, and there was no way off.

He must have been apprehensive, climbing the front steps of the American consulate. He wore his best suit, a gift from his new friend. You had to impress if you were to be considered seriously for such an important position. He was self-conscious of how badly he was perspiring and the prickly wetness seeping through his shirt.

The heavy door closing behind him seemed to bar his exit and, in the crowd of Chinese scurrying noisily in quest of a visa authorizing them to leave for the United States, he would have felt distinct, if only for wanting to stay.

When he finally got the attention of a harried American official and explained his purpose, he was surprised at how easily he was hired. Coping with a severe shortage of Chinese linguists, the Americans were grateful for Larry's services. Whatever vetting was performed was cursory. Neither resources nor conditions allowed for anything approaching thoroughness. His demonstrable ability to translate accurately was enough to get the job.

Ineligible for a formal security clearance, he would not be exposed to any classified material. He was asked to review the press, listen to radio broadcasts, read official pronouncements issued by the Communists and the government, and provide written translations. He gave the Americans his best effort. His new friend had insisted he do nothing less.

"As you serve them, so you serve us," he'd insisted, in case Larry's conscience needed swaddling. "Our aim, you know, is not to hurt the United States. It is to help China."

Larry was to apply himself to his task, to become the most accomplished translator on staff. The Americans were to have no cause to doubt that he was the most articulate, the one with the surest voice for the subtleties of both languages. Whenever someone had a difficult job, they were eventually to become confident that it must go to Larry. And if ever he found himself swamped, he should at least take a moment to glance over a document for the gist and recommend whether it warranted his attention or could be delegated to another.

All the while, from time to time, he would meet with his friend and let him know what he saw and heard. It was very innocuous; he wasn't privy to enough for it to be otherwise. But his friend seemed inordinately pleased.

As the Communists approached Shanghai, the American mission was ordered to abandon the mainland and relocate to Hong Kong in April 1949. Larry was invited to accompany them and keep his job.

His friend couldn't have been happier. No more conclusive proof that Larry had won the Americans' trust could be forthcoming. He urged him to accept the offer, while cautioning him that they would probably not speak to each other for some time. However, he would always remember Larry as a true friend, and as soon as possible he would send an emissary to continue the relationship on his behalf.

Larry responded that he would appreciate the remembrance.

In the never-say-never world of espionage, Larry stands, to date, as the only known example of a Chinese penetration operation. In other words, not an agent of opportunity, one recruited because he was already in a position of interest and influence, but an individual recruited from the outset to be run against an identified target. And it is accepted wisdom among China-watchers that Larry was a straight penetration.

How reasonable is it to assume that he is really the only one?

"History is a good predictor of the future with the Chinese," Magers concedes. "They don't generally operate outside their established box. Now, we may have defined the box incorrectly, but what they've done successfully in the past, they tend to do again."[20]

Magers's opinion allows for two possibilities. The first is that there have been other penetrations heretofore undetected. Or, if the Chin case is, in fact, unique, then there is greater variety to their methods than expected. Whichever, it points to a far more determined opponent than is usually accepted. Whereas they are expected to task passively, Larry was assigned to actively seek out employment with the US government.

Why did Larry go along?

We can closely — intrusively — monitor how a man behaves. But his motives are a jigsaw fractured into random pieces, all of the same color, that are nearly impossible to assemble into a coherent structure.

Among the least convincing myths about intelligence officers is that they are superior judges of character. Were that the case, they would take a far more impartial approach to people — the way a psychiatrist proceeds to examine a patient without a predetermined diagnosis. But intelligence officers come at everybody with fill-in-the-blank suspicion. I know you did something, I just haven't figured out what . . . yet.

The investigator's talent is distinguished by his recognition of the one maneuver on the chessboard that signals the strategy to which his opponent is committed to pursuing to the bitter end. He hears that slipped syllable that reveals the doubt someone feels when reciting a prepared excuse. He catches the hitched breath that precedes a true, reluctant confession. He sees that off-rhythm blink when he poses a question it was hoped he didn't know enough to ask. He instinctively feels the instant sweat surfaces on the skin, when spit evaporates off the tongue.

Never mind the lie detector, a good investigator will tell you. Guilt doesn't scare anyone; getting caught does. Confidence beats the lie detector, regardless of whether you're being deceptive or not. The good investigator shreds that confidence the way no mechanical device can. The polygraph can only measure the subject's reactions. It doesn't have eyes that can bore into him, coaxing him to say more. It doesn't have a voice that can ooze sympathy or sneer reproach, prying out explanations and rationalizations that require ever-further elaboration . . . and with every comment, something else the subject never intended to say is exposed. With what he says, what he suggests, the investigator implies the promise that any confidence you ever shared with anybody is vulnerable. He can make you regret every word you've whispered aloud to yourself in a dark, empty room; make you feel observed and overheard when you know there was no possibility.

That people lie is taken for granted. Lies are body armor borne to protect the secrets that are the product of our fear and humiliation. Intelligence officers are trained to isolate seams through which they can penetrate to the core and discover whether the secrets are public betrayals or merely private disgraces.

"Larry was intensely interested in money," asserts Paul Moore, when asked to ponder why he did it. "The money part comes first. He keeps score by money. Anything that is a gateway to making money is good. It really is all about the money."

Over the course of several hours of conversation, I press him on that conclusion, arguing that Larry's lengthy service to China suggests something deeper, especially considering that he was presented more with an opportunity than money at the outset.

"People rarely commit espionage for only one reason," he concedes. "Sure, he was loyal to China, but he constantly wanted to know whether something came with money attached. He gets the honorary rank of deputy bureau chief in the Ministry of Public Security. That's great. 'Does it come with a salary?' he asks. It doesn't, and he doesn't like that. From my experience, it was always about money.

"Yeah, there could have been some belief underlying it, but it's not so terribly likely. You have a continuum of services and relationships and money. Larry had many sides to his character. I'm not disagreeing that it might have been something more than money. In this instance, though, I believe it played the predominant role."[21]

Van Magers, too, puts the emphasis on money, "Even from the beginning, I think money motivated him. In 1948, he's ready to take his place in the world, but that part of the world he was prepared for ceased to exist.

It was a pretty good bet the Communists were going to come out on top. If he'd believed the Guomindang was going to win, he'd have gone with them. I think he was an opportunist. I never saw anything that would indicate there were a lot of principles involved."[22]

An opportunist, perhaps, but one who was remarkable for not wavering over decades. To date, Larry is the longest-surviving penetration agent in the very long history of espionage. At least, who has ever been revealed.

"At first, I think, he did it ideologically, to help Mao," Ken Schiffer counters. "As he gets into this thing, as often happens in espionage cases, it becomes one of many motives that work into the equation. He needs money, he wants to create a legacy for his family. He is flattered to have the Chinese doting on him. It makes him feel good. You know, without spying, who is he? He's not a famous CIA operative or anything else. He's just a translator. This gives him what his personality had been looking for — after the idealistic motive."[23]

Rudy Guerin, as well, mentions money, but goes on, "Everyone likes to be stroked, some people to the extreme. Listen, all these guys have character flaws, otherwise you just don't do this. They stroked him. That's why they have banquets and give you a phony medal and give you a title, if that's what you want. They tell you the president is aware of what you're doing. Makes you feel pretty good. Because maybe, when you go to your real job, people don't do all that for you."[24]

"Of course it was money," states Tom Carson. Then, he falters, remembering everything that transpired over all those years of risk and stress and uncertainty. "But it had to be more than that. He really didn't get paid that much in the scheme of things. We don't know exactly how much he got."

He pauses, willing himself into the mind of the man he'd hunted so long ago. "He was not a rabid Communist. He raised his children as Americans. His daughter said she was called a banana growing up, yellow on the outside, white on the inside."

Thinking how difficult it would be to see that kind of pain inflicted on his own daughters, Carson shakes his head. "If anyone says they know, well, they're just guessing."[25]

That's true. Because you never truly *know* anybody. Not to the point where they lose the power to shock. This applies to your most trusted confidants, to say nothing of casual acquaintances or, in this case, an adversary observed piecemeal from across a distance in snippets of conversation and intermittent sightings. Consider all the husbands amazed to discover the telltale clues of being cuckolded; the parents happening upon a child's drug abuse; the executive dazed by evidence of an adviser's fraud. Deceit is not the exclusive preserve of spies. They are simply more accustomed to it and better schooled to pull it off; more apt to test their mettle along that road.

Deceit is not unlike other human endeavors, whether noble or nefarious. It may begin in passion or curiosity or excitement. Then continue from habit or dependency or from the apparent absence of alternative. And end in disappointment or contentment or resignation. A continuum of action does not transpose to a continuum of purpose. Sincerity, like anything else, is corruptible. The corrupt always find grounds to exonerate themselves.

## *Pusan, Korea, July–December 1951*

The post–World War II map looked incongruously bleak and hostile to the victorious Western powers. The Iron Curtain had drawn across Central Europe, where, from their vantage point, it seemed impenetrable; yet coming from the opposite side, it gave the impression of an awfully thin veil against the Soviet Union's stated intention to foment Communist revolution the world over. To that end, Mao's triumph in China figured to be a decisive achievement. A monochromatic red stain blotched a massive swath of the map.

When Mao ventured outside his native land for the first time in December 1949 to visit Stalin in Moscow, the illusion of a cohesive Communist bloc was reinforced. In fact, their relationship was antagonistic, characterized by jockeying for the upper hand. Mao was determined to guard China's sovereignty at the same time that he connived to acquire the technology and resources he desperately needed from the Soviets to spur development.

Mao shunned relations with the West to convince Stalin he was a stalwart ally. In the most recent assessment of his reign, Jung Chang and Jon Halliday argue, "It is widely thought that it was the U.S. that refused to recognize Mao's China. In fact, Mao went out of his way to make recognition impossible by engaging in overtly hostile acts."[26]

What China lacked in industrial resources and production capacity in the aftermath of the Japanese and civil wars, it made up for in human capital. Stalin understood, and sought to exploit, this without undermining his undisputed leadership of the Communist world. Having no intention of committing Soviet troops to Asia, he was content to use the occasion of their meeting to parcel out Vietnam and North Korea to Mao.[27]

On June 25, 1950, the North Koreans attacked South Korea, storming across the 38th parallel, which marked the division of the peninsula. Accepted scholarship was that China was innocent, even unaware, of North Korean premier Kim Il Sung's scheme. In an early study on the subject, Allen S. Whiting writes, "People's Republic of China had a strong interest in the attack . . . but lacked direct responsibility for its initiation or outcome."[28]

Kim's forces quickly advanced against the ill-prepared and poorly drilled southern army. Though war-weary, the West was Communist-phobic and fearful that appeasing any sign of Communist belligerence would encourage more audacious aggression, as had been its experience with Nazi Germany. With South Korea on the brink of collapse, the United States brought the conflict before the UN Security Council, where each permanent member had the power of veto. The Soviets were absent, boycotting in protest over Taiwan occupying China's seat. Thus did the resolution calling for military intervention pass without dissent.

Under US command, a UN force was dispatched and reversed the tide. By October 7, it had pushed the North Koreans back north of the 38th parallel. The Chinese threatened to intervene if American soldiers proceeded any farther. Rather than halting, they pressed the advantage, approaching the Chinese frontier at the Yalu River. On October 19, Mao made good on his promise and Chinese "volunteers" entered the fray. Historian John Toland concludes, "China reluctantly entered the Korean conflict, not to further world communism but to protect itself from invasion by a powerful enemy threatening to use atomic bombs."[29]

Chang and Halliday contradict this premise. They contend, "Mao encouraged Pyongyang to invade the South and take on the U.S.A. — and volunteered Chinese manpower — as early as May 1949."[30] They quote a communiqué of March 1, 1951, from Mao to Stalin wherein he articulates his objective for the war: "to spend several years consuming several hundred thousand American lives."[31]

Thanks to the influx of the Chinese soldiers, the UN was quickly driven back. By the first week of 1951, the Communists were again in control of Seoul, the South's capital.

By the time the Chinese intervened in the Korean War and stood bayonet-to-bayonet across from Americans, Larry had insinuated himself as an important member of the US mission in Hong Kong. His translations were accurate and lucid, his work well respected.

Combat against Chinese soldiers meant not only casualties but prisoners as well. Many of those fighting as so-called volunteers were actually pressed into the Red Army. Often they were former Guomindang troops who had survived reeducation, but whose loyalty was never sure. Tossing them into the bloody battles was a convenient way to eliminate large numbers of them. Poorly equipped, inadequately dressed for the Korean winter, malnourished, and suffering intense psychological trauma from the relentless aerial bombings inflicted on their lines by the Americans, Chinese troops surrendered in droves. Indeed, Toland contends that the "majority of those surrendering were veterans of the Kuomintang who took advantage of the turn of the battle to 'come over' to the side of democracy."[32]

The Americans were desperate for native Chinese speakers to assist with interrogations of the prisoners. Among American citizens who had been security-screened for military intelligence and the State Department, and were qualified to conduct such interviews, few had the requisite language ability. One possible source of linguists, Taiwan, was purposely excluded from participating in the UN contingent so as not to further antagonize the People's Republic or give it the excuse of Taiwan's complicity in the belligerence to try to retake the island by force. Scrambling, the United States enlisted translators it was employing for nonsensitive jobs. Among them, Larry Chin. In July 1951, State sent Larry from Hong Kong to Pusan, at the extreme tip of the South. During a three-month tour, he estimated that he was involved in questioning between 100 and 150 Chinese prisoners.[33] He probably did not conduct any of the interviews on his own, but only served to translate on behalf of an American officer.

With the combatants locked in stalemate, on July 1 North Korea and China accepted a UN invitation to discuss a cessation of hostilities. Thus began the longest truce talks in military history, involving a total of 575 meetings over two years and seventeen days.

It took five months and sixty-five meetings just to reach agreement that the 38th parallel should be the line of demarcation, thereby denying either side territorial gains. That settled, the mechanics for exchanging prisoners of war stood out as the most divisive issue. Admiral C. Turner Joy, the chief of the UN delegation to the Korean Armistice Conference, went so far as to blame this one dilemma for "delaying a truce for over a year."[34] Making its case, the US attorney would hold Larry responsible for this delay and all ensuing casualties.

The UN position was that each prisoner ought to be allowed to choose whether he wanted to be repatriated or resettled elsewhere. In other words, North Koreans and mainland Chinese would have the opportunity to stay in South Korea or to seek asylum in the West. Of course, the same choice would apply equally to captured UN combatants. The Communists' position was uncompromising: All prisoners, without exception, must be repatriated. There was a huge disparity in the number of prisoners held by the two sides: According to lists exchanged in December 1951, the Communists held 11,559 soldiers, while the UN had 132,474, including 20,700 Chinese.

The UN's prisoners were held in camps on Koje Island, located off the southern tip of the peninsula. Here the compounds were violently split between Reds and Whites. Guards were confined to the perimeters; inside, near civil wars waged, with brutal beatings frequently inflicted. In an extreme display of revulsion at the prospect of returning to the Communist side, many prisoners resorted to mutilating their bodies with crude tattoos of pro-Chiang, anti-Mao slogans. With their politics indelibly gouged into their skin, they pleaded, sending them home was to condemn them to dire punishment at the hands of the authorities. Red prisoners responded by forcibly etching anti-American sentiments on some of their White enemies, thinking this would disqualify them from resettlement in the West.

The UN screened each prisoner individually regarding repatriation. Anyone who answered affirmatively when asked if he wanted to return home was slated for repatriation without further questioning. Those who responded negatively were asked whether they intended to resist repatriation forcibly. A negative response marked the prisoner for return. Anyone who said, Yes, he planned to resist, was asked a series of questions, culminating with, "Despite your decision, if the UNC should repatriate you, what would you do?" Finally, the prisoner "was listed for repatriation unless during the questioning he mentioned suicide, fight to death, braving death to escape, or similar intentions."[35] These multiple hoops were arrayed to encourage all but the most indomitable spirits to go home.

During talks at the border town of Panmunjom on April 19, 1952, UN negotiators informed their Communist counterparts that a poll of prisoners revealed approximately half did not wish to be repatriated. The Communists were absolutely furious and utterly intransigent — they would accept nothing less than the return of all prisoners. Heavy casualties were being inflicted and North Korea was being bombed to rubble. Still, "'Not a single one is to get away!' Mao's chilling mantra prolonged the war for a year and a half, during which hundreds of thousands of Chinese, and many more Koreans, died."[36] To say nothing of Americans and other nationals committed to the UN contingent.

----

By the end of 1951, Larry's stint in Korea was over and he was back in Hong Kong at his job with the US consulate. In April, he met with Dr. Wang (not to be confused with Wang, his college roommate), the head of the Beijing Red Cross Society. His position undoubtedly allowed him to travel more freely than a Chinese national with a less humanitarian title. He was more likely an intelligence co-optee than an officer.

At his trial, Larry testified that he held no fixed political views at this time. However, Dr. Wang's story influenced him. "I learned that he was almost executed because he was caught by the Guomindang so I was sympathetic to him. He told me that he was captured together with a number of his friends, and his friends were all executed, except him, because he was a medical doctor."[37] Larry believed he was a member of the Communist Party.

Recalling the sort of information he elicited from Chinese prisoners, Larry told his trial, benignly, "I would ask where they live and how many family members and how they do make a living and what kind of income they receive."[38]

But what he gave the jury was a sanitized and very much abbreviated distortion of the truth.

"Did you give him [Dr. Wang] any information about the condition of the prisoners of war as you found it?" Jacob Stein, Chin's lead defense attorney, asked.

"Yes. I told him how they live, what kind of provisions were provided them, what kind of food they eat and what kind of exercises they do each day." He added, "I told him that from my interrogations their living standard was real low in China, but in the camp their food was better than their home."[39]

The prisoners painted a picture of a desperate country, weakened by war and ruled by a government preoccupied with exercising power over — as opposed to caring for and feeding — its citizens. They described a country whose infrastructure had been badly damaged, whose industrial production had been ruined, whose agriculture was decimated. They may have shared an inkling of the fierce dictator Mao would become. Not flattering for China to learn that its citizens found conditions in a UN prison camp preferable to their homes, but it hardly makes sense as a reason to prolong a fruitless war.

For what purpose did the Chinese insist on the return of so many men who were blatantly antagonistic to their regime? Why not take advantage of the opportunity to be rid of this potential source of internal dissent? What was so important about getting the prisoners out of the clutches of the enemy?

There was one specific category of prisoner that the Americans absolutely insisted was to be exempted from repatriation, but in whose return the Chinese had special interest. American secretary of state Dean Acheson stated that any prisoner "who had rendered 'outstanding service' to the Unified Command and who, if returned to Communist control, might be killed, might be paroled."[40] *Outstanding service* is a euphemism for willingly sharing knowledge.

By the time Larry met them, those willing to talk would have been drained of all military intelligence. Furthermore, he lacked the appropriate clearance to sit in on the most sensitive interrogations. He participated once the only questions left to answer were in regard to conditions in China, as he testified.

However, as an intelligent man paying careful attention, he could well have discerned which prisoners appeared most cooperative. Larry surely told Dr. Wang all about those rendering "outstanding service." Nothing else explains why China was so frantic to get these people back under control. And to punish them. Those prisoners who ultimately did return to the mainland were not celebrated as heroic resisters, but were enslaved in Manchurian reeducation camps, where they suffered appalling conditions.

"We couldn't figure out what was the big deal about repatriation. I mean, what is the big deal?" Johnson recalls wondering at the time. "Now we know. They wanted them back because of everything they were giving away."[41]

Paying a source is an awkward matter, even when that source expresses interest in compensation. As a livelihood, snitching for money holds about as much respectability as sex for money. Best to concoct a plausible fiction to rationalize the furtive exchange of the rumpled brown envelope stuffed with greasy, well-used bills at the conclusion of a productive debriefing. Larry was first rewarded for his efforts when Dr. Wang paid him approximately two thousand Hong Kong dollars — the equivalent of between five and six hundred US — after his stint in Korea. Ostensibly, he was being compensated for the sale of some property his family owned in Beijing, Larry would explain. "Dr. Wang helped me by bringing the proceeds to Hong Kong."[42]

It was exactly a year after Larry met with Dr. Wang, on April 26, 1953, that armistice talks were reconvened at Panmunjom. They had been in recess for seven months with neither side willing to budge on the prisoner exchange issue. The impasse was breached by Zhou Enlai's proposal that all detainees demanding repatriation be exchanged forthwith, while talks proceeded on the disposition of the others.

Of course, other things — far more momentous than Larry's debriefing — were going on. The new American president, Dwight Eisenhower, suggested in his February 2, 1953, State of the Union address that he might consider using the atomic bomb against China. Mao, according to Chang and Halliday, welcomed the threat and intended to exploit it to pressure Stalin into giving him nuclear weapons.[43] On February 28, Stalin suffered a stroke; he died on March 5. While in Moscow for the funeral, Zhou was informed that the Soviets had decided to end the Korean War. Facing pressure from the Kremlin, Mao gave in on voluntary repatriation in order to move the talks ahead.

Agreement was reached on June 8 to move all resistant prisoners to the demilitarized zone, where they would have to meet with "explainers" from their home country who would take the opportunity to persuade them to return. Anyone who still refused would not be forced back. In the end, close to twenty-three thousand North Koreans and Chinese remained in the West, while thirty-five South Koreans and twenty-three Americans chose to stay with the Communists. On July 27, 1953, the armistice formally ending the Korean War was signed, and prisoner exchanges began the following week.

*Alexandria, Virginia, November 22, 1985*
"The thing about the prisoners of war," Johnson says later, "he thinks that's a throwaway. It ends up being the primary espionage count he's convicted on."[44]

Larry may have thought it was so long ago, so inconsequential thirty years after the fact. But it proved to be the decomposing corpse in the deep recess of his closet that could not be dressed up with a neatly stitched patchwork of pretense. Here was a clear act that damaged the national security of the United States in the midst of a military conflict. Americans were dying, and Larry was spying. Espionage is not legally defined by the harm that can be directly attributed to it. The act itself is the crime.

When Roth excused himself to phone Schiffer with Chin's admission about Korea, he knew he had a confessed spy. But without corroborating evidence, he didn't necessarily have a prosecutable spy.

A confession is a tricky thing. Police love it for carrying the authenticity of being spoken by the accused. Juries are hesitant to believe anyone would confess to a crime unless truly guilty. For both those reasons, defense attorneys find a confession troublesome — though it's far from an insurmountable obstacle to exoneration. Confessions can be dismissed on a variety of legal technicalities that attorneys are expert at manipulating.

The investigators were urged to press on. To get *evidence*. A piece of paper clearly anointed with a SECRET stamp that Joseph Aronica could wave dramatically under jurors' noses, declaring *this* very document went from the guarded precincts of the CIA, delivered to Beijing by Larry Chin.

Guerin was conscious of time passing.

While the FBI was careful to describe the proceedings as an interview, the distinction from an interrogation was subtle and growing less noticeable by the minute. This wasn't a function of atmosphere, but of legality. Once he'd admitted espionage, the question of whether he was in custody became salient. Theoretically, he retained the right to ask the agents to leave. Practically speaking, he had jumped off that precipice.

Armed with knowledge of a crime, were the agents now obliged to place him under arrest and, thus, advise him of his rights?

Concerned that this would alter the mood, they were loath to do so. Guerin was skillfully playing to Larry's hopes and quelling his fears. You really have to tell us everything in order for us to evaluate whether we can use you, he was goaded. Since Aronica had forbidden an arrest without his explicit authorization, the agents could argue that they had relinquished the power to detain him. Each time Larry excused himself to go to the bathroom, exiting the living room without an escort, was regarded as proof he was not in custody.

Getting Larry to keep talking wasn't difficult. He now believed it was in his best interest. He was engaging in an act not of contrition, but of salesmanship. The only way to sell the FBI on operating him as a double was to make sure they understood how important a spy he'd been all these years, to demonstrate he was far too valuable to be discarded in prison.

### *Kadena Air Base, Okinawa, May 1952*

Wang would have reacted gleefully when Larry told him he was offered a job with the FBIS on Okinawa. In fact, given Larry's inclination to self-promotion, he almost certainly declared that he was joining the CIA. Just four years after being recruited and gaining employment with the Americans, he had been invited into its most secret place. He earned the Ministry of Public Security great prestige in the constant competition waged among the organs of state.

If Larry was shrewd, he expressed some reservations about the position. Moving to Okinawa meant uprooting his young family. His daughter, Roberta, was barely two, and his son, Peter, only six months old. A lateral transfer from State to CIA would benefit China, but what of his career? A father had to plan ahead, after all.

Wang agreed wholeheartedly and set Larry's mind at ease with assurances that he could expect compensation for his sacrifices.

Whether Larry hemmed and hawed as a negotiating tactic, we'll never know. We do know he took the job and moved his family to the American Kadena Air Base. Among his benefits was home leave every two years at government expense. Home, in this case, was Hong Kong, as travel restrictions against Americans going to the mainland would have applied as well to him as a federal employee.

Wang would not have risked venturing to Okinawa, where Chinese agents didn't have the same freedom of movement they enjoyed on Hong Kong. The logistics of arranging a covert meet were impractical, especially given the large US military contingent, and unnecessary. Seeing Larry whenever he got back to Hong Kong would be sufficient.

Larry's job was to listen to radio broadcasts emanating from China and translate the content into English.

"Radio broadcasts were one of the very few windows during that period of time to [sic] the United States to determine, for example, what was happening on mainland China, what the Chinese intentions were in the Korean War, what its intentions were about invading Taiwan and about its development of an expanding military force as well as its political stability," Aronica explained to the jury at Chin's trial when he laid out the time line of his activities.

The specific broadcasts Larry monitored were not chosen at random, but judiciously selected by his superiors.

"The supervisor knew what should be translated based upon classified intelligence requirements of the United States," Aronica said ominously. Each time he returned to Hong Kong, "he secretly met with agents of the Chinese intelligence service and . . . gave them information about what he was doing at FBIS, how he was doing it, and what the US intelligence concerns were and how successful the US was in getting the kind of information we were seeking."[45]

What he described doesn't sound like much — listening to broadcasts issued by tightly controlled media that reflected nothing except what the state intended the public to hear — but intelligence requirements are highly classified for very good reason. From what an adversary is anxious to learn, a state can extrapolate what they might already know. Thus, by a process of elimination, if China was aware that the United States was directing all its resources toward learning the condition of its nuclear facilities, for example, China could ascertain that the US lacked intelligence sources in a position to report on them. Conversely, if the US suddenly seemed to halt efforts to ascertain the Communist regime's current intentions with regard to Taiwan, it could be a tip-off that it had a reliable source in place in the Ministry of Foreign Affairs keeping them informed. Hence, it's always just as important to disguise what you do know as what you don't.

Moreover, the prosecution established the continuum of his relationship with China. Regardless of the specifics upon which Larry reported, a pertinent point was that an American government employee was pursuing a clandestine relationship with an agent of a hostile state. If his access was limited by circumstance, his intentions were boundless.

Spying is deliberate.

On home leave in Hong Kong in 1956, Larry dropped a line to Dr. Wang on the mainland saying how nice it would be if they could get together.

Wang responded with enthusiasm at the prospect of seeing his old friend, but, alas, he found it impossible to travel at the moment. Fortunately he had a friend, Mr. Ou, who would be able to meet with Larry.

A change of handlers can generate difficult emotions in a source. The sense of security inspired by a familiar handler, not to mention established techniques for being handled, can be shaken. Suddenly the whole facade of the personal, one-to-one connection that is held in secret from the rest of the world is broken down and the spy faces up to the existence of a bureaucracy buzzing in the background, assigning and reassigning his friends.

Not so with Larry. He appeared focused on his own agenda, and to pursuing it without great bouts of sentimentality. If Ou was to be his handler, Ou it would be. And Wang was gone from his life.

Ou Qiming would continue to be his handler right up until Larry's final visit to Beijing in February 1985,[46] when they would see each other for the last time.

During his time on Okinawa, Larry met Chow Chin-yu, also known as Cathy, a base employee. Like him, she was married when they began an affair. Not much is known about his first wife, Doris Chiu. Personal history forms he filled out at the time show that they were married on the mainland in April 1949; she accompanied Larry to Hong Kong. Together they had three children. Their divorce was finalized on March 24, 1959. Cathy, who had been married since April 4, 1942, divorced her husband on November 30, 1962.

Searching through Larry's papers, agents discovered an angry letter Doris had written him complaining that the divorce settlement hadn't taken into account the "millions" he'd been paid to spy.[47] Though the sum is a wild exaggeration, it was never ascertained whether Larry had boasted about his secret venture, if he'd carelessly let it slip, or if she was somehow a participant.

Attempting to learn who might have been aware of his espionage, Aronica would ask after Doris.

"She might have known, but I wasn't sure," Larry replied.[48]

Since she had never lived in the United States, the FBI didn't pursue her during the course of its investigation.

## Santa Rosa, California, 1961

In the aftermath of hostilities in Korea, China moved up the CIA's priority list. While the USSR was not to be displaced from the top slot, it is worth noting that the Soviet Cold War never resulted in direct military confrontation; the United States and China actually traded shots.

Larry's skills remained in demand. He was offered a transfer to the FBIS bureau in Santa Rosa, California, where, as Aronica would explain in court, "he did basically the same thing he had done in Okinawa. Again, his supervisor would tell him what to translate based upon the classified intelligence requirements of the US intelligence community. Again, the radio broadcasts continued during that period to be one of the few windows that the West had into what was going on in mainland China."[49]

It was an ecstatic moment, a professional achievement that bespoke his worth to the US government and foretold his value to the Chinese. More so, it was the realization of the dream nurtured the world over: a ticket to America.

And not a ticket punched after days or weeks sealed down in the dank, stinking hold of a decrepit freighter. Off-loaded on a desolate stretch of coastline in the dead of night to decide on your own which direction would bring you to the nearest shelter. To shuffle along, the skin on your feet peeling away in chunks from being immersed so long in seawater. Hoping for nothing better than a menial job — or several menial jobs — paying for barely food enough on one day to fuel the halfhearted trudge to work the next. To disappear into a leaky, vermin-infested room in a ghetto where you hope to pass unnoticed, among all the others whose hooded eyes betray their desperation to become invisible.

Not Larry. He would fly comfortably into San Francisco with a government job, as good as any middle-class American.

Before making the move across the Pacific, he took home leave to Hong Kong. There, he informed Ou of the good news.

The Public Security officer could barely contain himself. Larry's success belonged to him. It would bring accolades, perhaps even the chance to visit the West.

Ou was wary of one thing. Larry had been among the Americans now for a dozen years, working and socializing with them every single day, whereas Ou only saw him every couple of years or so. The fear with all undercover agents is that they will cease to distinguish between their enemies and their true friends. As with a child, you send them out into the world without any assurances how they will return. Will it be with their values intact or corrupted? Do they remain yours or give themselves to another?

Ou had no specific cause to doubt Larry's integrity, just the ever-present reluctance to trust fully that is the intelligence officer's natural inclination. He was at a disadvantage in discussing the Americans with Larry because he didn't know them firsthand. They could be seductive, he knew, with their undisciplined lifestyle. With a good salary and a nice home, Larry might become blind to the bankruptcy of their society. It is easy to become lazy and fall into the trap of mistaking the instant gratification of material pleasure for an end goal. The goal, Ou insisted, was to fashion China into the proletarian state they all, collectively, desired. Larry had to be mindful that, whatever joys came to him in California, he was privileged to accept them as rewards for his perseverance on behalf of the people. He had to behave like an American for the cause of China.

Ou struck a conciliatory tone regarding America. The bitterness of Korea had dissipated. Relations with the Soviets were deteriorating. Utopian ideas of international Communist solidarity were in tatters. If anything, national boundaries were hardening against ideological currents. Maoism was not Stalinism was not Leninism was not Titoism. Helping China wasn't synonymous with hurting America, he affirmed.

But his pep talk wasn't necessary. Larry wasn't conflicted.

Santa Rosa is just fifty-five miles north of San Francisco. It is temperate, predominantly middle class, and overwhelmingly white. It's the kind of orderly community where government prefers to set up its offices. It doesn't impose a huge cost-of-living burden, and it promises a tranquil environment in which to raise a family. In these respects, Santa Rosa bore a striking resemblance to suburban Virginia.

For Larry, it was a positively idyllic setting. He couldn't believe the affluence, nor the unostentatious way in which it was borne. Every home was equipped with the latest appliances — refrigerator, washer-dryer, television set; each family owned at least one car, and some had two. Government employees, with their job security and steady paycheck, found credit readily available. Satisfying the acquisitive impulse was the easiest thing in the world.

Spying is liberty.

It excuses every lie.

And spies lie a lot. The fact of being a spy can be used to rationalize every deception. You lie to build cover. You lie for self-preservation. You lie when it isn't necessary just so you'll be better when survival depends on it coming as second nature. You end up hiding something of yourself from everyone you know. But it's different things with different people in different circumstances. Until your life is so enfolded in a labyrinth of lies, the truth never escapes.

Larry was thirty-nine, with the comfort of a stable job. He settled into a cottage at 91 Barham Avenue. This was his first time away from the East. He felt liberated. And California on the cusp of the 1960s was an amazing place to be liberated.

He arrived in Santa Rosa alone in January 1961, followed by Cathy in June 1963. They were married in Reno on August 5 in typical Nevada style, with much haste and little ceremony. The next year, they moved to 1438 Heather Drive. His two oldest children, Roberta and Peter, soon joined them.

Cathy was a typical stay-at-home Chinese wife. She was competent enough in English to make her way, but not enough to assert her independence outside the home. Which was all right with her. She was thrilled to be living in America.

At work, Larry was popular for his proficiency and helpfulness. Socially, he was popular for his charm and exoticism. It wasn't, after all, every day that you met someone from Beijing. Many of the young secretaries who'd never ventured far from home were captivated by his stories about growing up in China. He enjoyed recalling his homeland for them. He loved the novelty of being fascinating. It eased the homesickness that would well up unexpectedly from time to time and make him feel utterly isolated no matter how many people were around.

"One of the principles of Chinese intelligence is that tomorrow is more important than today," Moore explains. "They're always calculating an operation in terms of what might happen next. It's the opposite of the Western approach."[50]

At some point, senior officials in Beijing deemed Larry a trump-card source: His intelligence could trump other sources. He was counted on to authenticate or refute what they gleaned through other channels.

A serious debate ensued at the highest levels of the government as to whether Larry should be operational or held in reserve to be activated only in the event of war. Less than a decade removed from Korea, the conflict in Vietnam was growing in intensity, Taiwan was still a constant irritant, and China feared America's nuclear arsenal.

"You could always work up a scenario where they would actually go to war," Moore suggests. "I think it was quite credible."[51]

Every human source operation is fraught with risk. Despite the most stringent precautions, the greatest care, the strictest adherence to agreed-upon procedure, each time a spy misappropriates a document to make an illicit copy or poses a question that reaches outside the parameters of his need to know or glances at the papers exposed on an adjoining desk, he could unwittingly initiate a chain of events that would ultimately trigger his downfall.

The decision to make Larry operational was taken by Zhou Enlai himself. Responsible for foreign affairs as well as serving as something of an intelligence czar to the Politburo, Zhou must have concluded that the benefits derived from a continuous stream of information — presumably including advance warning of aggression — outweighed the risk of getting caught. Also to be considered was the uncertainty of trying to establish secure contact with a dormant source only after the eruption of hostilities. And once Zhou gave the okay for the operation, it is only reasonable to conclude that he took an interest in its progress and Larry's output. Indeed, he exercised overriding control on the case; not, of course, on a micro level, but in terms of broad oversight. This comes as no surprise, given the repercussions that could reasonably be predicted in the event the United States discovered a Chinese spy within its intelligence service. It would be a very foolhardy minister of public security who would suffer Zhou's wrath were he to be caught unawares in an international scandal of such magnitude.

Spying is tradecraft.

Spying is witchcraft.

With Larry in the United States, the operation assumed a new level of complexity. Not only would he be farther from home, but he'd also presumably access greater quantities of interesting material. He would still have the opportunity to go to Hong Kong. Records later assembled by the FBI showed that in fact Larry took home leave in September–October 1961 and March 1965. Only upon becoming a naturalized American in 1965 was he no longer eligible for home leave. Nonetheless, he returned to Hong Kong in May–June 1966, January 1967, February–March 1968, and March 1970, just prior to transferring to Rosslyn. These trips allowed Ou the opportunity to debrief Larry and top up his enthusiasm for the mission, but not to reap maximum benefit from running a penetration of the CIA.

Larry could hardly be expected to load up his suitcase with a year's worth of pilfered documents; the risk of getting caught crossing international boundaries was excessive and avoidable. Furthermore, his trips were too sporadic to fully exploit the advantage of having him on the spot providing intelligence more or less as it happened. Even with the most rapid turnaround, documents take time to process, analyze, and distribute to the officials who need to see them. Year-old intelligence is little more tantalizing than month-old pastry.

In addition, international travel — even to destinations such as Hong Kong, against which there were no restrictions — left paper trails. If nothing else, he couldn't reasonably travel to Asia on a weekend, so leave applications had to be filed. Valid passports maintained. Customs declarations submitted.

For security reasons, single-line control was imperative. That is, Larry would continue to be run directly out of Beijing, as opposed to being assigned a handler in the United States. No intermediary was informed about him. Absolutely no contact with anybody was permitted to occur on US soil. But he did need a convenient method for communicating with Beijing, preferably one that allowed him to instigate contact when he saw fit, without engaging in a complicated exchange of signals.

Traditionally, the Chinese abstain from the trappings of tradecraft. They don't usually do those things that are so meticulously contrived to disguise espionage that they could be mistaken for nothing else. You won't find one of their officers rooting around between the rocks in a park to free the discarded soda can that contains a secret message from an agent. You won't witness the nearly invisible brush pass, designed to put two people alongside one another for just the instant it takes for one to slip a sheaf of paper or roll of film or microcassette to the other. Nor will you intercept letters that, if examined closely enough under the microscope, will reveal the most delicate of microdots in the faint period at the end of a sentence in the midst of a long, unassuming paragraph.

Espionage as God intended it.

No skulking. Nothing elaborate. Just simple reliance on the extravagant normality of the situation to make anything nefarious seem inconceivable.

But this case demanded an exception. Just as this case was unique for involving a directed penetration, so it was unique for the copying of documents and the employment of a courier to handle the volume of material Larry was passing over.

Happily, the United States shares the world's longest undefended border with Canada. Americans and Canadians were not even obligated to carry passports when crossing to one side or the other. Any photo ID — most commonly, a driver's license — was enough to be greeted with a friendly welcome and a quick wave through from Customs officers. The volume of traffic at the busiest crossing points meant that formal records were nonexistent in the era before computers.

From San Francisco, it's only a two-and-a-quarter-hour flight up the Pacific coast to Vancouver where, a later search through Chin's papers would reveal, he traveled in May and June 1967. It is only reasonable to speculate that both trips were occasions to transmit intelligence to his friends.

### Alexandria, Virginia, November 22, 1985

The agents were increasingly anxious to cut to the chase, while being cautious not to betray any hurry. Every tick off the clock reminded them that the courts are disposed to consider overlong interviews as coercive.

"We wanted to get up to current intelligence," Rudy Guerin explains. "What did you give up? Is there anyone out there who's in danger now? Were you able to get information on CIA sources or FBI sources? What is your contact procedure? Have you met anyone here in the US? We're trying to get as much as we can as quickly as we can, because at any moment the lightbulb might go on: Whoa, I've said enough."[52]

Guerin pulled from the file folder several FBIS documents related to China from the 1970s and early 1980s. Showing them to Larry, he asked, "Would this be something like what you would pass?"

Chin looked them over. "Yes."

Guerin had him sign his initials on each one.[53]

This was circumstantial, as opposed to evidentiary. They were establishing a pattern of behavior, but not corroborating a verifiable act of treason.

Documents *like* that, sure. But Mr. Chin, did you hand *these* documents to agents of the Chinese government? No, sir, I did not.

"He was very cagey about the documents," recalls Johnson. "We could never get him to identify a particular document. Maybe he knew that saying *I gave that one* would have hanged him. He seemed to know he couldn't give us that. Or maybe he'd passed so many, he really didn't know."[54]

Larry was clever and self-controlled throughout. Never was it, Hey, I was wrong, I'm sorry, I wish I'd never done it. No, it was, Hey, you got me, how can we resolve this thing? Let's make it about how I can help you, not how you're going to hurt me.

He was the classic overanxious buyer in a bidding war with high-pressure salesmen. He sold himself on a deal that had never been offered. It was a fatal error. They were playing out a variation of a slapstick negotiation routine, where the seller gets the buyer so turned around that the buyer begins arguing for a higher price. He fell victim to the conceit that he was the smartest guy in the room.

*United Nations, December 1968*

At the height of the Cultural Revolution, Larry lost direct contact with Beijing. Between January 1967 and March 1970, he only went to Hong Kong once, in February–March 1968. He learned afterward that Ou, along with the entire unit of which he was a part, had been exiled to a farming commune to undergo intensive criticism and reeducation. It was the common story of the time. They needn't have done anything. Obedience could be a transgression equal to disobedience. In a society where either action or inaction might be equally regarded as evidence of disloyalty, depending on the inclination or fervor of the local Red Guards, safety was nonexistent.

The upheaval suffered in the ranks of the Ministry of Public Security, as in other sections of the government, was immense. Entire offices and bureaus, in major centers and regional outposts, were closed and staff dispatched to communes for reeducation and hard labor. Adding to the degradation of Public Security officers, in particular, was that they sometimes shared their fate in the company of common criminals. Further insult was inflicted toward the end of the Cultural Revolution, when the criminals were as likely as not freed before they were.

Applying a very Chinese approach to turmoil, Larry was philosophical and bided his time. The Cultural Revolution was bound to be temporary. The mayhem couldn't continue indefinitely. Since it wasn't a revolt against the Communist regime, the party would restore order in due course. People would return to their posts. Or they would be replaced.

Kang Sheng had assumed control over the Ministry of Public Security. "Under his supervision, however, the secret police did little more than purge his enemies, guard him and his allies, and suppress popular discontent. He could boast of no major victories in the world of espionage to justify his claim of being a specialist in intelligence and security," report Byron and Pack. Adding, with regard to the most important agent under that service's control, "Chin's work did not reflect much credit on Kang's skills as a spymaster. While Kang was riding high, Chin lost contact with his CCP handlers and had to resume his espionage activities on his own initiative after the Cultural Revolution ended and stability returned to China. Kang and his comrades were preoccupied with events at home, virtually to the exclusion of the outside world."[55]

While China was in chaos, Larry's career with the CIA reached a crossroads in 1968, when the agency announced plans to close the Santa Rosa office come 1970.

Suddenly he faced the uncertainty of unemployment and the reality that he had limited marketability as a linguist. Roberta and Peter were fast approaching college age. His youngest son, Homer, now living with him as well, was fifteen. Their education alone was going to up his cost of living significantly. They were bright kids, and he took great pride in their ambition to become doctors.

Out of necessity, he made application for a job with the UN's translation bureau.

A reference — consulted in connection with a security screening investigation — who had known Larry for nearly thirty years told the FBI that "the applicant [Chin] would prefer to continue his employment with the United States Government, but if his job is terminated, he believes the applicant would take a position with the United Nations."[56]

On December 11, Larry was informed by the UN that he had been accepted onto the list of candidates to fill vacancies in the Chinese section as they opened. Moore speculates that the Chinese would have been unhappy. "They had lots of people at the UN. A translator-level penetration of the UN doesn't give them anything. Larry was a penetration of the CIA. That's the pinnacle."[57]

Were he cast out from the US intelligence community, as he expected, he'd no longer be of any use to China, in any event. Therefore, he had to find an alternative to secure his livelihood first. Perhaps, once at the center of international diplomacy, he could convince Ou that he was still useful.

The matter became academic when his preemployment medical uncovered that he had diabetes. For insurance purposes, the UN wasn't prepared to engage him until he could demonstrate that the disease was under control.

In his closing argument at trial, Jacob Stein drew attention to this episode. "He was all set to take that job. . . . The fact that he wanted to go to the United Nations where he would have no access to classified material absolutely contradicts the [US] government's position."[58]

However, this ignores Chin's own testimony in response to his attorney's questions when he stated explicitly that he applied to the UN only because he believed his FBIS employment was to be terminated.[59]

### Rosslyn, Virginia, April 1970

As it happened, Larry was offered the chance to continue his employment at FBIS headquarters in Rosslyn, marking a great leap forward for his spying. Not only was he placed in a position to mingle with intelligence officers from the Directorate of Operations in nearby Langley — those men and women running secret operations against China — but he was granted a top-secret clearance. Now he could be assigned highly sensitive material to translate. Now he could spy in earnest.

The FBIS clearly held him in high esteem. With skilled Chinese linguists anything but abundant — and few, if any, who could boast more than two decades of government service — he was warmly welcomed into this more clandestine milieu. During his trial, Larry expanded on how anxious the CIA was to have him cleared: "I had to fulfill a period of five years of citizenship in order to get this clearance. At that time, the bureau in Santa Rosa already closed, so in order for me to fulfill the five years, the agency continued to be open, leaving me there with an editor and engineer, and I worked on that basis as a skeleton staff for five months before I got my five years' citizenship qualification. Then I got clearance."[60]

An internal memo from the chief, Personnel and Training Branch, bears this out: "If Security regulations had allowed, FBIS would have converted Chin to Staff [permanent] status in January 1965 when he became a US citizen."[61]

Larry describes himself as having become disillusioned with Communism. "I was so pleased that I was in the free world, and I was believing in the

Western way of life. This hit me most hard in the year of 1960 when there was a purging of intellectuals in China, and many of my friends were persecuted, and some of them committed suicide." He provided the names of three individuals by way of illustration.[62]

Larry was referring to Mao's infamous Hundred Flowers Campaign. Recognizing that the People's Republic was stagnating, Mao came up with a scheme to embrace intellectuals and scientists, who had heretofore been treated as adversaries because they were mostly products of the pre-revolutionary bourgeoisie. In May 1956, Mao issued his famous call for "letting a hundred flowers bloom" in culture and "a hundred schools of thought contend" in science.[63] Interpreting this as a call for open debate, intellectuals responded enthusiastically. Too much so for the comfort of the regime, which — perhaps thinking it would inspire only praise for having bestowed the gift of free expression — was taken aback at the harshness of the criticism and the relish with which it was articulated. Mao responded by reverting to a hard line and, in July 1957, began a propaganda assault against his critics, who suddenly found themselves branded counter-revolutionaries, anti-Communists, and rightists. Hundreds of thousands were banished to hard-labor camps, prison, or internal exile.

Controversy over this campaign persists even today. Historian Jonathan Spence insists that the Hundred Flowers Campaign was not a cynical plot by Mao to trick his critics into exposing themselves.[64] On the contrary, Jung Chang and Jon Halliday contend that Mao was indeed deliberately "setting a trap, and that he was inviting people to speak out so that he could then use what they said as an excuse to victimize them. Mao's targets were intellectuals and the educated, the people most likely to speak up." He confided to a few intimates that he was "casting a long line to bait big fish."[65]

Before Larry settled into Alexandria in April, he took a trip to Hong Kong in March. Ou had been rehabilitated, returned from exile to his old position. As if nothing had ever happened, they met for the first time in more than three years. For those who had emerged relatively intact, the

prevailing instinct was to repress the memory and the shame of whatever criticisms they'd experienced. The sooner they could go back to their
routine, the sooner they could forget.

"The Chinese practice continuity," says Magers. "They may preach
something different, but then they go back. Whether it's a comfort level
or something else, I don't know. But you have examples of families in
a Beijing *hutong*, neighbors for generations. And the kid of one family
becomes a Red Guard and struggles the parents of the other family. Well,
when it was all over, they went back to living beside one another. This
was true in the intelligence fraternity. How do you compartmentalize
all that? I don't know. But things went back pretty much to how they
were."[66]

Outwardly, at any rate. It was imperative to reclaim one's position, to
regain trust. Having seen how quickly and brutally the leadership could
change the political climate, neither victims nor victimizers could confidently predict the next shift. Inwardly, however, everyone must have been
left dizzy, as if they'd been blindfolded, spun around like tops, and forced
to hazard which direction to head for safety.

If Ou Qiming had been a true believer, a die-hard Communist, his
faith must have been dealt a blow of considerable force. How could he
retain his belief in an ideal that had been wielded as such a blunt weapon
against him? I imagine Larry pondering the very same question. After all,
he had been off the mainland for more than twenty years. Whatever he
might once have felt about Communism, he had never for a minute lived
in a Communist state. However much he may have admired Mao and
the Chinese Communist Party, he had never depended on their tender
mercies. Living soft in the United States, Larry only had memories of a
privileged upbringing in a corrupt China and those passionate academic
debates about the rebirth of a better, just China.

Among the members of the Ministry of Public Security's offensive counterintelligence unit banished to the countryside was Yu Zhensan.

Under cover of ideological dogma, the Cultural Revolution was all about settling scores. In an atmosphere where every accusation resulted in punishment, revenge was being exacted at all levels of Chinese society. The more highly placed your enemies, the worse you fared. Mao put Jiang Qing — "a persecution zealot"[67] — in charge of the Cultural Revolution Small Group to direct the purges. Kang Sheng was appointed her adviser. Dr. Li Zhisui, Mao's personal physician and confidant, wrote of Kang, "I associated him with the dark side of the party, with all the dirty work that had to be done, delving into people's pasts, finding new enemies, suggesting new targets for attack."[68]

Recall the speculation that Kang and Jiang were instrumental in getting Yu started on a career in the Ministry of Public Security. The hallmark of the Communist Party's longevity has not been consistency, but a volatile succession of purges and rehabilitations, of officials falling in and out of favor for reasons that defy coherent explanation. Which, of course, is fully intended. People who devote all their energy to staying in line behind their leader are not inclined to forge their own path.

One of the old grudges Jiang nursed was against Fan Jin, Yu's mother, the woman for whom she had been discarded by Yu's father. She seized the opportunity of the Cultural Revolution to exact her revenge. The Red Guards were brutally and enthusiastically efficient when directed against selected targets. Though the details are scant, it is believed that Fan Jin was struggled severely.

One benefit security officers claim, as a matter of course, is protection for their families. Having a son in Public Security, for example, ought to be enough to ensure an old woman's peace. But when that son was exiled from Beijing, his fate uncertain, she was left defenseless, and Yu powerless even to implore his onetime benefactors to take pity . . . not that Jiang and Kang were known for the quality of their mercy. He lost tremendous face in his mother's eyes. She never forgave him for her ordeal. The experience left him embittered — both for his own degradation, and for the humiliation of failing to shelter his mother.

*Alexandria, Virginia, November 22, 1985*

The protective barriers built up around the national security apparatus are designed to keep intruders out. Those who are openly admitted into the fortress are deemed trustworthy, and thereafter subject only to the most perfunctory scrutiny. Thus, contrary to the external appearance of impregnability, for those who have crossed the moat with dry feet, extracting classified intelligence is not particularly difficult.

Larry shrugged and told his interviewers that he simply stuffed documents under his shirt at the end of the day and walked out with them. Safe at home, he used his Minolta camera — not some James Bond miniature disguised as a fountain pen or cigarette lighter, but a regular camera — to snap photos of each page. For instance, on March 1, 1981, he wrote in his diary, "Films taken (6)," presumably referring to enough material to fill six rolls of film. The following morning, he'd return with those same documents inside his shirt. He waved and exchanged greetings with the security officers at the front gate. He knew employees were not subject even to random searches.

In keeping with China's cautious approach, Larry insisted that he never pilfered any documents classified top secret; he believed these were too tightly controlled to be removed from the FBIS premises. This, of course, is distinct from saying that he never reported on the contents of the top-secret documents he was able to scrutinize in the office.

Relatively few documents were classified to that level, in any event. In part, this is a function of efficiency. Intelligence agencies the world over are organized according to geographic compartments. Within these compartments, *need-to-know* must be defined relatively broadly. In order to fully analyze conditions in a region, an employee must have a solid background, a comprehensive understanding of context. Only then can he reasonably interpret the more specific incidents with which he is preoccupied.

The first criterion that distinguishes superior analysts is that they read *everything*. Every tidbit about the subject in which they are expert interests them. The more they access, the greater success they'll enjoy binding disparate bits of information into some cogent assessment of use to decision makers. A respected and experienced analyst such as Larry Chin would thus have been encouraged to look over classified intelligence to compare with the open source material he was translating.

Consequently, secret documents — which represent the most common classification within an intelligence agency — circulate relatively freely inside a unit. According to Executive Order 12356, which defines security classifications for the entire federal government, the unauthorized disclosure of secret information could "reasonably be expected to cause serious damage to the national security." Even the disclosure of material classified as confidential "could reasonably be expected to cause damage to the national security," as per the order.

TOP SECRET would be stamped across only that intelligence associated with the most sensitive information — that which identifies sources and methods. Readership would be carefully restricted and monitored. Top-secret files have to be signed out; if procedures are adhered to properly, at any given moment their whereabouts are known. Misplacement would be quickly noted. According to the classification guidelines, the unauthorized disclosure of top-secret material "reasonably could be expected to cause exceptionally grave damage to the national security."

"The Chinese approach is very much glass-half-full," insists Moore. "They're delighted with what you give them. For sure, we would have pressed him to find a way to get top secret out securely, but not the Chinese."[69]

Tick tock.

Larry had been talking for hours. He'd paused to go to the bathroom. He'd received a couple of phone calls. Though he'd spoken to the callers in Chinese, he was on the phone so briefly that he must have just said he was busy and would call back later.

Each interruption caused the agents to hold their collective breath. Breaking the flow of his monologue, at any moment the circuit might pop and he'd realize he'd volunteered enough to establish his potential as a double, if that was their interest. Further revelations would only serve to incriminate. When he returned to pick up where he'd left off, they exhaled slowly to conceal their relief, urging him along with their close attention and methodical note taking.

It would be counterproductive to bombard him with an aggressive barrage of questions. As soon as they appear confrontational, it's going to hit Larry that he's talking himself into a very deep hole. They have to keep everything conciliatory. Steer Larry to establish his bona fides as their agent; don't drive him to confess to crimes against the United States.

As time passed, the agents were growing increasingly anxious. Except for the direct admission relating to the Korean War, they hadn't elicited a tangible bit of spying they could present to the US attorney. He had admitted to a long-standing relationship with a known agent of the Ministry of Public Security. By any standard of common sense, it was confirmed that Larry Chin was the spy that PLANESMAN had alleged. Yet by evidentiary standards they had built a sand castle well below the high-tide line.

### Toronto, Ontario, 1970s

Ou received the good news about Larry's impending move to Rosslyn with relief. Still shaken and feeling vulnerable from the blistering venom spewed during reeducation, Ou was eager to have his importance in the system reaffirmed so quickly.

All those years Larry spent in Okinawa and California had yielded quantity, which always goes a surprisingly long way toward impressing management. It usually took some creative writing to assert its quality, however. Nonetheless, even the lowliest intelligence falls into the category of good-to-know, particularly when sources are few and far between. A lot of careers could be launched and held in orbit simply on the existence of a reliable agent in the CIA. Perhaps that was what ultimately saved Ou from the worst excesses of the Cultural Revolution. Perhaps his punishment was limited to admissions of flawed thinking, but no more, because someone, somewhere had cautioned his tormenters that, for unspecified reasons, he was not to be pushed too far.

Larry's relocation necessitated new procedures to replace his contact in Vancouver. On March 28, 1981, he recorded in his diary, "Canada flt see Lee," in reference to a flight to Toronto to meet his new courier. Once he'd collected enough rolls of film, he passed them over — undeveloped — to Mr. Lee. Mr. Lee would service Larry exclusively. It goes without saying that he never knew Larry's identity or the nature of his activity.

Mr. Lee is a pivotal character in this plot. His identity remains a tantalizing mystery. He could be anybody and, at the same time, was nobody. He might have been a waiter in a sooty Chinese restaurant off Toronto's bustling Spadina Avenue. He might have run an import–export business out of one dilapidated room atop a strip mall in the burgeoning Chinese community in Scarborough, east of the city.

He was simply a co-optee. Approached by an acquaintance, a favor was requested of him. *Guanxi* demanded he comply, if possible. As it happened, the favor was not a great imposition. Periodically, he would have to meet a man who would hand him a package, the contents of which need not concern him. His responsibility was simply to collect the package.

He was chosen for his reliability and because he lived in Toronto, the ideal location for Larry's contact. Toronto International Airport, in the suburb of Mississauga, had daily flights to and from the US capital region. Larry could fly into Toronto, meet Lee, and be back home within several hours, without anybody ever knowing he'd left the country.

To minimize superfluous contact, meets were arranged well in advance. As in, *Mr. Lee will be at such-and-such a location at a particular time on irregular days every month*. If Larry had something to pass along, he only had to show up and deliver. If not, Mr. Lee would be available the following month, or the one after that. This allowed Larry maximum flexibility while ensuring fairly rapid transmission whenever he should come across something timely. It appears they met at various locations in Mississauga — once at a shopping center, for instance, and another time in the lobby of an airport hotel.

How Mr. Lee got the material back to China has also never been verified. He may have delivered it to someone from the Chinese consulate in

Toronto, who sent it to Beijing by diplomatic bag. Or he may have delivered it to an accommodation address, from whence it found its way to an official establishment and the protection of the diplomatic pouch.

As soon as it became practicable, the FBI sought the assistance of the Canadian Security Intelligence Service, but to no avail. Larry hadn't been under suspicion prior to his travels to Toronto and, thus, had never been placed under surveillance. Trying to locate Mr. Lee after the fact based on nothing but a commonplace last name proved impossible.

### Beijing, February 17, 1972

Referring to China in an article titled "Asia After Viet Nam," in the October 1967 issue of *Foreign Affairs*, Richard Nixon wrote, "There is no place on this small planet for a billion of its potentially most able people to live in angry isolation."[70] This was the first tentative allusion that he might be farsighted enough to see that the refusal to recognize the Communist regime was an untenable policy.

However, the analysis of an out-of-office politician is a far cry from the policy implemented by a sitting president. As Henry Kissinger, who has been both intellectual commentator and policy formulator, offered, "The analyst runs no risk. If his conclusions prove wrong, he can write another treatise. The statesman is permitted only one guess; his mistakes are irretrievable."[71] Once elected the next year, Nixon would get the opportunity to implement his idea.

Even if he was convinced of the wisdom of establishing a high-level dialogue with China, he needed to be confident that any overtures toward that end would be received favorably and not be manipulated into a source of embarrassment for the American government. The same held true for the Chinese. With a long legacy of entrenched hostility, either side was reluctant to make conciliatory gestures that wouldn't be reciprocated for fear of appearing weak.

Based on that article, Nixon would recount in his memoirs: "sophisticated observers were able to see that I was raising the curtain for the

China initiative that became the centerpiece of my administration's foreign policy."[72] There's a potent dose of hindsight in this comment. Does he count the Chinese among those observers? Would Mao, who spoke no English, or, more likely, Premier Zhou, who was fluent, pull out a back issue of *Foreign Affairs* once Nixon was elected and confidently say, *Good news, here's a president ready to dialogue with us?* Or, if they were even aware of this article (and they probably were, since *Foreign Affairs* has long served as a publication through which the policy elite have expressed their views), would it have been sufficient to undo Nixon's well-earned reputation as an ardent and unyielding anti-Communist?

The two countries had yet to overcome the harsh feelings engendered by the Korean War, and the 38th parallel remained (and remains) among the most heavily fortified and tense borders in the world. China still resented America's recognition of Taiwan. The US was entrenched in Vietnam and viewed the conflict as a further attempt by the Communist bloc to extend its control, while China feared America's intentions for, again, sending troops to fight in a country with which it shared a frontier.

Kissinger explained the dilemma at length. "The opportunity was that China might be ready to enter the diplomatic arena and that would require it to soften its previous hostility toward the United States. In such circumstances, the Chinese threat against many of our friends in Asia would decline; at the same time, by evoking the Soviet Union's concerns along its long Asian perimeter, it could also ease pressures on Europe. But for such possibilities to be clearer, we needed some communication with the Chinese leaders. If we moved too quickly or obviously — before the Cultural Revolution had fully run its course — the Chinese might rebuff the overture. If we moved too slowly, we might feed Chinese suspicions of Soviet–American collusion, which could drive them into making the best deal available with Moscow. As for the Soviets, we considered the Chinese option useful to induce restraint; but we had to take care not to pursue it so impetuously as to provoke a Soviet preemptive attack on China. And at home we had to overcome a habit of mind that had seen in the People's Republic either an irreconcilable enemy or a put-upon country concerned only with the issue of Taiwan."[73]

The United States and China had been meeting at the ambassadorial level in Warsaw for years. These talks, however, involved little substance, amounting mostly to rhetorical expressions of grievance. Periodically the Chinese would suspend them in protest of some slight or other, such as on February 18, 1969, when the Chinese ambassador canceled a meeting with his American counterpart after China's chargé d'affaires in the Netherlands sought asylum in the US.

Then, on March 2, Soviet troops attacked Chinese forces along their disputed Ussuri River border. Over the coming months, the Soviets massed forty divisions along the four-thousand-mile frontier. This development exacerbated the Sino–Soviet rift that had been growing for years. At the same time, it was also the first solid evidence of a split in the Communist bloc observed by the Americans, who had previously dismissed all indications as a ploy to lull them into underestimating the impetus to world revolution as decreed by Leninist dogma.

"If we could determine what we suspected — that the Soviet Union and China were more afraid of each other than they were of the United States — an unprecedented opportunity for American diplomacy would come into being," wrote Kissinger, who was then Nixon's national security adviser.[74]

Mao confided his thinking to Dr. Li Zhisui: "Didn't our ancestors counsel negotiating with faraway countries while fighting with those that are near?"[75]

On April 1, China sent an important signal. Defense Minister Lin Biao, speaking before the Ninth National Congress of the Chinese Communist Party, abandoned the conventional reference to the United States as its principal enemy, instead calling the US and Soviet Union equal threats to its security.

Thus began months of symbolic pronouncements that depended on subtle interpretation if they were to have the intended effect. And as Kissinger admitted, "The isolation between America and China had been so total that neither knew how to contact the other, or how to find a common vocabulary through which to assure the other that rapprochement was not intended as a trap."[76]

On December 3, 1969, in an effort to reopen the Warsaw channel, the American ambassador passed a message to the Chinese chargé that the United States was prepared for serious talks. Upon learning of this proposal, Mao reportedly said, "Nixon must be sincere when he sends word that he is interested in talking with us."[77]

On December 11, the ambassador was invited to visit the Chinese embassy. A formal agreement was reached on January 8 to resume regular meetings. Kissinger calls the 134 meetings that ensued "the longest continual talks that could not point to a single important achievement."[78] Except that two intractable ideological enemies were speaking, and that was no small feat.

Frustrated that China "ignored the few low-level signals of interest we sent them," Nixon was more explicit in his First Annual Report to the Congress on United States Foreign Policy in February 1970: "It is certainly in our interest, and in the interest of peace and stability in Asia and the world, that we take what steps we can toward improved practical relations with Peking." He later commented, "The leaders in Peking clearly understood the significance of the language in this report."[79]

That same report also stated, "We will regard our Communist adversaries first and foremost as nations pursuing their own interests as *they* perceive these interests, just as we follow our interests as we see them."[80] Aside from the provocative reference to *adversaries*, it is significant that the United States admitted that Communist behavior was not intractably at odds with its interests.

Years later, Nixon reflected, "The China initiative had nothing to do with my attitude toward communism. My decision was based on my belief that the security of the United States would be served by developing better relations with one Communist power that was not on good terms with the other, the Soviet Union — a much more formidable adversary."[81]

As the United States calculated how to exploit tensions between China and the Soviets, so the Chinese had to calculate whether reciprocating America's overtures served its national interest. They were, after all, staring down the business end of forty Russian divisions. Were they best off trusting their longtime opponent or mending fences with their erstwhile ally? How confident ought they to be that they fully appreciated the Americans' motives? Were there implications to opening a dialogue at the highest levels that escaped their notice?

Americans see themselves as benevolent, and are confused when the rest of the world fails to share that vision. Years after leaving office, Kissinger acknowledged, "American leaders have taken their values so much for granted that they rarely recognize how revolutionary and unsettling these values can appear to others."[82]

From China's vantage point, the United States was deeply threatening. Yes, the US feared Communist expansionism. But so, too, did China fear Western influence. The Chinese people had a long and degrading history of foreign occupation that had only ended during the lifetime of its current leaders. They were, naturally, going to receive any Western approach with trepidation.

In April 1971, China took a bold step by inviting the American Ping-Pong team, against which it was competing at a tournament in Japan, to visit Beijing. The team accepted, thus beginning what came to be known as Ping-Pong diplomacy. On April 14, the day the team was welcomed by Zhou Enlai in the Chinese capital, the United States announced that it was lifting a trade embargo against China. On April 27, Zhou delivered a secret message through a Pakistani emissary that China would be willing to host an envoy of the president, or even the president himself.

In their damning biography of Mao, Chang and Halliday argue that the chairman had coveted relations with the United States since Stalin's death in 1953 as a way to access advanced technology. The bitterness ensuing from the Korean War prevented any immediate rapprochement. Subsequently, he had to keep his distance as he promoted Maoism as an independent ideological force around which the third world could rally in counterweight to the superpowers. When he finally decided to extend an invitation to Nixon, "The motive was not to have a reconciliation with America, but to relaunch himself on the international stage."[83]

It was agreed that Kissinger would slip clandestinely into China while on a diplomatic visit to Pakistan in July 1971 to pave the way for an official visit by Nixon. The United States was adamant that these talks be conducted in absolute secrecy. In fact, Nixon argues, "Our delicate negotiations with China would have collapsed if my preliminary diplomatic messages to Chou En-lai or Henry Kissinger's trip to Beijing in 1971 had become public. Opponents of the new relationship in both countries would have sabotaged our moves toward a rapprochement."[84] Contradictorily, Kissinger states, "We learned later that the Chinese were extremely suspicious of our desire for secrecy; perhaps they saw it as a device to allow us to reverse course quickly."[85]

On July 15, all the covert preliminaries covered, Nixon went on television to inform the nation that he would go to China. The announcement represented a dramatic turnabout in American and Chinese foreign policies. Whether they would become allies was uncertain, but they would seek enough common ground that they need no longer be enemies.

On February 17, 1972, Nixon stepped off *Air Force One* at the Beijing airport and shook Zhou Enlai's hand.

"When our hands met, one era ended and another began," he wrote grandiloquently.[86]

"Mao had not only got Nixon, he had managed to conceal that this had been his objective. Nixon was coming thinking that he was the keener of the two,"[87] Chang and Halliday write, insinuating that the chairman had actually duped Nixon. Furthermore, they quote Zhou mocking Nixon, comparing him to "a loose woman 'tarting herself up and offering herself at the door.'"[88]

Nevertheless, rapprochement constituted the kind of radical shift leaders are reluctant to undertake. As Nixon and Kissinger would stress repeatedly in their writings on the subject, and as books about Mao and Zhou have affirmed, both sides were only behaving as their interpretation of self-interest dictated. Trying to do what you believe is in your best interest does not negate the risk of being wrong. The wild card is always the sincerity of the other side. Was there any conceivable way that this initiative could be exploited by one side to the other's disadvantage?

It was specifically in this regard that Larry proved directly helpful to Zhou and Mao.

"He provided a lot of stuff on that," affirms Moore, referencing, in particular, a secret Presidential Review Memorandum prepared for Congress that spelled out in detail Nixon's plan for opening up to China. "There must have been a number of drafts that circulated all over creation for comment and input. I'm not sure how it got into Larry's hands, but if you have friends, all sorts of funny things happen. I could imagine, since Larry is a useful guy and very capable, he could have found himself in a room where they were discussing this and that."[89]

Purportedly, he actually saw specific documents, although nothing was definitively identified as the *one* he handed over. He may have reported on a conversation or he may have seen a report, or even had his opinion solicited on a particular draft.

At a time when the United States was contemplating its most daring policy initiative toward China since, well, ever, it doesn't seem unreasonable that he might have been invited to some working skull sessions. His interpretation of signals emanating from China could have been solicited by Americans who found the whole enterprise maddeningly cryptic.

Indeed, he would boast, "I am an expert in Chinese affairs. I knew about the Chinese mentality. I knew the Chinese society. I know the politics and the bureaucracy in China, which, coupled with what I learned from newspapers and magazines, I would know exactly what is happening in China."[90]

Guerin showed him documents related to Nixon's plan.

"If I had access to that, I would have passed it," Larry said cagily, careful about fingering particular documents.

"He tells us that he *would* have passed documents related to Nixon's position *if* he had seen them," Schiffer recounts. "Well, we were prepared to show that he had signed as having seen them."[91]

In one of the volumes of his memoirs, Kissinger reports on an exchange he had with Mao on February 17, 1973, that really makes sense if considered in light of Larry Chin's presence. It bears quoting at length.

Mao was discussing how "maneuvering for petty advantage is short-sighted and that we should do nothing to undermine mutual confidence. 'Let us not speak false words or engage in trickery,' he insisted. 'We don't steal your documents. You can deliberately leave them somewhere and try us out,' he joked, though he gave us no clue as to where we might carry out this test and how we might know that the Chinese had not taken advantage of it. There was no sense in running small risks, Mao was saying. And while he was at it he questioned the utility of big intelligence operations as well. Indeed, he considered intelligence services generally overrated. Once they knew what the political leaders wanted, their reports came in, 'as so many snowflakes.' But on really crucial matters they usually failed."[92] This was published before Larry's arrest. In the books he wrote afterward, Kissinger made no further allusions to Chinese intelligence.

A later defector source from China said that Larry is upheld as a hero in the People's Republic for his role in advancing Sino–American relations. This defector indicated that Zhou wanted to go forward, but Mao was plagued with uncertainty.

"Mao was not convinced Nixon was sincere. The best information we have is that only when Chin told them it was legitimate were they prepared to proceed," Magers says. "Now, there were other things going on. The US was consulting with the French about its intentions. Some of this was shared with the embassy in Beijing, though it wasn't very extensive. Boursicot had this, and it corroborated what they were hearing elsewhere. Notwithstanding, there is no question that Chin was far, far, far more important than Boursicot."[93]

Ken Schiffer is equally unequivocal: "China trusted Nixon's motives based on the information Chin passed them."[94]

In her analysis of the event, Professor Margaret MacMillan makes a very cursory reference to Larry, acknowledging, "The Chinese also had a spy in Washington, in the CIA."[95] Though she says that she found the notion that such a penetration was in place rather intriguing, she pursued the issue no farther. Moreover, given how tightly controlled was all information about Nixon's intentions, she is skeptical that Chin would have been in a position to learn anything of significance.

"The process was in a very delicate stage, and rumors were not even circulating within State or the National Security Council, so it seems rather unlikely to me that a relatively low-level employee of the CIA would have had access," she says.[96]

Of course, there was much happening simultaneously. There were those Soviet troops mustered across the Ussuri River. There was Mao's desire to import advanced technology. There was the anomaly of the world's most populous state denied its rightful place at the United Nations. There was Nixon's conclusion that America's interests were better served by engaging China than isolating it. These were the essential factors.

To fully appreciate the complexities, one must take into account how incongruous were the respective worldviews of the Chinese and Americans.

Even the most unwavering American proponents of realpolitik approach the world with optimism about the underlying reasonableness of human nature. Admitting self-interest as a valid motive, they assume this invariably means that peace is preferable to conflict — and ultimately that truth is more beneficial than falsehood. That's why Americans are more likely to refer to hostile states as adversaries than as enemies, a softer term that suggests competition rather than outright enmity. It's why Americans are stunned when a president refers to an "evil empire" or "axis of evil," with its implications of irredeemable wickedness. Conflict is supposed to be the anomaly, a situation that arises when the balance is temporarily thrown into disequilibrium. This outlook is indicative of people who anticipate rewarding lives and who see hostility as an interruption in the pursuit of life, liberty, happiness. Of their government, they demand wholehearted effort to maximize the conditions under which these objectives can be met.

Between the Ussuri River crisis of 1969 and Nixon's visit in 1972, America's perception of the dangers it faced was out of all proportion to its power. The Soviet Union, it feared, was recklessly adventurist and determined to expand its nuclear arsenal — to what end? To backstop a ground assault in Europe? To launch a preemptive strike against the continental United States? American ground troops were committed to Vietnam, causing the nation terrible anguish. Reaching out to China was a logical policy to reduce international tension and improve stability.

China's rulers perceive the world differently. Conflict is accepted as a natural state of affairs. Chinese encounters with foreigners have, more often than not, been traumatic. Over its long history, it has endured a succession of invasions by land and by sea. Suffering leaders who believed — or at least acted as though — their mandate was sanctioned by heaven, few Chinese were rewarded with much better from hard work than mere subsistence. Most Chinese experienced the world as a harsh place of little promise. With a stoic outlook, they hope sacrifice brings a better life to the next generation.

Confidence is a precious luxury when adversaries come to negotiate in the international arena. They approach warily. Outward displays of friendship are all the more spooky for the apprehension that they are false, and throats will be slit should the chance arise.

Where does Larry fit into this complex constellation? How decisive was his role? Were not all the arguments in favor of rapprochement so compelling that the advantages to China of overcoming its reluctance to trust the United States were obvious? Was it not an untenable position for America to act as though the most populous nation on earth was without a legitimate government?

"I think Larry Chin mattered because Mao had the ability to say yes or no, we will have Ping-Pong diplomacy, we will open up," Magers responds. "The Chinese were looking at the world from such an entirely different perspective. They were convinced, for example, that the West had a cure for ALS [popularly known as Lou Gehrig's disease, with which Mao was afflicted and of which he eventually died], but were not sharing it because they didn't want Mao to recover. I recall when the first Chinese delegation to the UN came in the middle of the General Assembly session in 1971.

They reported back how impressed they were to see the African American and Hispanic American hotel employees secretly take out their copies of Mao's *Little Red Book* and show them underlined passages. But, they reported, the most amazing thing was how clever the Americans were: The night the delegation arrived in New York, the American government brought every car in the northeastern US and put them on the road leading from the airport so they would be fooled into thinking there could be that many cars in New York City. They believed it!

"From the perspective of 1971, they knew so little about us. In retrospect, how could they be so blind? Well, they were just coming out of the Cultural Revolution. None of us had a good window. Remember, for years we denied the reality of the Sino–Soviet split. If American officials could be so blind, certainly Chinese officials could have doubted rapprochement.

"I think the fact they had someone they trusted telling them the overture was legitimate added credibility."

Wouldn't it have happened anyway?

"It would have happened some time in the future," he says. "But political careers in the West are short. Nixon could open up China. [President Lyndon] Johnson could not have. [President Jimmy] Carter could not have."[97]

MacMillan concurs with this assessment: "Nixon's visit occurred because both sides came to the conclusion at the same time that it was a good idea. Yet it took individuals, four men in this case, to make it happen. Nixon and Mao, Kissinger and Chou. Two men who for all their faults possessed the necessary vision and determination and two men who had the talent, the patience and the skill to make the vision reality."[98]

Nixon's credentials as a Communist baiter allowed him the political maneuverability to improve relations with China that would have been denied his Democratic predecessor and successor, with their more liberal reputations. Nixon was not susceptible to being chastened as soft on Communism. Furthermore, the most ardent opposition to his efforts would be from within his own Republican Party's ranks and, therefore, more easily quelled. Mao was apparently untroubled by Nixon's anti-

Communism, allowing, "I like to deal with rightists. They say what they really think — not like the leftists, who say one thing and mean another."[99]

"Perversely, Larry actually did some good for the United States," Paul Moore concedes. "There was this dance going on, but you need two to tango. The US needed to signal its intentions. And it needed for China to interpret these signals correctly. This was the part the US couldn't control. Between the talks in Poland, the Ping-Pong diplomacy, et cetera, nobody really knew what to believe. The significance of Larry Chin was his access to special material on China at FBIS. When the government decided to change its policy, it was written up. It was all tightly controlled, but Larry got access and told the Chinese.

"Whether he actually passed them a document, he passed them the contents of the document. So they had verification from their trump-card source of what they were seeing through other channels. This was going right to the top. Mao was very impressed with him. Once, when he was frustrated trying to find out about some internal party rumblings, Mao yelled, 'I have a better idea of what comes across Nixon's desk than I do what's going on in Shanghai.' I assure you, this is the kind of remark that filters down the line."[100]

That he had a positive influence on rapprochement would become the cornerstone of Larry's defense.

Under questioning from Jacob Stein, he lectured, "At the time, there were two factions in China. One is a pragmatic faction which would like to direct China to develop its economy. And another faction is Maoist faction, which would follow the doctrine of Mao Zedong, which would lead China through politics.

"The pragmatic faction was Zhou Enlai. . . . I am very much in favor of Zhou Enlai's faction . . . because he is more practical. He wanted to build Chinese economy, improve the livelihood of the Chinese, and his subordinates are Western-trained and wanted to give greater democracy to the people."

"Did you form any objective with respect to this clash between groups under Mao?" Stein inquired.

"Yes. I would hope that if I could in any way influence the Zhou Enlai faction, I would certainly do it."

"Did you do it, did you influence that faction?"

"Yes."[101]

It was a popular conception of the time that Zhou stood apart from Mao and the rest of the Communist Party. He was definitely distinguished by his sophistication and the debonair mannerisms he'd adopted while a student in Paris, making him someone with whom Europeans and Americans felt immediately comfortable. If Mao came across as a loutish peasant, spewing the cumbersome rhetorical jargon in which the maniacal ideologue finds comfort, Zhou appeared to be the reasonable philosopher, who appreciated that ideology organizes thought but needs to be adapted when facing real-world conditions.

When dealing with an alien culture, human nature compels us to seek out, and then cling to, whoever creates an impression of familiarity. Because we interpret our brand of civilization as the norm from which others deviate, it is wonderfully reassuring to find that man in a strange environment who seems to emulate us, who curbs the excesses we fear in his culture in favor of behavior to which we can more easily relate.

However, we know that Mao's rigidly totalitarian state demanded conformity and was quick to punish deviation. To affect a preference for Western style risked incurring accusations of preferring Western thought. Such obvious anti-Maoism was tantamount to treason and was — quite literally — deadly. Common sense, therefore, argues that Zhou's display of the sort of individuality others couldn't have gotten away with was sanctioned — that his superficial nonconformity disguised a deeper loyalty he never gave Mao cause to doubt.

Above all else, Zhou was *the* great survivor of the People's Republic. A veteran of the legendary Long March of 1934–1935 and a resident of the primitive outpost that the Communists inhabited in Yan'an when the Japanese occupied China, Zhou's standing in the party was solidified in its earliest days. His uncanny ability to escape the periodic purges that claimed so many of his contemporaries and to win Mao's confidence — or at least maneuver himself into a position from which he couldn't readily be removed if ever Mao had misgivings — speaks volumes about Zhou's political savvy and knack for consistently siding with the victors, or making himself scarce, when disputes flared.

Chang and Halliday trace the idea that Zhou represented a more liberal element all the way back to the waning days of the civil war in 1949 when Mao was concerned about a last-minute American intervention to save the Nationalists. Mao arranged to pass a message to President Harry Truman that indicated a split in the Communist Party, with a pro-Western faction led by Zhou. Given American backing, it suggested, Zhou might succeed in influencing its foreign policy. They call the ploy a "hoax," but it served to create the lasting impression that Zhou was less hard-line than others within the party.[102] They go on to say, "The real Chou was not the suave diplomat foreigners saw, but a ruthless apparatchik, in thrall to his Communist faith. Throughout his life he served his Party with a dauntless lack of personal integrity."[103]

The idea that Zhou led a faction opposing Mao is ridiculous. Dr. Li offers, "I realized that Zhou Enlai was Mao's slave, absolutely, obsequiously obedient. Everything he did was designed to court favor with Mao. Everything he did, he did to be loyal to Mao."[104]

Gao Wenqian, who was Zhou's official biographer at the Central Research Office for Documentation of the Chinese Communist Party, wrote, "Zhou Enlai almost never made a mistake. This was the key to his ongoing success over many decades and throughout turbulent times. . . . He was almost entirely self-effacing. He knew how to mend the broken pieces of crockery that Mao shattered from time to time. Zhou's genius for self-abnegation and the deft and artful way that he had of cleaning up a nasty mess aggravated Mao, the master, and piqued his pride. They were the odd couple, but this was no domestic comedy. On some level, Mao hated his servant, who, he knew, was not only far too smart, but also inscrutable in his devotion, and he always kept his eyes half-open for the chance to humiliate him."[105]

The point being, it is fallacious to presume that Zhou and Mao disagreed about opening up to the United States. They worked in concert. Though Zhou was clearly the skillful diplomat employed to implement the policy, Mao was the ultimate authority who sanctioned it. And if China needed Larry Chin to boost its confidence in order to proceed, it was not to reinforce a Zhou faction competing against a Mao faction.

Larry insisted that he had been able to positively influence the Zhou faction. The Vietnam War was raging, he reminded the jury; China was stuffing North Vietnam's coffers with money and supplies while American forces on the ground supported the South.

"I came across some classified information," he explained. "One of which was a special report delivered by President Nixon dated February [1970] stressing his wish to improve relations with China."

"Is that report public knowledge now?" Stein queried.

"It is public now, but not at that time."

Asked how he came across it, Larry replied, "There are classified documents circulated as reference materials for people working there [FBIS headquarters]. And one of the reference materials was this report by Nixon to the Congress."

His response seems less than candid. Since the entire business was guarded under such rigorous security, it doesn't figure that any related documents were circulated as casually as he implies. He was trying to create the impression that he had seen it as a matter of course. That, in fact, it had enjoyed a wide readership.

Though acknowledging that what he saw "was a special report from President Nixon to the Congress," Larry swore that the "document was circulated in the bureau through desk to desk."

Asked by Stein to summarize the report in question, Larry replied in surprisingly poor English, "That report refers to China in state of enemy, stating that the culture Chinese people, the historical ties between the Chinese and American people, and one most important phrase was that the United States will take steps it can to establish practical and cooperative relations with China."

"What was your reaction to that document?"

"I was astounded by this about-face on the part of President Nixon."

"What did you do with that document?"

"When I saw that, I thought if this information is brought to the attention of the Chinese highest leadership, it might break the ice and start a turn from hostility to friendship."

"Who did you want to see that document?"

"I wanted Zhou Enlai to see it."

"Why?"

"Because he is the pragmatic faction who would like to develop Chinese economy according to the Western system, and he would certainly like to reestablish friendship and cooperation with the United States."

"So what did you do? Tell us the time, place, and circumstances."

He snuck the document out of the office, surely down the front of his shirt as he had done on so many other occasions. That night, he photographed it at home. The next morning, he returned with it to work. As per the instructions provided by Mr. Ou, Larry went to a pay phone and called Mr. Lee. He identified himself as Mr. Yang and told him he had something to give him. That weekend, he caught a flight to Buffalo, where he rented a car for the two-hour drive around Lake Ontario to Toronto. Mr. Lee gave him directions to one of the nondescript strip malls that dot the expressways north of the city.

An anonymous middle-aged man window-shopping, minding his own business among a crowd of people. He sees an acquaintance. They greet each other casually with pleasantries. In a handshake, a roll of film is passed without being remarked upon. Each continues on his way with a nod and a wave.

Larry went on to tell the court that China had effectively cut itself off from information emanating from the outside world.

"The leadership of China was impossible to receive real information which would reflect the true intentions of the United States. There was such a tremendous suspicion and paranoia, the feeling that no true approach would be valued or assessed as such. Whatever it heard would be interpreted as propaganda or as a deceptive approach," he explained. "For this reason, at that time, I thought that now I have a direct link with the core and heart of the highest leadership of China. That would be comparable to a hotline now between Moscow and Washington. To reach directly to the heart with the true situation in the world and in the United States. I think someday I can play a very important role in this situation. So that is why I accepted Mr. Ou's offer to have this link through Mr. Lee."

"Why didn't you go to your superiors and tell them just what you just told us?" Stein wondered.

"Well, there is a code of secrecy and I would be working under that regulation, and anyone that broke that regulation would certainly be fired."

At this point, Stein took the opportunity to read into the record several positive evaluations from Chin's superiors. In October 1972: "The high level priority requests to provide on the spot interpretation and translation of volumes of written material generated by President Nixon's trip to the PRC were met commendably and promptly by Mr. Chin." He was praised for being "an all-round linguist and intelligence officer. A real asset to the Agency and one that would be difficult to replace."

"Did you ever hold back in the devotion that you gave to your job?" Stein asked.

"No."

On cross-examination, Aronica cut right through the fatty tissue of post facto justification and probed the throbbing heart of the matter. "What you had been doing at least for eleven years, from 1970 until 1981, was stealing documents from the CIA and giving them to the Chinese?"

"That is right," Chin agreed.

"You knew that whatever documents you were to supply or whatever information you were to supply to Mr. Lee or directly to Mr. Ou would go to the highest levels of the Communist Party in China, is that correct?"

"Yes."

"And to the highest levels of the government of the People's Republic of China and the Central Committee of the Politburo?"

"Yes."

"Zhou Enlai is a Communist, was he not?"

"Yes."

"A high official of the Communist Party and a high official of the government of the People's Republic of China?"

"They are identical."

"And when you passed these documents that you had stolen out of FBIS headquarters your intent was to help China, is that correct?"

"My intent was to help China and the United States to reestablish good relations."

"Was your intent to help the Chinese, the People's Republic of China?" Aronica emphasized the admission that would ensure a conviction.

"Yes, in the meantime help the United States, too."

"Answer if you would, Mr. Chin, my question. When you passed the documents was it your intent to help the People's Republic of China?"

"Yes."

As Aronica hammered away repeatedly, Stein was moved to object, causing the presiding judge, Robert Merhige Jr., to come to his rescue, "I suspect the answer is fairly obvious. You did do it with the intention of helping China and, as I understand it, the intention of helping the United States, is that correct?"

"That is right."

"You had a dual purpose, is that what you are saying?"

"That is correct."[106]

Recalling the case, Aronica is contemplative. "I think, bottom line, he believed in what he was doing, in the Communist Party. Helping both sides was a rationalization when he got caught, but that's nonsense. Maybe on some level he believed it, but was that his motive? No way."[107]

Magers remarks, "You offer a justification when you recruit somebody to spy, something to hang the fig leaf on. To some extent, Larry did help China–US relations. In so doing, he compromised an awful lot of things and cost American lives in the Korean conflict. You can compartmentalize. If I were Larry Chin, I would want something to enable me to justify my actions."[108]

*Alexandria, Virginia, November 22, 1985*
Telling truths that have been concealed for so long is an emotionally draining exercise. Listening to them brings surges of adrenaline you fight to contain behind a sympathetic and encouraging mask. For both parties, the interview was exhausting.

Once Larry explained his role in bringing China and the US closer together, he gave the agents every indication of winding down.

One gaping blank area on his landscape was Vietnam.

"He didn't volunteer to us anything about Vietnam," Magers recalls.[109]

Two factors mitigated his ability to report, at least about the early phases of the war. The first relates to his being posted in Santa Rosa. During that period, prior to obtaining his clearance, he was denied access to operational data that might have revealed insight into America's intentions. Second, there was that period coinciding with the Cultural Revolution when his handlers were out of touch.

Neither excuse covers the crucial period between 1970 and 1975 when Nixon struggled mightily to extricate the United States from the most contentious international adventure in its history. He applied the entire spectrum of instruments, from hellacious bombing campaigns to diplomatic overtures, in search of an exit strategy that preserved America's dignity and upheld its military stature in the eyes of Cold War adversaries and friends alike.

Certainly China had an interest in America's activities and objectives in Vietnam. Given the claims that have been made regarding Larry's access — both authorized and inadvertent — and the volume of documents he made available, it is hard to conceive that he neglected to pass over intelligence concerning Vietnam.

In the interest of establishing the long continuity of Chin's espionage, Aronica did raise the matter briefly while questioning the defendant.

"You carried on these activities [spying] while the United States was fighting in Vietnam and the Chinese were supporting the Vietcong?"

"Yes. At that time, I was distressed about this so I wanted to help the People's Republic of China and the United States to make friends instead of making enemies."

"While we were at war with the Vietcong and the North Vietnamese . . . you were stealing documents and passing them to the Chinese?"

"That is right."[110]

And he left it at that.

To this day, nobody can state for certain the exact volume of material Larry turned over to Chinese intelligence. It can only be surmised that thirty-three years of active and enthusiastic espionage netted an absolutely massive amount of paper. Sources have suggested that there were banks of file cabinets at Ministry of Public Security headquarters reserved exclusively for his output. One estimate had it that thirty translators worked full-time for three months to handle all the documents he supplied. This may be apocryphal, as other people in a position to know have indicated that, for security reasons, nothing he passed was ever directly translated — although, one would expect, it needed to be at least paraphrased in Chinese so that high officials who couldn't understand English might be briefed.

As the agents pressed him to fill in the blanks with more specifics, Larry began to balk. Rather than leaving when he hinted that he was getting hungry, Johnson suggested they all dine together. Being diabetic, Larry needed to keep to a fairly strict dietary regimen.

Even in the most confrontational interviews, sharing a meal is the great rapport builder. The break allows the interrogators to bestow something upon the suspect, and the rigidity of role-playing can relax a bit.

"What would you like to eat?" Terry Roth asked. "We'll order in."

Larry expressed no preference.

"How about Chinese," Roth offered, whether in a demonstration of cultural sensitivity that would have made senior managers across the bureau proud or a show of irony is unclear.

Larry agreed, expressing a preference for seafood.

Roth went to the phone and actually called down to Carson and Schiffer to have them place the order. That way, the delivery went to the apartment where the pair were holed up, and Schiffer brought it to Larry's door.

While they waited, they continued talking, though it became clear that Larry had finished with his outline of events.

The agents asked whether he would mind if they searched his apartment, not yet letting on that they were armed with a search warrant.

He hesitated. "I'm not sure what my rights are."

Johnson, the lawyer, pulled out a copy of the US Constitution from his briefcase and advised him of his Fourth Amendment rights. "Mr. Chin, if you don't want us to search yourself, your house, your office, or anything, all you have to say is, *I don't want you to search.* And we won't."

"Well, then, I would prefer you didn't."

Johnson nodded.

Roth asked Chin if he'd consent to sign a written statement attesting to what he'd just told them.

Larry smiled at the idea, but refused to put his signature to paper. Thinking ahead, perhaps, he imagined he had retained some last vestige of deniability. Or he was just pleased to demonstrate some defiance to buoy his sinking feeling that all was lost. "That would be evidence coming from the horse's mouth, and I would be the horse."[111]

Once the food arrived, the agents steered the conversation away from the sordid business of treason to a subject closer to Larry's heart: gambling. Chin, they knew from their investigation, was an avid gambler who made regular pilgrimages to Atlantic City and Las Vegas. Blackjack was his game. Like all serious gamblers, mathematical evidence aside, he was convinced he had devised a system to beat the odds.

However often luck might desert, the system should eventually prove foolproof, he was convinced. No matter how disappointing the losses, each represents just another cobblestone along the path to the big win. Each bet holds out the promise of easy riches. It's all about hope . . . and the deck can never be stacked too high against that.

The FBI was already aware that China had paid Larry on several occasions. Without going into exactly how much or how often, he saw no harm in volunteering the system by which he had arranged for some of his payments.

It wasn't enough just to conceal the source of his additional income — he had to hide that he even had extra money. Intelligence services are supposedly vigilant to inexplicable lifestyle changes on the part of employees. The emphasis is on *supposedly*. Aldrich Ames, the longtime Soviet spy, wasn't shy about turning up at the Langley parking lot in his Jaguar. He satisfied his colleagues' curiosity by claiming that his Colombian-born wife had come into an inheritance. With his overseas family ties, Larry could probably have made a similar claim. However, he was far more discreet than Ames, eschewing such lavish displays of consumption. Besides, he had a better story than a onetime windfall. He boasted about his proficiency at the gaming tables. He even claimed to an acquaintance that his proficiency resulted in his being barred from a number of casinos.[112] The truth of the matter, his own records would reveal, was that he had paid out $96,700 between 1976 and 1982 to satisfy debts to several casinos.[113]

Courtesy of his frequent visits, the casinos regularly offered him high-roller junkets with complimentary airfare and hotel stays. It is believed that over some periods, he would go to Vegas once, even twice a month. They readily extended him credit.

Larry would request, say, five thousand dollars in chips. He'd gamble away two grand of that, and cash in the remaining three thousand. When people asked about his trip, he'd tell them it went very well: He'd won three thousand dollars. Meanwhile, within a week or so, the casino would send him a letter requesting repayment of his five-thousand-dollar debt. He would promptly wire the Bank of Hong Kong, where the Ministry of Public Security deposited payments in his personal account, and have them transfer the money directly to the casino. The arrangement was flawless, giving him a plausible excuse for the money and an effective way of slipping cash in from overseas.[114] An entry in his diary for January 30, 1979, confirms this arrangement. Larry wrote, "HK Bank asked send $ to Sands 35K." The amount is shorthand for thirty-five thousand dollars.

While Johnson and Roth were talking to Larry, Guerin was on the phone with Schiffer, giving him a detailed account of everything Chin had said. Schiffer, in turn, was relaying the information over to Justice officials and Joseph Aronica for a decision on whether his men could make the arrest. While they debated how to proceed next, Schiffer instructed Guerin to ask Chin to surrender his passport.

Larry rose and headed to the bedroom.

"Hang on, Mr. Chin." Guerin had an uneasy feeling. "Terry, why don't you just walk with him."

You never know when a cooperative suspect might be overcome with regret and become desperate to undo what he's said. Guerin couldn't know exactly when, or if, it would hit Chin that the agents hadn't commented on whether they thought he'd be an effective double. He wanted to preempt any crazy ideas Chin might get about killing himself or coming at them with a weapon.

Larry had no such inclination. He returned and handed a passport to Guerin.

"Mr. Chin, this is expired."

Larry feigned surprise. "My other one must be in the other apartment."

"Never mind, we'll get it later."

Meanwhile, a variation on the old *guanxi* debate had erupted. What to do next?

Schiffer was decided. Arrest him on the spot.

"We got what we're going to get. Let's take it and get out of here," he insisted.

While Guerin was on the phone waiting for a decision, Roth went to the bathroom, leaving Johnson alone with Larry. They were sitting side by side on the sofa. Night had fallen, and they could see the lights of Alexandria shimmering out the window. It was the sort of simple, worldly beauty toward which you'd grow complacent if you glanced upon it every night with no reason to expect it wouldn't be there tomorrow.

Larry was looking out the window. He took it in dreamily, registering the entire panorama, reflecting on the long journey from war-torn China to a high-rise condo in suburban Virginia.

The American dream. The immigrant's dream of America. It could come true. This was it, everything he'd ever wanted. This view encompassed it all.

He shuddered involuntarily. "You know, money is the root of all evil," he mumbled.

"In my opinion," Johnson recalls, "it was one of those few moments of honesty, and he was telling me right there why he'd done it. You could see, it was a very heartfelt thing."[115]

The American justice system makes a vital distinction between arrest and conviction. An arrest confirms suspicion and the existence of enough evidence of guilt to warrant taking an individual into custody and bringing him to trial for a crime. Once the trial begins, however, the defendant is presumed to be innocent, and the fact that he has been charged with an offense is not supposed to prejudice that presumption.

The only hope for an individual who knows he's guilty is insufficient evidence or some other source of reasonable doubt. In Larry's mind, however, the very fact of arrest was a declaration of his fate. He was waiting to be judged, not by twelve good citizens of Virginia, but by three FBI agents and whoever it was they kept calling.

By any measure, the interview had been a spectacular success. They absolutely had enough probable cause to charge and arrest him, which had not been the case when they knocked on his door.

Aronica hesitated. Did they have enough for a successful prosecution?

They had an admission of espionage. They had two concrete instances when information had been given to a foreign — and hostile — government, the most recent of which had occurred fifteen years ago. They had a witness of sorts, but he wasn't going to be available to testify. Indeed, he was not even to be acknowledged before the court. There was no video of Larry removing documents from FBIS premises. There was no exchange of money witnessed. There was no instance of harm coming to a specific agent of the American government that could be attributed to Larry Chin. All of this is to say that Aronica was not being unreasonable to want more.

"Whenever you go before a jury, you roll the dice," he explains, from his experience of more than thirty years as a prosecutor and criminal defense attorney. "You want to make sure you've got everything lined up. This is a high-profile case. And his lawyers will argue, Was it a confession, wasn't it a confession? We looked at it one way, that he was admitting this stuff; but when a guy says he transmitted this *kind of document*, but you can't show the jury a particular document, a SECRET stamp across it, and say, *This is what he passed*. You've got to be able to prove something."[116]

Some of the headquarters people were also reluctant. Chin had served up an intriguing outline, but in espionage, as in the exploration of deep space, what is observable is dwarfed by the immense darkness beyond. Furthermore, that which is unknown is somehow more intriguing and, seemingly, more important than what is known. If only we can get our hands on what eludes us, whatever that is. Could they learn more about operations or agents in present danger? Could they find out about operatives currently in the United States?

Perhaps yes, but quite probably no.

Carson was pissed. "If we don't arrest him now, he's gone."

It was suggested that it might be advantageous to watch him for a while. Now that he had been accused, maybe he'd panic. Perhaps he had an emergency contact at the embassy. A surveillance photo of Chin in the company of a Chinese official would be a useful exhibit in court.

Maybe if they scheduled an appointment to return the following day, Larry would be inclined to talk more, to serve up more specifics, perhaps even identify a document that would sink nails into his coffin.

Schiffer fumed, "He's a flight risk. He has all kinds of avenues to run. We don't have his passport. There's no way in holy hell we will assume responsibility for keeping him under surveillance. We don't have the manpower."

He reminded them of Edward Lee Howard, whose escape was fresh in the bureau's corporate memory. Though Larry hadn't demonstrated any ability in tradecraft, he had never had occasion to do so and nobody knew whether he was trained in countersurveillance.

Maybe he'd consent to move to a hotel for the night. Sit on him until morning, then pick up the interview.

"No, sir." Schiffer wouldn't back down. "If an arrest isn't authorized tonight, it's on you."

Faced with what amounted to an ultimatum, it was finally agreed. Larry Chin would be arrested.

Schiffer turned to Carson and said, "It's your case."

In the tradition of the bureau, the case agent gets the honor of making the arrest.

In a tip of the hat to the Year of the Spy, William Wang, the special agent responsible for coordinating the Special Surveillance Group that was on the scene in case the order was given to follow Larry, handed Tom his handcuffs: the same pair that had been used to hook up John Walker when he was taken into custody. One day they will be proudly displayed in the museum at FBI headquarters, an artifact of Cold War espionage.

Guerin hung up the phone and waited by the door. Roth and Johnson sat with Chin. The television was on, they'd run out of small talk, and Larry was done with big talk. He must have been wondering why the agents didn't put their notes in their briefcase and be on their way. They were the party guests who had long outstayed their welcome. He was too polite, or too frightened by this point, to suggest that he'd like them to leave. He might have thought they were debating a strategy to exploit his double-agent potential. He was probably reviewing his performance in slow motion, the way you'll replay a car accident in your mind, agonizing about how you could so easily have swerved or applied just a touch more pressure on the brake and avoided the whole mess.

Or maybe it dawned on him that he'd said far too much. He wished he could suck every word back down his throat, into the depths where he'd kept them secure for three decades. Maybe Johnson was right after all, and he should have followed legal advice not to talk. Maybe he wasn't the smartest guy in the room.

It was 10:37 PM. Everyone was tired.

Guerin let Carson and Schiffer in at their soft tap. He grinned widely. Carson's smile was more grim.

Roth and Johnson rose when the agents came into the room. Larry followed suit, not encouraged by their demeanor.

It was a moment of great emotional ambiguity for Carson. Up until now, he'd only seen Chin from a distance, like a character in a movie. They had never before locked eyes, which is the moment at which human beings actually become real to each other.

To Larry, Carson meant nothing. He was unaware of the sleepless nights Carson had devoted to him. He had no idea that he'd been an apparition in his every waking thought for close to three years. He was oblivious to the anxiety he'd produced, that he was the instrument of Tom's torment.

Larry was the counterweight on the scale against which Tom weighed everything else in his life. Good husband, good father, decent man, dedicated agent all stacked up featherlight against Larry, smug and aloof and carefree. Larry scorched his self-esteem the way a high school bullying causes a lifetime's humiliation for the most successful of men.

"I was relieved that we'd been proven right in who we chose to investigate and that we had come as far as we had," Carson says of his feelings in a measured tone.[117] Sometimes the long, hard fight to reach a goal makes it all the sweeter. Sometimes it leaves you beaten so raw, you can't be sure whether you've won or lost.

Carson approached solemnly. "Mr. Chin, you are under arrest."

Chin's arms hung limp at his sides and his head drooped as if suddenly too heavy for his neck to hold upright.

Carson took Larry's right wrist and slipped the cuff into place. He paid him the courtesy of securing the bracelet to his left wrist in front, rather than twisting his arms behind his back. The man before him didn't have much fight or flight in him.

They patted him down for weapons or any contraband or valuables that would best be left in the apartment rather than seized at the jail. Guerin and Schiffer couldn't contain smirks when they pulled out Larry's oversized wallet and discovered five hundred dollars in cash and a valid US passport.

"I forgot," he mumbled with an apologetic shrug.

Carson read him his rights, giving him the caution about remaining silent after he'd already talked himself out and reminding him that he could have legal counsel present for any questioning now that the questioning was done. Larry nodded when asked if he understood his rights.

"Please call Cathy and tell her I won't be home," he said.[118]

They led him to the elevator and down to the parking lot, where a large contingent of agents was milling about. They would proceed upstairs to execute the search warrant, spending the rest of the night combing through Larry's apartment. An inveterate pack rat, he violated the first rule of any criminal enterprise: Destroy whatever might incriminate. Larry didn't have a criminal mind — or else was so arrogant that the possibility of getting caught never merited serious consideration. Consequently, he held on to everything. The agents bundled up boxes of documents. They found diaries, hotel and restaurant receipts, airplane tickets. He made notes of deposits and transfers of funds from one bank to another. He kept letters written in Chinese. Their bearing on the case couldn't be evaluated until each one was translated. There would be thousands of pages to review.

Larry was guided into the passenger-side backseat of the unmarked car. Carson slammed the door and walked to the other side. Johnson drove with Schiffer beside him. They pulled away with the slow deliberateness of a hearse starting off on a final journey.

Larry looked up at his apartment building wistfully. His father would never believe how his son had prospered in life — that he'd put his own children through medical school and ensured a comfortable retirement. It was quite a success story.

As the car pulled out onto Duke Street, he lowered his head. They turned onto the expressway toward Arlington, where Larry would be booked into the county jail for the night.

The voice of Assistant Director Buck Revell came up over the two-way radio. "I want two agents in the cell with the suspect," he ordered tersely.

Schiffer keyed the hand mike, "What for?"

"Because we don't want a suicide."

"What makes you think he'll commit suicide?"

"No specific reason."[119]

Carson looked over at Larry, who betrayed no reaction to the conversation from the front seat. He could certainly hear, but wasn't necessarily listening. Or maybe, with the distortion caused by the static burping into the gaps in the exchange, he didn't make the connection that they were discussing his situation.

Schiffer replied that prisoner security was properly the jurisdiction of the Arlington County officers; the bureau shouldn't interfere.

He received no further objection.

When they arrived at the jail, Carson helped Larry from the car and took him by the right elbow, Johnson on his left. Tom explained that he would be processed here and arraigned before a judge in the morning. Larry didn't respond. He looked somewhat dazed, a combination of fatigue and stress and the dawning, terrifying reality that he was a prisoner. Over the course of several hours, he had lost control over his life. To his ear, each door they passed through on the way to booking closed with the concussive clang of heavy iron-barred cell doors.

Putting someone in custody is a paper-heavy exercise. Arlington County is the central short-term holding facility for detainees awaiting court appearances. While Alexandria has its own jail for those arrested by the city police, individuals taken in by state, county, or federal officers end up in Arlington. A typical night's haul is mostly made up of domestic disputants, drunk and disorderlies, a drug possessor or seller. A rancid collection of losers and pukers, some sullen, others ranting. They were deposited on the benches facing the booking desk by arresting officers, who mostly resented the burden of excessive bureaucracy for minor offenses.

None of the prisoners awaiting processing was especially dangerous. Few were even cuffed. For the most part they understood that good behavior was the path to easiest treatment. Seeing the motley crew from a distance, a middle-class citizen would consider crossing the street. Johnson took Chin and steered him over to a bench.

Larry stretched out his neck to neatly readjust the collar of his coat before stiffening his posture, a pose of frightened dignity.

The severely intoxicated man beside him roused himself and turned to look at the interloper on *his* bench, breaking the drool chain that had attached his bottom lip to his chest. What hair wasn't sticking up at wild angles, as if being pulled by forces of static energy, was sweat-plastered to his scalp and neck. His jaw was stitched with red, oozing scratches from the fight he'd made the mistake of starting. He stank of the alcohol he'd consumed and the gutter he'd fallen into. His pupils undulated crazily among the rivers of capillaries discoloring his eyes.

He looked Larry up and down, taking in his nice clothes and gentlemanly bearing. He assumed the cunning expression of the rat who's found the cheese at the end of the maze.

"Hey! Hey!" he called out, unable to articulate even a single syllable without slurring.

Larry stared at his own hands with intense concentration, willing the drunk back into semi-consciousness.

"I'm talking to you!"

Larry leaned diffidently as far to the side as he could, cringing against the invasion on his personal misery, this further ignominy.

The drunk lifted a hand to Larry's shoulder and gave him a shake. "Hey, man, you look like a lawyer. I'm talking to you! Are you a lawyer, man? Seriously! Man, are you a lawyer? I am really fucking messed up, man. Can you help me? I need a lawyer! Somebody get me a fucking lawyer! A lawyer!"[120]

Carson was out of sight, taking care of the paperwork. Johnson saw the exchange and shared a laugh with one of the county cops over Chin's distress.

Larry began contemplating what incarceration was going to be like. He considered whether he had the strength to withstand years in the company of drunks and degenerates and, worse, the violent predators who would rob him of any few possessions he may be permitted. He summoned all his self-control to keep from being sick with fear. Cowering weakly in a corner, holding down the nausea day upon day upon month upon year.

After depositing the paperwork with the jail authorities, Carson returned and led Chin in for photographs and fingerprints. When all that was completed, Larry was officially in the care of the county for the night.

There are those veterans of the criminal justice system who look upon some soft county time as three-hots-and-a-cot, as in three meals and a bed to sleep in. To people who rarely get up in the morning with such lofty guarantees, and with the exception of the stone junkies and booze-hounds who hurt unbearably without their elixir of choice, a little lockup can be a good thing.

But not so for one jerked out of comfort and tossed in a cage. Not so for Larry Chin. It is fairly routine practice to put a first-time arrestee who shows any sign of being unable to cope under a suicide watch until the authorities are sure he has acclimatized.

With the warning from the assistant director fresh in his mind, Carson went directly to the duty officer. "Look, this guy's not a drunk, he's a citizen. Make sure he has a blanket and keep an eye on him tonight. We'll get him first thing in the morning."[121]

The county jail doesn't have a wide range of accommodations or a lot of officers on duty for close supervision of individual prisoners. Larry was held in the drunk cell because it's the one directly in front of the desk officer, and so is constantly under watch. Though nothing could be done about the smell or the lack of privacy, the officer would make sure that Larry wasn't bothered by other inmates and that he didn't do anything desperate.

# — 7 —

# The Preliminaries

*Alexandria, Virginia, November 23, 1985*

As promised, Carson and Schiffer retrieved their prisoner first thing in the morning.

Larry looked gaunt. He had escaped further harassment during the night, but the assorted shouting, complaining, farting, and retching that form the soundtrack of the open-all-night-for-business drunk tank, along with the crackling of his own thoughts, kept him awake, as tense as a high-voltage wire.

The agents handcuffed and escorted him out to their car. They drove in silence back to Alexandria, to the federal courthouse serving the Eastern District of Virginia. Under the circumstances, Carson and Schiffer didn't want him to say anything. Having advised him of his rights, the agents wanted to avoid any complications.

Larry was brought before Judge Brian McCoy. Aronica appeared for the state; Peter Meyers was retained for the defense.

Chin was charged with conspiracy: "To knowingly and willfully, communicate, deliver and transmit to a foreign government, that is, the People's Republic of China and to representatives, officers, and agents thereof, documents, photographs, and information relating to the national defense of the United States with the intent and reason to believe that the same would be used to the injury of the United States and to the advantage of the People's Republic of China."

The defendant pleaded not guilty.

Judge McCoy ordered him held over for the grand jury. The grand jury is an intervening stage between arrest and trial. The panel neither sees the

accused nor hears a defense. It is presented with the charges, an explanation of the offense, and a brief synopsis of the facts against the defendant.
Jurors do not ascribe guilt or innocence. They merely rule whether there
is enough substance to the allegation to warrant bringing the matter to
trial.

Agreeing with the prosecution's contention that Chin posed a flight risk,
the court denied bail.

Larry Chin was remanded to the Prince William County – Manassas
Regional Adult Detention Center.

## *Prince William County – Manassas Regional Detention Center, Manassas, Virginia, November 1985–February 1986*

The detention center accommodates all classifications of detainees awaiting trial and sentencing. Because of the seriousness of his crime, Larry was
confined in the maximum-security unit. Under strict supervision, he was
placed in a two-man cell on a block with between thirty and thirty-five
other inmates. Upon sentencing, prisoners are dispatched from this local
jail to the appropriate state or federal penitentiary. Chin stood to end up
in the latter. A harsher, more disturbing environment, where frustration,
rage, and a good deal of fear shape the days.

Prince William – Manassas doesn't even rank when discussing tough
penitentiaries.

"My jail is probably like your average high school," insists Glendell
Hill,[1] who was director of inmate services back when Larry was incarcerated. A former Manassas city police officer — in fact, the first African
American officer in that department's history when he joined in 1969
— he became superintendent of the prison before returning to policing as
sheriff of Prince William County.

Truly, from the outside it doesn't look much different from a high
school. A squat, brick building with slits of windows, its only distinguish-
ing feature is the barbed-wire-topped chain-link fence that surrounds the
perimeter.

"Certainly," Hill continues, "confrontations occur between people once in a while. It isn't easy being housed with complete strangers without privacy. I haven't had anyone seriously hurt by another inmate."

He describes Chin as a model prisoner, which can be taken to mean that he didn't pose a disciplinary problem that would make him especially noticeable to the staff.

Uprooted from his sedate comforts, he now sat in the company of murderers, rapists, and thieves. Prison constitutes a society unto itself. While younger, more street-savvy offenders view guards as adversaries, Larry most likely appreciated them as protectors. Being an elderly Asian, unaccustomed to violence, he couldn't look to any segment of the population for obvious allies. It would quickly become apparent to him that he'd do best to pass unassumingly, inconspicuously. Nothing about him made him a particular target. Then again, you never know. Inadvertent slights or envy become the basis of hostility; grudges fester easily, seeping wounds constantly being picked at and irritated in the damp claustrophobia of detention. Trying not to offend without seeming weak is a swaying tightrope that is hard to steady.

Despite the nature of his crime, he wasn't considered a high-profile inmate who would attract unwanted attention from other inmates.

"Most of these guys have never heard of espionage," jokes Hill.

Prison life is a bleak sequence of routines. Maximum-security routine is the bleakest, subject to the tightest regulation, the least freedom of movement, the least variety of activity to fill the day. Interaction among inmates is firmly restricted. Wherever you have to go, you must be accompanied by an escort. Chin was confined to his cell, except for recreation. Hill recalls that he was an accomplished Ping-Pong player and passed much of his rec time playing.

The shock of confinement reverberates. The constant monitoring unnerves. The close quarters provoke. The loneliness is a relentless throb. Helplessness and hopelessness are the remorseless artillery pounding at your hold on who you could have been before ending up here. Without some entrenched faith in reprieve, release, or redemption to fend off the assault, it's easy to succumb to how overwhelming the situation is.

What to do with all the empty hours? Idle time. Time for ideas to gestate and die. Time to conjure up dreams to go unfulfilled. Time to regret. Time to be afraid. Time for shame.

Time to reflect, suggests Hill.

Not a good thing, that, if it only serves to drive home the wreckage of your life. Spending uninterrupted days, months, years in your own company is intolerable torture if the pervading sentiment is self-loathing. Your mind wants to escape to other places, to memory, perhaps. But all it does is fast-forward and rewind through interminable might-have-been scenarios.

Locked away, his mail and phone calls subject to screening, Larry couldn't contact his friends, nor could they get an encouraging word to him, had they been so inclined. The newspaper reported his arrest and published details of the allegations contained in the affidavit filed in court, but that was all.

Had Chin confessed? If so, how much? The Ministry of Public Security, he imagined, would be frantic to learn.

With his contact to the outside world constricted to visits from family and lawyers, Larry fretted over how to get a message out. He realized his legal position was precarious. By arresting him and publicizing his capture instead of proposing to employ him as a double agent, the FBI made clear that it had no further use for him and was content to secure a long prison term. His best hope was to convince China of his undying loyalty and constant friendship, then wait for rescue.

He needed to fashion a message that would be convincing and, above all, communicated directly from him in such a way as to leave no doubt that it was his words, uncoerced and unscripted by American intelligence. There was one way, only. To go into open court and reveal how he'd spun his story with the aplomb of a master pitchman. What he was selling wasn't aimed at Americans, but at his far-off Chinese comrades. It was a huge go-for-broke, no-hedge gamble, Larry knew. But he was a gambler, convinced with crazed certainty that the next card, the next spin, the next roll, held victory, salvation. The worst possibility was to deny fate by refusing to play. Nothing else stands in the way of eventual success.

*Washington, DC, November 23, 1985*

"Now the work begins," Schiffer told Carson, reality quickly dissipating any inclination to celebrate the previous night's success. They may have finished first in their division after a long hot summer's season, but they hadn't achieved anything before laying claim to the World Series crown. Nobody scores off an arrest that goes sour in court.

First thing that morning, Guerin, Johnson, and Roth sat down together to prepare a comprehensive report of the interview. Using the notes taken by Roth and Johnson, and their collective memory, they reconstructed it as close to verbatim as possible. They spent more than ten hours at it.

All the material seized during the search was deposited around Carson's desk like so much debris gathered from the site of an airplane crash. He would have to sift through it all, reconstructing what happened and pulling from the wreckage those salient points that indicated Larry's guilt.

"How we put the case together was crucial," Carson says. "How do we make sense out of everything to get a conviction? We know what we know, but to prove it? That's another bag of worms."[2]

The FBI had confronted Larry with all the indicators of espionage it had, and he'd corroborated every point. He had admitted being a spy, though by pleading not guilty he seemed to contest the confession. That was a matter to be debated in front of the jury.

The search had turned up the extensive diaries Larry kept. Read sans context, they emitted not a whiff of criminality. However, as contemporary confirmation of the events covered in the interview, they were powerfully supportive of the government's claims. For example, when he told the FBI he had gone to Toronto in order to pass classified documents to Mr. Lee and his diary contained an entry for just such a trip, it would be difficult for him to refute the reasonable conclusion that he had, in fact, gone to Toronto and performed an act of espionage. If a contemporary diary entry placed him in China or Hong Kong at the same time that a confidential source had said he was there meeting with intelligence officers, the prosecution's reconstruction of events would gain credibility. Chin was meticulous about noting financial transactions, which supported the contention that he was being paid by the Chinese and the money was being held for him in Hong Kong accounts.

Similarly, during the interview he specified that when photographing classified documents on behalf of Public Security, he used a Minolta camera. Well, the agents recovered a receipt for the purchase of a Minolta camera. Now, the possession of that camera does not constitute evidence of espionage. But by proving the existence of the very camera to which he referred, it added credibility to his overall statement, the point of which was to allege espionage.

With secrecy no longer an issue, financial records were sought from Hong Kong so as to prove that deposits were made as Chin had alluded in the interview. The legal attaché, the FBI liaison officer at the American mission in Hong Kong, was tasked to take photographs of the hotels where Chin had stayed. Better than words, pictures would bring immediacy to the story when displayed before the jury.

The Ministry of State Security station chief at the Chinese embassy unfolded that morning's *Washington Post*. He scalded the back of his throat as his first cautious sip of tea became a shocked gulp. "Ex-CIA Analyst Held as Spy; China Allegedly Got Secrets," read the front-page headline.

The implications for his career were ominous. He had never heard of this Larry Wu-Tai Chin the paper spoke about. Had no clue whether he was a Chinese agent — nor, under the circumstances, did he want to know. Whatever the truth, he could already feel telltale winds foreshadowing a hurricane-force shit-storm. Before risking any more damage to his blistering esophagus, he hurriedly dressed and left for his office to begin drafting an urgent cable to Beijing headquarters to advise them of what had transpired and seek direction.

The ambassador, too, had been surprised when he read the news.

However, he reacted with more equanimity. Perhaps even with a little mirth at his covert cousin's misadventure. It would, however, quickly turn to anxiety over having to deal with another ministry's pratfall. He fired off his own cable to superiors at the Ministry of Foreign Affairs requesting immediate guidance.

Predictably, the State Department summoned a Chinese representative to Foggy Bottom for a formal dressing-down that very day. To appear himself, the ambassador might imply that his government had something for which to apologize. Minister Counselor Wang Li and First Secretary Qiu Shengyun went to absorb the rebuke from Acting Assistant Secretary for East Asia/Pacific (EAP) John Monjo and Acting Director EAP Chris Szymanski. At least the Chinese officials could deny any knowledge of Chin without a word of a lie.

Monjo officially notified them of Chin's arrest. It followed, he assured them, "extensive investigation" — which, he noted pointedly, "is continuing."

The American government was aware that Chin's activities dated back to the 1940s and continued to the present. "We are aware of the manner in which your intelligence services directed and handled this individual," he continued gravely. He specified that Chin was being charged with acts of espionage.

"We are deeply disturbed by this case and the long involvement of Chinese intelligence services in it," he concluded.

If espionage is an affair that reeks of cheap motels, diplomacy is a perfumed parlor flirtation. Nonetheless, the double entendres are well understood and just as crude after their own fashion. To be deeply disturbed was to be royally pissed off. Whether pissed off manifests as harmless, though uncomfortable, sulking or some kind of tangible punishment would remain undecided until State evaluated all the ramifications.

Wang replied as expected, with indignation. He denied any knowledge of the case and, therefore, "could not accept the charge."

He went on to say that he would bring the matter to the attention of his government and reserved the right to comment further at a later time. He did, however, make the point that it was not China's practice to carry out such activities.

"The policy of the government of the People's Republic is to promote Sino–US relations, in the past and in the future," he asserted. He then pouted that it was "not helpful" for the Americans to have gone public with the matter even before notifying his government.

Monjo explained that State hadn't issued a formal announcement; rather, it is the nature of the American judicial system that charges are filed as a matter of public record.[3]

Facing questions from the American press in Beijing, Foreign Ministry spokesman Li Zhaoxing stated, "We have nothing to do with that man. The accusation made by the U.S. side is groundless."[4]

Thus is the game played, and Larry must have expected no different.

The most senior ranks in the Ministry of Public Security understood the difficult and distressing truth: Their man was gone. Top Politburo members who had for years been briefed according to Larry's intelligence without being privy to his identity would learn, yes, Chin is ours.

News of a lost agent has the same effect within an intelligence service as a plane crash among the air traffic controllers handling the flight. The momentary hollowness of disbelief is quickly filled by a rockslide of panic, which settles unsteadily into utter helplessness.

Public Security officers were left with no alternative but to scour press reports for clues on the specifics of the Americans' accusation and the nature of the evidence against Chin.

The overseas accommodation address to which Larry had sent letters would be considered compromised. Assigned exclusively to him, its being blown wouldn't have any impact on other operations. Despite being known to Chin only by a generic surname, proper tradecraft dictated that Mr. Lee be treated as if he'd been compromised. He would be told nothing; he simply never heard from Mr. Yang again, nor were any further favors requested by his friends. Whatever benefits he earned from his cooperation went unaffected, so he recognized he'd done nothing to undermine his *guanxi*. If he followed the media, he was undoubtedly startled to realize the importance of the affair in which he was implicated. Concerned about how much effort might be devoted to identifying him, he ended up looking over his shoulder for quite some time, but was eventually relieved that he seemed to have attracted no attention.

More distraught than anyone was Ou Qiming. He had done well in his career — having risen to deputy chief, First Division, Second Bureau of the Guangdong Provincial Security Bureau — in no small measure because he ran so influential a source. He worried: Might he be suspect for Chin's apprehension? Just as a homicide investigation begins with a close examination of the victim, his intimates, and his acquaintances, so, too, investigating the loss of an agent begins with scrutinizing whoever was aware of the case. That index finger pointed directly, Ou was well aware, at himself. But of course, not exclusively. There was also, for instance, Miss Wong.

But above all: Yu Zhensan's absence was cause for foreboding around the office. He was several days beyond his authorized leave before his superiors became alarmed. Things happen, after all, though they were hard-pressed to think of an acceptable excuse for not calling in to request permission for an extension. Chin's arrest was the first signal that Public Security had a true crisis on its hands.

Officers were sent out on a furious hunt to find Yu. Family, friends, the most offhand acquaintance, all were questioned — none too gently. It seemed like every counterman at any noodle stand he'd ever passed was brought in for interrogation. His home was ransacked. Border posts all around the country were given his picture. Police at every airport, every bus and train station, were alerted. Not a trace.

Yu was gone. Disappeared, along with every secret ever entrusted to him. Each now as worthless as stocks during the Depression. Larry's arrest was the best clue to his fate. What was most disturbing was that Yu shouldn't have known about Chin. Assuming he did, managers faced the same conundrum as their counterparts at CIA who were trying to ascertain what Larry gave up: reviewing his cases and writing those off as tainted was straightforward. Finding all that he had no business knowing — but did — was as dispiriting as dragging a deep lake for a missing child.

Even when her last footprints lead to the water's edge, you hope against hope that she didn't sink to the bottom.

Colleagues were questioned. Not to be blamed, they were promised, but so we can get a handle on this thing.

It's unknown whether Miss Wong came clean about Yu's advances and how she spurned him. The potential relevance might have dawned on her, and she knew better than to volunteer and leave it to her superiors' speculation whether she bore any responsibility. Nobody on this side of the Pacific seems to know if Miss Wong suffered any consequences.

Whether it's conjecture or something more substantive, I have been told that Ou emerged unscathed. How Yu came to expose Larry was troubling, but the timing of the arrest was such that no other culprit was plausible. Furthermore, assuming it operates internally like all other intelligence services, Public Security recognized the counterproductive nature of bringing additional turmoil upon itself.

The Americans picked up no maydays to the ships at sea. Single-line control meant that Larry's arrest couldn't imperil any other agents. The anomaly of an overseas agent run by the domestic Ministry of Public Security (though by now merged with the Ministry of State Security into a single entity) meant that those agents under its control had no more connection to the old State Security than a CIA source had with the FBI. If China anticipated increased vigilance from American counterintelligence, it wasn't indicated in its behavior. To all appearances, the Chinese reaction to Larry's arrest was business as usual.

*Alexandria, Virginia, January 2, 1986*
Having successfully indicted Chin on one count of conspiracy to transmit defense information to a foreign government — Title 18, US Code, Section 794 (c) — the prosecution returned to the grand jury in the new year to level more charges once it had the opportunity to review the evidence culled from his diaries and the mass of other papers seized from his apartment.

Two additional indictments were handed down for transmitting defense information to a foreign government — Title 18, US Code, Section 794 (a). In formal and precise legal language, the indictment charged, he "unlawfully, willfully, and knowingly" delivered to the government of China "information relating to the national defense of the United States with the intent and reason to believe that the same would be used to the injury of the United States and to the advantage of the People's Republic of China." In general terms, it claimed that he communicated classified material gathered from the FBIS. It detailed his known travel to Toronto, Hong Kong, Macao, and Beijing, linking it to meetings with agents of China's intelligence service. Essentially, this was intended to establish tradecraft and clandestine behavior consistent with espionage.

From a legal standpoint, "national defense" is a "generic concept of broad connotations," the US attorney argued in a trial memorandum. "For information to relate to the national defense, it is *not* necessary that it be vitally important or that its disclosure could or would be injurious to the United States, although it is necessary that the government have safeguarded or attempted to safeguard the information." Thus, for example, a document classified in order to protect sources could be defined as related to the national defense. Also, the "goals and objectives of United States intelligence" falls broadly into the definition of national defense.[5]

As far as documenting explicit acts of espionage, the indictment harked back to 1951, when Chin "agreed to and did provide information to the PRCIS [People's Republic of China Intelligence Service] concerning the location of Chinese prisoners of war in Korea and the information that the American and Korean Intelligence Services were seeking from the Chinese POWS during the Korean Conflict." This he did for two thousand dollars. It also drew attention to Chin's September 17, 1983, trip to Hong Kong, during which he identified a fellow FBIS employee as susceptible to recruitment (that being Victoria Lowe).

To prove guilt, the prosecution would have to demonstrate *intent* or *reason to believe*, on the part of the accused, that the information would be used to the detriment of the United States *or* to the advantage of a foreign state. In plain language, it meant that even though the accused might not have intended either outcome, he had reason to believe it would transpire as a result of the action of revealing protected material to a foreign state. Hence, it would be insufficient for the defense to argue that the defendant hadn't intended to injure his country.

Whether the information could be used to the detriment of the United States *or* the advantage of China was a crucial distinction for the prosecution. The Supreme Court has held that the effect of transmitting information need only be one or the other, not both. Therefore, it would be sufficient to prove that China gained some advantage from the information it received, regardless of whether any demonstrable damage was suffered by the US. The actual crime is the disclosure of information.[6]

Cited among the methods employed to conceal the conspiracy, as well as its "success and profitability," the indictment pointed to "filing false tax returns which failed to report income earned from espionage activities and failed to report CHIN's Hong Kong financial activities; and, failing to report to the Secretary of the Treasury CHIN's interest in Hong Kong bank and financial accounts." Having reviewed his financial records, the prosecution documented a number of financial transactions, including deposits to a Hong Kong bank account:

- of HK$50,000 deposited on December 28, 1978;
  January 15, 1980; and January 16, 1981;
- of US$40,000 on July 22, 1981;
- of HK$174,000 on April 3, 1982; and
- of HK$100,000 on December 21, 1982.

On June 18, 1983, a gold account was opened in Chin's name at a Hong Kong bank. The initial deposit was of two hundred taels, or 240 ounces, of gold, worth approximately ninety-eight thousand dollars US.

Three separate counts of transmitting classified information to a foreign government — Title 50, US Code, Section 783 (b) — related to Chin's trips to Toronto. For each occasion — January 5, 1979; June 2, 1979;

and unspecified days in July 1980 — he was charged with unlawfully and
knowingly communicating to Mr. Lee "classified information concerning the West's assessment of Chinese (PRC) strategic, military, economic,
scientific and technical capabilities and intentions derived from overt and
covert human and technical collection sources." However, it is revealing
of the prosecution's case that nothing more definite was alleged. In other
words, it intended to prove that the three meetings with Lee that could
be corroborated were for the purpose of conveying classified information,
but it was not prepared to stipulate the substance of that information.

Six additional charges were laid for filing false tax returns during all
those years for which it was established that Chin had failed to declare
income from his employment on behalf of Chinese intelligence. With
reference to 1979, it was specified that he had neglected to report the sale
of securities he owned in Hong Kong and Shanghai banks. The charge for
1980 didn't spell out a particular sum. Between 1981 and 1984, he was said
to have substantially understated the income he earned from interest, per
Title 26, US Code, Section 7206 (i). The Fifth Amendment that protects
against being compelled to make a self-incriminating statement extends to
withholding the precise source of one's income, in the event that it derives
from illegal activities. Nonetheless, that income must still be included on
a tax return.

For the years 1980 to 1984, he was charged with failure to disclose his
interest in financial accounts in a foreign country, identified as Hong Kong
— Title 31, US Code, Section 5322 (b).[7]

If convicted on all counts, Larry Chin faced 133 years in prison, plus
heavy monetary penalties for the tax related offenses.

"The key to the case," Carson notes, "was getting that interview admitted.
If we got it in, we thought we had the case won. If not, we might have had
to drop the charges."[8]

The very same day the indictment was handed down, Chin's defense
team, Stein and Gary Kohlman, filed a motion to suppress this most
damning piece of evidence.

The fifty-eight-page brief (at the preliminary hearing, Judge Albert Bryon Jr. would remark, "I am surprised that you could find fifty-eight pages in a supplemental memorandum to talk about voluntariness of confession, but somebody did") begins by detailing the security procedures in place at the Watergate at Landmark apartment complex to prevent visitors from arriving unannounced. Nevertheless, three FBI agents did manage to appear at Larry's door "unexpectedly." It inaccurately states that, upon opening the door, he was advised by the agents "that they were there because he (Mr. Chin) had been charged with distributing classified information to the People's Republic of China." In fact, they gained admission on the pretext that he might assist them with an inquiry into a leak to China.

The door through which they proceeded to enter afforded "the only exit from the apartment." One of the agents "indicated where Mr. Chin should sit by placing his hand on Mr. Chin's shoulder." The agents positioned themselves on either side, and directly in front, of him. He was "completely confined." Larry also reportedly noted that the men were armed.

"Mr. Chin at that point reasonably believed that he was under arrest," the brief asserts. A mistaken belief doesn't become true just because you really, really believe. People aren't under arrest until they are so informed or until some action on the part of a law enforcement officer indicates that their liberty is infringed, such as when he refuses to leave when so asked or hinders suspects from exercising their freedom to proceed.

Over the course of a five-and-a-half-hour interrogation, according to the defense, "At no time was Mr. Chin able to speak with an attorney. He was never informed of his rights. Nor was he ever told by the agents that he was not under arrest, or that he was free to leave and free to direct the agents to leave." When the interrogation was over, it went on, "The agents then performed the two functions they intended when they arrived: Mr. Chin was transported to jail on a charge of espionage, and his apartment was searched."

The brief harangued the agents for having "repeatedly *warned* Mr. Chin that 'this was the only opportunity he had,' 'his only chance to cooperate,' and *threatened* to 'present the case to the Department of Justice' if he *dared* to ask them to leave" (emphasis added). Thus, "For each time the agents went through the motions of telling Mr. Chin that they would leave if he wished to remain silent and/or speak with an attorney, they actually made it crystal clear to him that he could not realistically exercise those choices."

The defense's contention was that Chin was in custody, thus deprived of his freedom, from the outset, but was never advised of his rights, as required by law. Since, they argued, "statements elicited in the absence of *Miranda* warnings [so named in reference to the landmark *Miranda v. Arizona* case of 1966 that established the precedent] are inadmissible even if voluntary," Larry's statement to the agents ought not to be admitted as evidence.

Moreover, referring to Larry's musing, "Maybe I should seek legal counsel," the defense cited precedents where the courts had ruled that any ambiguity about whether a suspect was asserting his rights had to be clarified before questioning could continue, or ought to be interpreted in the suspect's favor as an assertion of his rights. The defense claimed that Larry's remark "constituted an assertion of his right to counsel and required, therefore, that the three agents terminate their interrogation."[9] The reasoning follows that his statement was inadmissible because his rights were not respected.

Crucial as was Chin's statement, the prosecution conceded in its responding memorandum, "It has long been settled that an accused may not be convicted on his own uncorroborated confession." The definitive precedent was set by the Supreme Court in a case heard in 1951, wherein it ruled, "It is necessary, therefore, to require the Government to introduce substantial independent evidence which would tend to establish the trustworthiness of the statement."

To this end, the US attorney declared his intent to deliver expert testimony to show that Chin's actions were consistent with known intelligence-gathering methods employed by the Chinese. Charts depicting the chronology of the case and the web of financial transactions accompanying it were to be presented to the jury, along with photographs of locations where various events transpired and of diary and passport entries that would corroborate statements made by Chin.[10]

## Alexandria, Virginia, January 3, 1986

A preliminary hearing was convened at the federal courthouse before Judge Bryan to address pretrial motions, notably to determine whether Chin's statement to the FBI should be suppressed.

The first order of business was to arraign the defendant. The defense acknowledged receiving a copy of the indictment and waived a formal reading of the charges. Stein entered a plea of not guilty on his client's behalf. He elected trial by jury. All parties accepted February 3 as an appropriate date for the trial to begin.

The government began by calling Mark Johnson.

It had been decided that Johnson would carry the bulk of the testimony concerning the interview. Guerin exempted himself because he had other cases going that he worried would be compromised should his name or picture appear in the paper. One can only imagine that they had to do with human source operations he was running against Chinese intelligence. Roth, with the most courtroom experience of the bunch, was decidedly not enthusiastic about testifying. Of all the agents involved, he had the least expertise in the history and tradecraft of Chinese intelligence and didn't relish having a clever defense attorney turn him all inside out on these intricacies. He would, however, appear at the preliminary hearing.

This was maybe the highest-profile case he'd ever have a hand in, so Johnson was enthusiastic about the opportunity to take the stand, get his name in the paper. If the trial went well, it could only help his career.

Aronica began by having Johnson set the stage for the interview with Chin, explaining how he, Guerin, and Roth came to enter his building unannounced. They were received very cordially, he asserted.

Aronica then had him provide a detailed account of the interview. Johnson was forthright concerning his controversial remark about being

an attorney, putting in context that it was accompanied by an admonish-
ment that Chin need not speak with them, that he could seek legal counsel
or ask them to leave at any time. He told the court that Chin was further
advised that if they left, the investigation would continue and the evidence
they had collected would be submitted to the Justice Department, which
would be informed of his refusal to cooperate. He presented the interview
as an opportunity — but one that an attorney would undoubtedly advise
him to pass up.

Recognizing that the "I'm a lawyer" comment was a glaring problem
that the defense would not overlook, Aronica chose to confront it head-
on, asking Johnson, "Why did you identify yourself as an attorney?"

"Because I wanted to make perfectly clear to Mr. Chin and emphasize
the fact that the statements that he made to us were voluntary, that he
didn't have to talk to us, and that if he wanted us to leave, we would go.
By stating that I was an attorney, I thought I was adding emphasis to those
statements."

"Did he ask you to act as his attorney?"

"No."

"Were you offering to act as his attorney?"

"No."

Enough demonstrably false confessions have been signed that the court
is suspicious of overlong interviews. The sheer pressure of being questioned over the course of hours can be enough to weaken a suspect's psyche
to the point that he may confess for no other reason than to put an end
to it. Being accused of lying, more so than of a crime, by officers who are
not shy about their disbelief, who prod and cajole you to agree with their
truth, who offer respite if only you'll stop insisting on your innocence, can
become strangely enticing. Johnson referred to the log the agents kept
during Larry's interview to demonstrate that he began cooperating after
only fifty minutes.

Having, he hoped, defused that issue, Aronica moved on to whether
Larry was in custody while he was talking. Johnson described how Larry
freely fixed himself tea alone in his kitchen, went to the bathroom on

several occasions without an escort, and was allowed to answer the telephone. He pointed out that, at no time, did any of the agents physically touch Chin. At the agents' behest, dinner was ordered and the four of them ate together.

Johnson claimed he had no idea whether Chin was going to be arrested until Carson and Schiffer showed up at the apartment at 10:37 PM, at which point Chin was advised of his rights. He was informed that a search warrant was being executed. He was led from his home to a waiting car.

On cross-examination, Stein would hammer repeatedly at the sequence by which Chin was advised of his rights, agreed to speak, and was formally placed under arrest. If he was in custody, it was essential for him to have been explicitly instructed that he was under no obligation to speak in order for what he said to be admissible in court. Any doubt on this point would allow Stein to argue that his statement was improperly obtained. He knew his client was in trouble if his confession was ruled admissible.

Stein commenced by scrutinizing how the agents obtained entry to Chin's apartment complex. His insinuation was, clearly, that they had behaved in a covert manner to evade prior announcement of their arrival.

"You had a way of getting to Mr. Chin's apartment without calling him ahead of time," he declared accusingly. "Was it your intention to knock at Mr. Chin's door without any forewarning to him?"

"I'm not sure I understand your question," Johnson hedged.

"Did you consider that the element of surprise was favorable to you in your assignment?"

"I don't think I considered the element of surprise. I just thought that we would go to the door and knock and talk to him that way. That's just how we decided to do the interview."

"The matter of legal counsel had not come up until he mentioned the word *legal counsel*," Stein challenged. "That's true, isn't it?"

"That's correct."

"And when he announced that he might need legal counsel, you announced that you were a lawyer."

"No."

"At some point you did announce that you were a lawyer."

"Yes."

"Had you discussed with the Department of Justice whether you were going to tell Mr. Chin that you were a lawyer?" Stein inquired sarcastically.

"I didn't discuss anything with the Department of Justice," Johnson said defiantly.

"Well, when Mr. Chin raised the question about a lawyer, in whatever words he raised it, you were not obliged at that point to tell him you were a lawyer, were you?"

"No."

"But you chose to do so, didn't you?"

"Yes."

"And you gave him certain legal advice, didn't you?"

"No."

"You told him that he could cooperate or he could not cooperate, correct?"

"No. You are changing the format all around. He stated, I am not sure of my legal rights. I am not an attorney. And in the same conversation, right after that, I said, Well, Mr. Chin, I am an attorney. And you do not have to talk to us if you do not want to."

"Now, when you said that . . ."

"Can I finish?" Johnson demanded.

"Yes."

"I stated that I am an attorney and you do not have to talk to us if you do not want to. If you want us to leave, you merely have to ask and we will go. And the fact that you are talking to us is completely voluntary. You can call an attorney anytime you want. That's what I stated, I am an attorney, and that's the context that it was stated in."

As Stein continued to bore down like a drill bit into a pulpy tooth, Aronica objected.

Judge Bryan cautioned against being argumentative before cutting Stein off altogether: "I think we have explored this particular area enough."

Not long after, Stein returned, "Up until the point where you said that you were a lawyer, Mr. Chin had entered a denial to all accusations, isn't that true?"

"Yes."

"And his admissions or whatever they are, took place after you gave him a supposition concerning what would be the attitude of the Department of Justice under certain conditions?"

"I never gave him a supposition as to what the attitudes of the Department of Justice would be. I can't tell what the Department of Justice will say."

One final time, he tried: "Let me see if I can capture this. You said that the reason you told him you were a lawyer was because you wanted to emphasize what his rights were."

"No. The reason I told him . . . ," and Johnson repeated himself until Bryan interrupted with exasperation, "Yes, I think I've heard this three or four times."

Aronica proceeded to call Terry Roth to the stand.

"At any point during the interview, did you threaten Chin in any way?"

"No, sir."

"Coerce him in any way?"

"No, sir."

"Was he forced to answer any questions that he didn't want to answer?"

"No, sir."

"Was there any yelling, screaming, or pounding on the table?"

"No, none of that."

"Did any of you touch Chin during the course of the interview?"

"No, sir."

"How was the interview conducted?"

"During the entire time it was really rather low-key, matter-of-fact. Everyone stayed extremely calm during the interview."

"How about Chin?"

"Probably the calmest of all."

Roth reiterated Johnson's testimony concerning Larry having been invited to call an attorney if he so desired and that he was free to ask them to leave.

Stein's tactic on cross was to tear into the agent's assertion that this would be Larry's only chance before his case was brought to the Department of Justice.

"We told him that this was his only opportunity," Roth affirmed, "and if he didn't cooperate or talk to us that night, that we would not be coming back to seek further interviews with him."

"And nobody said to anybody at the Department of Justice that Mr. Chin has decided to stay and talk and we are wondering now what your reaction is?"

"I personally did not."

"You don't know if anybody else said that, do you?"

"No, sir."

"He has availed himself of the opportunity and now we are wondering whether you would be lenient with him. No one said that, did they?"

"I don't know what discussions were taking place with the Department of Justice."

Bringing his questioning to a close, Stein asked, "You know what an interrogation is?"

"Yes."

"This was an interrogation, wasn't it?"

"I would prefer to call it an interview."

"I understand that. But it was an interrogation."

"If you want to use that term, I suppose you could."

The only witness called by the defense was Larry Chin.

He walked stiffly to the stand. His dark suit was a little baggy from the weight he'd lost over the past five weeks on a jailhouse diet. He was composed as he swore to tell the truth.

Stein began by having him describe the procedure by which visitors gained entry to the grounds of his apartment complex. The purpose was to show the judge that the FBI agents had purposefully circumvented those procedures in order to get to his door unannounced.

Stein brought out the fact that Chin was aware the agents were armed. He also put his dependence on oral medication to treat his diabetes on the record.

He then proceeded to dissect Johnson's ill-considered "I'm a lawyer" remark.

"What did you say when Mr. Johnson said he was a lawyer?" Stein asked.

"I said, then what should I do?"

"What significance, if any, was it to you that Mr. Johnson said he was a lawyer?"

"Well, at that point, I realized he was a lawyer, then he had certain ethic code to follow, so whatever he says would carry the weight of legal advice."

"Did he say anything to you which you took as legal advice?"

"He mentioned if I cooperate, there would be one consequence; if I do not cooperate, there would be another consequence. So I think that was his legal advice."

Stein went on, "Did the subject of calling a lawyer come up?"

"I was the one who first *demanded* to have the assistance of legal counsel" (emphasis added).

"Did you ever call a lawyer?"

"No, I did not."

"Why not?"

"Because Johnson said he was a lawyer, so I thought he should be aware of all the resource of a lawyer, so if he was a lawyer, I did not have the need."

Having established that Chin was thoroughly confused regarding his right to, or need for, counsel, Stein went back to the arrival of the agents.

In Chin's testimony, they weren't invited into his apartment, "they just came in, three of them."

"Did the door close behind the agents?" he asked, ominously.

"That is right." Chin nodded.

To advance the idea that Chin was in custody, Stein had him recount how he was "directed" where to sit. Around 9:00 PM he expressed a desire to return to his other apartment, but was told he could only do so if accompanied by an agent. He says that his housekeeper came by, but was turned away at the door. Chin called Cathy to tell her he couldn't come home for dinner and another call from a friend was cut short when Chin told him he was tied up.

The defense reiterated that the FBI's intent, from the first, was to arrest Larry and search his apartment.[11]

This was not, at all, so. "Without his confession, we really didn't have very much," Rudy Guerin acknowledges today.[12] The FBI had presented shadow puppets in the guise of monsters and Larry had projected upon them his fears of the truth. He assumed his back was to the wall, so he reluctantly fell into his interrogator's arms.

Satisfied, Stein had no further questions.[13]

Aronica rose for his first exchange with Chin. Asked his impression of him, Aronica replies, "I thought Larry was a very bright guy. Scheming, cunning. Look, he was able to get away with this for thirty years. He was very careful. A very disciplined guy."[14]

He was impressed by Chin's composure. A lot was riding on how the judge would rule on the admissibility of his statement, yet he appeared to be calm and sure of himself.

The prosecutor led Chin through his educational background and outlined his work history with the American government. When he began enumerating his real estate holdings, Judge Bryan interrupted, "What is all this?"

"Your Honor, just to show that he is familiar with the English language, that he is sophisticated." Aronica requested the court's indulgence.

Bryan again intervened when Aronica addressed how extensively Chin had traveled the world.

"You were advised, were you not, during the course of the interview that you did not have to talk to the agents?"

"I was not advised at all," Chin argued.

"Are you saying that you were not advised of that?"

"Not in that respect," he prevaricated.

"You were not advised that the agents would leave if you didn't want to talk to them?"

"Well, they might have said that, but I didn't remember."

"You didn't remember," Aronica repeated sarcastically. "I don't have anything further, Your Honor."

Immediately upon hearing closing arguments, Bryan ruled that the interview was not custodial. "Certainly a reasonable person would have felt that he could terminate the interview at any time. He was not only told that, but the atmosphere of the interrogation corroborated that. . . . This just was not custodial unless you are going to say that whenever a police officer interrogates you there is an element of confinement. That theory has never been adopted by any court so far as I know."

With respect to whether Chin's statement was voluntary, he ruled, "There is, of course, no overt coercion, threat, manhandling, or even touching of the defendant. Nor do the other aspects of this session, interrogation, are they revealed to be such as to cause whatever he says to be involuntary."

On Johnson's remark, he argued, "The injection of the subject of a lawyer, in my opinion, doesn't make it involuntary when you consider in what context the subject of a lawyer came about. . . . The alternatives that followed, while importuning, are certainly not such that you could say that they were coercive or caused the statements to be made involuntarily. Nor is the statement that this is the last opportunity to talk to us. That was, again, importuning, but there is nothing wrong with that, and there is nothing coercive about that."

He accepted that the agents didn't intend to arrest Chin from the moment they arrived, but only after hearing what he said. Had he refused to speak with the agents, they were going to exercise their search warrant. Whether they might have arrested him based upon what it uncovered was moot, because that, too, implied that he wasn't being arrested on the strength of what the bureau knew prior to contacting him. Thus, Judge Bryan denied the motion to suppress the statement.

*Washington, DC, February 1, 1986*

It hadn't been much of a Christmas for Tom Carson.

Since the day following the arrest, his job had been to comb every scrap of paper seized from the apartment for any notation that corroborated Larry's statement and what PLANESMAN had alleged. At the same time, it was important that he be focused and concise about what he drew attention to, not to overwhelm the jury with detail it couldn't absorb. Simplify, don't confuse, the issues. Forty-three pages of diary entries — some of which were recorded on bank deposit slips — were ultimately entered into evidence. All were in English and in Larry's hand. Tom had the pages blown up and highlighted the relevant entries in orange.

Diaries give insight into the person who keeps them. They show the reader what that person thought was important or momentous about his life. Each entry represents some event or incident that he wants to memorialize. They are intimate reminders. *I was here and this is what I did.* And, as a reader, you know that every remark is significant in some way because it isn't meant for any eyes but the diarist's.

Chin's diaries began in 1961. The first highlight documented his departure from Okinawa on September 21 for Hong Kong. He returned to Okinawa on October 23, where he remained for three days before heading to California. He was entitled to the month in Hong Kong as part of his home leave allowance. However, put in the context of PLANESMAN's accusations and Larry's own admissions, a month spent in a city where Chinese intelligence enjoyed its freest reign off the mainland just prior to taking up a job with the CIA in the United States, where China had no official presence whatsoever, takes on a darker hue.

What to make of the October 19, 1964, entry: "CPR [Chinese People's Republic] A-bomb"? Did he feel pride at his homeland's arrival as a military megapower? Or did it have something to do with his work at FBIS, in the sense that he was tasked to pay close attention to any Chinese media reports related to the matter? Farther down the same page under 1965, he wrote, "2/7, 8, 11 US bombs DRV [Democratic Republic of Vietnam]." For February 17, 1979, he noted, "Chinese launches attack into Viet." FBIS-work-related? An event warranting his attention on behalf of Public Security? Or perhaps merely noted for his own purposes: an American atrocity against fellow Asians, fellow Communists, that justified his clandestine work?

He was fussy about spending, noting when he purchased a car, made repairs to his home, bought a stereo — the routine of middle-class life. In 1966, on February 25, he wrote, "Nudist movie bought SF [presumably San Francisco]."

Some inclusions are difficult to interpret. On January 18, 1966: "Political confab. 'inevitable.'" On March 3, 1966: "Visit Magaret Lee, Redwood City." Should that read Margaret? Was she among his mistresses? March 23, 1966: "CCP rejection, 'fabrication charge.'"

From Christmas Day until December 30, 1977, Larry was in Las Vegas. He claimed to have won nine hundred dollars at the Frontier casino. At this time, he began to invest in real estate, putting down a fifteen-hundred-dollar deposit for three local properties. Two weeks later, he was at the Sands, where he claimed to have won $1,750. At the end of January, he put a down payment of $2,995 on another residence, which he immediately rented out. In March, he returned to Vegas, apparently with a mistress: "Entertain Nancy Tu, 3/14–17." On the twenty-third, back in Alexandria, he sent five thousand dollars to Cheetah Corporation to purchase ten units. He records that he flipped those properties later that same day for a five-thousand-dollar profit.

At the time of these transactions, he was earning, according to his own records, $24,799.

In 1979, he began buying row houses in Baltimore, including 10 North Streeper and 449 North Milton in the east-side neighborhood just above Patterson Park. He paid $20,500 and $17,500, respectively. In August, he went on a selling spree, disposing of five Baltimore residences for a total of $100,700.

Because a circumstantial case depends on jurors recognizing how a disjointed jumble of dots can be connected to outline a picture of the defendant's criminal activities, it is critical that their attention be concentrated on relevant information and that they be made to see how actions that may seem innocent out of context actually prove the charge. Thus, the quirky entries from Larry's diary that couldn't be directly tied to the accusations he faced were left aside.

Carson put together a chart, headed CHRONOLOGY, that highlighted the indicators of espionage upon which the prosecution wanted the jury to focus. Aronica would place this chronology on an easel in the courtroom as a constant reminder of the points supporting his case.

# — 8 —

# The Trial

*Alexandria, Virginia, February 4–7, 1986*
Neither side attempted to plea-bargain.

The US attorney is always interested in convicting high-profile defendants, and spies are an especially exotic sort. The FBI was anxious to expose the China threat. Nothing would more effectively — not to say publicly — drive home the point than to convict a spy in open court.

Why the defense wasn't more assertive in avoiding a trial through a plea arrangement is only puzzling if one assumes that the government had an ironclad case.

"Chin didn't think he'd done anything wrong because, he argued, whatever he'd done had been helpful to the United States and all this nonsense," Joseph Aronica says with undisguised scorn. "He denied criminal intent to injure the US. Maybe the defense thought the jury would buy in to this, that he was really helpful."[1]

In terms of simple fairness, the defense couldn't have hoped for a better arbiter than the Honorable Robert Merhige. Over the course of his thirty-one years on the federal bench, his wisdom was overwhelmingly confirmed by higher courts, which overturned less than 5 percent of his rulings, a remarkably low rate.[2]

John R. Pagan, dean of the University of Richmond School of Law, Merhige's alma mater, called him "one of the most significant trial judges of the 20th century."[3]

A native of Brooklyn, he was in private practice in Richmond when President Johnson appointed him to the bench in 1967. In the early 1970s, Merhige became one of the most hated men in Virginia when he ordered the integration of the state's segregated school system. It was a decision that took moral and physical courage. He and his family were threatened and placed under the constant protection of US Marshals. His dog was shot dead outside his home. He would not be cowed.

If Merhige was known for something other than his integrity, it was for his rocket docket, keeping proceedings moving forward with maximum haste.

The morning and a good portion of the afternoon on the first day of the trial were given over to jury selection. Once the requisite twelve citizens — nine women and three men — were empaneled, the judge invited the advocates to deliver their opening statements.

Aronica offered a succinct outline of Larry's duplicity, careful to paint it in tones that made it appear as damaging as possible to American interests.

Of the Korean War prisoners, he emphasized that the American military was anxious to extract "battlefield-type intelligence. This included order of battle, identification of units, routes of approach, supply routes, and airfields." When discussing Larry's responsibilities as an FBIS monitor, he stressed how the determination of what needed to be translated was based on "classified intelligence requirements of the United States," including Chinese intentions regarding Korea, Taiwan, and, later, Vietnam, its military posture and capabilities, and its political stability.

As a matter of law, the prosecution contended that Chin's motive was irrelevant. Consequently, Aronica didn't spend much time discussing it, except to note for the jury, "Chin was paid for his services, and paid very well. . . . By July of 1981 when Chin retired after a career as a modestly paid civil servant, Chin had amassed approximately thirty rental properties. In addition Chin used money from his foreign bank accounts to pay his gambling debts."

Chin's access, he stated, included intelligence collection guidelines, reports about covert activity, operational sources, methods, and tradecraft, reports from American agents in China, intelligence personnel directories, finished intelligence analyses, and reporting from other US and foreign intelligence agencies.

"In fact," Aronica specified, "Chin translated from English to Chinese the instructions on how to use American secret writing techniques used by American agents in China."

Aronica was adroit about dropping extremely precise details on the jury in the exact fashion that the FBI had done with Chin, in order to suggest, *If we know the minutest trivia, we must be even better informed about the broad sweep.* For instance, regarding Chin's first meeting with Mr. Lee at a Toronto shopping center, he pointed out that they had arranged to meet "inside the north door," though he never identified the shopping center itself. With respect to Chin's photographing documents, he referred expressly to the Minolta camera. These references served to establish the depth of the government's knowledge of Chin's activity.

Ou Qiming was frequently drawn from the shadows. He was identified as Larry's longtime handler. Approximate dates of meetings between the two during Chin's travels to Hong Kong, Macao, and China were brought up. Clearly, the prosecution was trying to put it in the jury's mind that its information emanated from a source with exceptional access. By accentuating these apparently private meetings, Aronica implied that Ou may have been an informant.

Then, as if to steer the jury from speculation about how the FBI came to initiate its investigation, he said, "The government will prove its case through Chin's confession to special agents of the FBI on November 22, 1985. That confession will be corroborated by documents seized pursuant to search warrants of his residence and his office on that same day and the next early morning."[4]

Jacob Stein rose to present his rebuttal. He politely introduced himself to the jury.

He conceded that the facts outlined by the prosecution were not in dispute. Only how they ought to be perceived.

Yes, Larry participated in interrogations of Chinese prisoners during the Korean War. This was his assigned duty. Hearing their accounts of conditions in mainland China, how the Chinese soldiers compared life in captivity favorably to life under Communist rule, was "part of an educational process for Mr. Chin," Stein insisted.

Yes, Larry met a Dr. Wang following his stint in Pusan. Yes, too, Wang was a Communist. But that was incidental to his being with the Red Cross, so, naturally, he was concerned with how Chinese prisoners were treated. "And Mr. Chin told Mr. Wang [*sic*] how the prisoners were being treated. That is, they were being treated better in American captivity than they were as Chinese civilians." No harm done. Score one for the Americans.

Jump ahead and Stein explained that Larry became aware of a split between Mao and Zhou Enlai. He was determined to see the latter prevail "because he felt it was a very important decision that was going to be reached of worldwide significance." Stein offered no details about the factional dispute; nor did he enlighten the jury as to how a victory by one over the other might impact the world.

"He did have access to some information, and some information was transferred," Stein allowed. "But now we come, do you know to what was that information [*sic*]? There are only two people, really, who know what that information was. One of them is Mr. Chin.

"Now, Mr. Ou knows what Mr. Chin gave him. And it will become apparent in this case that the government has a very big supply of information from Mr. Ou. We have been informed by a witness list that Mr. Ou will not testify."

There you have it, he was saying, the devious Mr. Ou, betrayer of his longtime associate. But Mr. Ou, snake that he is, has not the courage to appear in open court and testify before the good people of Virginia. He will cower out of sight, too ashamed to face the accused here before the light of truth, where justice is measured for all.

Mr. Chin, in contrast, will, Stein assured, stand before you and testify himself.

"In many criminal cases, defendants choose not to testify for one reason or another. And many defendants who don't testify are acquitted, some are convicted," he reasoned. "In this case, Mr. Chin has chosen to testify, and will explain to you exactly what information he gave to Mr. Ou."

Stein turned the jury's attention to Nixon's overtures toward China in 1970. Chin took it upon himself to transmit secret documents concerning the president's intentions to recognize the People's Republic to Mr. Ou.

"The evidence will show Mr. Chin was not a mole, that is, he was not intent on taking information which would be harmful to the United States and transferring it to China. The evidence will show Mr. Chin was taking information which put the United States in the best light possible to establish confidence on the part of the faction he really wanted to succeed."

The crucial question, Stein tried to convince the jury, related to Larry's motive: "Was his motive a desire to bring about what we know actually did take place?"[5] His confusing syntax must have had the jury wondering what he meant to suggest, precisely, had taken place.

Mark Johnson was again called by the prosecution to recount the pivotal interview. Through his testimony, the jury learned about the story Larry related to the three agents who had knocked on his door.

Carson, who sat beside Aronica at the prosecution table, took the stand to present the evidence gathered in the search. Referring to the chronology Tom had prepared as a visual aid, Aronica led him through a narrative of Chin's activities, to the extent the government could corroborate them. The only direct reference to espionage was a line dated 1952: "Provides POW information to PRC — Paid $2,000.00."

After that, it takes a little more imagination to follow the story. There is a succession of travel. Home leave to Hong Kong, 1952–1961. Four separate trips to Hong Kong, September–October 1961, March 1965, May–June 1966, January 1967. After each, the remark, "Paid Money." Each trip was corroborated by blown-up photos of pages from Larry's passport showing port-of-entry stamps. The allegation that he received payment was supported by Larry's statement and corroborated by diary entries or receipts found in his apartment.

Then the jury saw references to a variety of other trips, to Vancouver, Hong Kong, Seoul, Niagara Falls, and Buffalo between May 1967 and September 1978. In the midst of this is a line that reads "1976–1981 Removed Classified Documents from FBIS" — with respect to which, the FBI could cite Larry's statement that, following a hiatus brought on by the Cultural Revolution, he regularly photographed documents for his Chinese friends.

In 1979, 1980, and 1981, there are his trips to Toronto. Six verifiable deposits to his Hong Kong bank account are highlighted, totaling HK$424,000 plus US$40,000, plus the purchase of US$98,000 in gold.

His July 1981 retirement from the CIA is referred to as the "Career Intelligence Award Ceremony at CIA Headquarters, Langley, VA." to exploit it for all its ironic effect. Then there are his other travels to Hong Kong, Macao, London, and, twice, to China. The trips to the Far East were rendered more tangible by posters showing stylized maps with arrows depicting Larry's to-and-fro movements and photo insets of the hotels where he'd stayed, the Sintra, Park, Dong Fang, and Grand in Hong Kong and Macao; the Qianmen in Beijing, from which he'd imprudently purloined his room key as a souvenir.

Another exhibit introduced by Aronica was a page from Chin's address book listing Tseng Chi-ping, 33 Boundary Road, 3rd floor, Kowloon, Hong Kong. It was superimposed on a board alongside a photograph of the building with a yellow frame around a third-floor window and a close-up of the doorway. This was the accommodation address to which Larry wrote when he needed to signal a meet.

"That's the real-life spy stuff," Carson insists.[6]

The thousand-pound elephant stomping and trumpeting his way through the courtroom was the predicate for the case. How did the FBI come to suspect Chin? Because Larry confirmed all their allegations during the interview, the agents were able to cleverly refer any thrust in that direction back to his own comments.

Thus, to the obvious question, How did you know he was spying during the Korean War? they could truthfully respond, Because Larry told us.

How did you know Larry met with Chinese intelligence agents during his trips to the Far East? Because he told us.

How do you know Ou Qiming was an officer of the Ministry of Public Security and his assigned handler? Because he told us.

How do you know he shared secret information in advance of President Nixon's trip to Beijing? Because he told us.

Ultimately, there could be no more compelling answer.

During cross-examination, Johnson was asked whether he "checked with Mr. Ou about the documents" Chin had passed to Public Security. He replied truthfully, "No."[7]

Stein asked Carson whether the search of Chin's apartment had turned up any classified documents. In fact, it had turned up but a handful, all of which were so innocuous that the prosecution decided not to refer to them. A review conducted by the chief of the Classification Review Division shows that they included five partial performance appraisals, which are technically classified confidential to protect employees from identification; official FBIS travel orders for Chin, again, technically classified, but only because his name appears as an employee; notes on Chinese military terminology likely prepared by Chin, restricted to official use only, and therefore not actually classified; two cables classified confidential, but containing no classified information; and two documents, still heavily censored, marked secret. As well, some Foreign Press Digests published by FBIS were recovered. These are classified confidential, despite being derived from open sources. They are routinely classified because they reveal government reporting requirements and are compiled by analysts with access to classified material whose assessments may unintentionally reveal insights into their classified reading.[8]

Carson hesitated, looked over to Aronica, but had no alternative. "Yes."

Aronica immediately rose in objection.

A procedure for dealing with classified material had been agreed to during pretrial motions. For the document to be made available to the defense, it would have to be reviewed by the government and assessed according to national security guidelines. In the event that the defense was permitted to review it, only the attorneys would be granted access. They would not have the opportunity to study it with their client.

Merhige called the attorneys forward for a bench conference.

Perhaps Stein was surprised by Carson's reply — there's the old legal cliché about never asking a question to which you don't already know the answer. Larry might have assured him that the FBI could not possibly have retrieved anything incriminating from his home. On that basis, he may have been less than enthusiastic about proceeding with this line of inquiry.

Merhige sustained the objection.

The jurors exchanged glances. They looked at Carson, wondering what secret had just been withheld from them.

"I knew exactly what they were thinking," Carson says: "*It's so sensitive they can't even talk about it.* I can't understand what the defense was thinking. From our perspective, it just would have been embarrassing if we'd gone through the process to declassify those documents, only to have them see how inconsequential they were."[9]

On the stand, Carson heaved an inaudible sigh. Had observers noticed, they could have misinterpreted it as relief that national security had been upheld. In truth, it was relief over not having to reveal that the few concrete examples of classified documents in Larry's possession were so trivial as to risk making any further reference to classified documents and the presumption that their revelation could damage national security seem preposterous.

The reason Aronica hesitated when it came time to make the arrest, and why the case was deceptively complex to assemble, was that it depended on circumstantial evidence. There would be no Perry Mason moment when the entire courtroom heaved a collective gasp at an eyewitness's incontrovertible testimony, no presentation of a gun still smoking. In the absence of a direct connection between the accused and the alleged crime, the prosecution needs to assemble so persuasive a preponderance of evidence as to make its explanation for what transpired dispel any reasonable doubt. Which prompts the question that haunts every prosecution: How much doubt is reasonable?

Intricate tradecraft has been developed and refined over centuries for the sole purpose of enabling spies to burrow their way to an opposing nation's treasure trove of secrets undetected. Information is taken as invisibly as oxygen is exchanged for carbon dioxide between the inhale and exhale of a breath of air.

It wasn't enough to know what Larry had done.

"You've got to be able to prove something," Aronica explains. "You have his relationship with the Chinese. You had his admission. We had the *type* of classified information he said he provided, but not *this* piece of paper going over. We had a rather broad conspiracy. We only brought one count that dealt with a specific transaction, that being during the Korean War, where he was very specific about what he betrayed. So we got General Stilwell."[10]

General Richard Giles Stilwell was a most imposing figure. Son of the legendary General Joseph Stilwell, who had led American forces in China and Burma during the Second World War, Richard followed his father's footsteps into the army and off to the Asian theater. He served with military intelligence during the Korean War and went on to command a regiment. Later he would serve as supreme UN commander for forces in South Korea and as an undersecretary of defense.

He strode into the courtroom with a refined military gait, his posture ramrod-straight. When he swore to tell the truth, he left no doubt as to his sincerity. This was a man who didn't take an oath idly. He bore his responsibility toward his country, not as a burden, but a debt that he owed willingly for all it gave to him. Though he was retired, the soldiers who had served under his command were still his men; those who had fallen on his watch, eternally given to his care.

Aronica, who began his career as a military lawyer with the Judge Advocate General's Office, laughs, "I have a kind of a loose demeanor in court, but I was told that as soon as he took the stand, I straightened to attention."[11]

Stilwell's bearing alone gave authority to his testimony. Stein later recalled, "One of the press people in the courtroom tapped me on the shoulder and said cross-examining him would be like cross-examining George Washington."[12]

Stilwell gave a brief primer on military intelligence and the importance of interrogating prisoners to determine orders of battle, strength of forces, logistics, the location of supply posts and airfields, and, in this case, how Chinese troops were transported to the front lines so far from their home bases.

He told the court how a dossier was built on each prisoner from the time of his capture at the front until he reached the prison camps in the far south, where Chin was posted. The prisoner underwent a series of interrogations as he moved farther back from the line, beginning with the purely tactical, which would be extracted as quickly as possible; moving on to the more strategic, which was less perishable; and eventually, as Larry had told the bureau, dealing with the general conditions inside China. Each prisoner's dossier accompanied him throughout his internment and was of use to interrogators in determining whether the individual was cooperative or recalcitrant. In either event, these files contained complete records of the interrogations.

Stilwell explained how repatriation of prisoners became the sole impediment to an armistice, and caused the war to be prolonged by another two years. Years during which the United States suffered additional casualties. Years for which Chin could not possibly argue that he had acted for the advantage of both the United States and China. Years during which he was not a conduit to encourage better relations between the two countries.

The first time he was paid by Chinese intelligence, Aronica would stress in his closing summation, was for spying that contributed to large numbers of American servicemen being killed.

It was a harsh charge, and one that the defense would scramble to refute.

Aronica put another authoritative witness on the stand: John Stein, the CIA's deputy director for operations — the man who oversaw the agency's covert intelligence gathering. Afterward, Stein admitted to reporters that he could not recall another espionage case in which so high-level an intelligence official had appeared in open court.[13]

The deputy director testified only in generalities. He did make the point on cross-examination that "some 90 percent" of final intelligence reports, including those that were destined for the president's attention, were derived from open source material.[14] It was important for Jacob Stein to elicit this fact because it contextualized any argument the defense could make to the effect that the great preponderance of Larry's access was to unclassified data.

However, Carl Ford Jr., the CIA's national intelligence officer for East Asia, responsible for preparing sensitive National Intelligence Estimates, the briefing books for the president and his cabinet, would state, "It really doesn't matter whether that information we report to the president is unclassified 95 percent and 5 percent classified. The fact that the CIA or State Department or DIA [Defense Intelligence Agency] tells the president this is the case is really important in itself because it gives you a sense of what the president knows and how he is going to react in various situations."[15]

Cy Braegelmann, who first met Chin when he arrived in Rosslyn in 1970 and was his supervisor at FBIS, claimed that the China section handled an average of fifty classified documents a day. Both he and John Stein admitted, under cross-examination, that they had never seen any documents that Chin was alleged to have given to China.[16]

Ford testified to the importance of FBIS's role during the period when China was closed to Western observers. "We relied very heavily on the radio broadcasts and the newspaper reports to give us sort of a flavor, a sense of what was happening on a day-to-day basis in China."

And those who, like Larry, spent most of their time monitoring open information, would have to be broadly indoctrinated in order to be effective at their jobs. Said Ford, "Despite the various strict rules on security clearances, need to know, and access to information, once people are cleared within the fraternity of intelligence operations, analysts, collectors, whoever it might be, we have to talk among ourselves. There has to be a free flow of information so that we all are learning from each other and that we are concentrating on the proper things."

Ford suggested that, with enough information at one's disposal, human sources could be put in danger, "If you put all of those information reports out on a table over a long period of time, it is possible to begin to try to trace back who the source of the information is."

Internal CIA directories, to which Larry would surely have access, can be essential tools in identifying clandestine officers. "An important counterintelligence principle is to identify who the opposition is. It is sort of the key to everything else. If you can find out who is doing it, then you can begin to improve your own security. That is the way, obviously, we work and other intelligence agencies around the world work."[17]

Merhige lost patience as Aronica's attempts to tease out Ford's testimony elicited only repetition. He interrupted the prosecutor's examination: "Can we sum it up, Mr. Ford, by saying from an intelligence standpoint, that the more we know and the less a foreign government knows the better off we are; and the more they know and the less we know, it is to our disadvantage? Isn't that a sum up of everything that we have been talking about?"

"Absolutely, Your Honor. In fact, in general, you are right on target," Ford replied.

"I didn't mean to say my suggestion encompassed everything. There are other factors, too. But that is the general principle, and you could testify for the next seven hours and end up with the same thing."

"Correct."

"You asked the last question," Aronica broke in to mollify the judge.

"Oh, but if that were only true." Merhige rubbed his forehead.

Stein would call Howard Spendelow to the stand. A professor of Chinese politics at Washington's Georgetown University, he had run (and continues to run) the Advanced Area Studies course on China for the State Department since 1980. The course is required training for American government personnel preparing for assignments in China and is intended to instill familiarity with the region's history, politics, economy, and culture. Though not a government official per se, his academic expertise coupled with this apparent official endorsement lent gravitas to his testimony.

Spendelow has an easy smile and light eyes that are untroubled by ulterior motives. He speaks gently, with sincerity and appears to expect the same in return. He looks upon espionage with a combination of amusement and indulgence, a kind of boys-will-be-boys shrug and a lopsided grin. If he gives it a second thought, it would be that of the academic inconvenienced by the denial of documents relevant to his research.

The defense had contacted him out of the blue, he recalls. "The argument they wanted to get out of me was that nothing Mr. Chin revealed wasn't, in fact, already in the public domain.

"I was led to believe that I saw the entirety of what the prosecution was prepared to have discussed in open court. As far as I could tell, it seemed to be the kind of analysis that could be put together by a careful reading of the *People's Daily* and was known to anybody observing China in that period. It was pretty standard political science stuff concerning domestic developments in China. I didn't see anything to suggest that he'd jeopardized the security of agents."[18]

Spendelow recalls making reference to the Gang of Four while testifying and that Merhige reprimanded him for abusing his access to classified documents. He was surprised, since this clique had long since come under public scrutiny following Mao's death a decade earlier. But such are the vicissitudes, and the power, of the whisper. Tuck common knowledge inside a secret and it becomes privileged, the unpolished grain of sand within the gummy guts of the oyster.

"Dr. Spendelow is an academic," Aronica rebutted derisively in his closing. "Dr. Spendelow is not in the intelligence community. He is not familiar with the intelligence community. When asked about the documents he read and gave us an opinion on, I asked him, Was he aware whether any of that information came from covert sources or involved methods of intelligence gathering? And he said, Well, no, I didn't, because I didn't see the covert sources listed, like for example, our agent in Beijing, our agent here, our agent there."

Aronica paused triumphantly. "Maybe you find that kind of attribution in academic journals and in research papers, but you don't, ladies and gentlemen, see that in intelligence reports. You don't list what your assets are, where they are, when the information is given. So you can take his opinion for whatever it is worth. The government believes it is not worth much in this area."[19]

The jury would find it easy to be dismissive — contemptuous, even — of an academic opinion when set beside the commentaries of John Stein, General Stilwell, Ford, Braegelmann, and Agents Johnson and Carson, all of whom had impressive titles and had personally matched wits against Chinese intelligence operatives. By comparison, this outsider's judgment seemed flawed because he expressed no clue as to how the intelligence community functioned.

Asked to respond to Aronica, Spendelow is philosophical. "I would disagree that I don't have any sense of how the intelligence community gathers evidence and how important it is to protect sources, or the difference between its reporting and academic footnoting. I'd just say that I saw nothing that seemed to me to have come exclusively from covert sources or anything seriously threatening."[20]

On the third day of the trial, Larry rose with great formality when his lawyer called him to the stand. Sitting in court had been exhausting for the concentration exacted in measuring every gesture — involuntarily rubbing his chin, licking dry lips, a quivering of his leg, a restless shift of his torso — for whether it conveyed guilt or innocence. Now at least he would get to speak, to explain the positive outcome of what the jurors might, naturally, mistake for harmful actions.

According to Larry, his involvement with prisoner interrogations in Korea brought forth nothing more sensitive than revelations about living conditions in China, none of which would have surprised Chinese officials, though they would have been chagrined to have their shortcomings exposed to the enemy.

Stein then reviewed the role Larry played in advising the Chinese about Nixon's intentions vis-à-vis rapprochement. Larry explained how he sought to benefit Chinese–American relations.

"What selection process did you use with respect to the documents you gave to Mr. Lee and Mr. Ou?" Stein said, encouraging Larry to put himself in the best possible light.

"I have two criteria. One is the information about American analysis of Chinese situation showing American understanding of China, the United States' interventions toward China, and the US view of how, and in what way, China can develop its economy and can play a role helping the United States against the Soviet Union. Now, another criteria is whatever information about China which has to do with the Soviet Union, like the Soviet threat against China or Soviet preparations and attitude toward China."

"What was your objective in adopting that criteria?"

"My objective is to influence the faction which is practical, which is pro-Western, which is opposed to politics and bureaucracy in China, to improve the Chinese people's livelihood, to improve the economy, and to establish cooperation with the United States and the Western world."

"Why is it that you took money if your objective was as you described it?"

"For one thing, it was offered to me, and if I rejected, if I had rejected the offer, the mission, and also the money offered would be a way of their controlling me, so to speak. So that they can evaluate my work with some kind of a control. And also, of course, money can somehow improve my style of living."

"You used the word *control*. What controls were exercised over you by Mr. Ou?" Stein sounded as though he wasn't happy with Chin's response. His own witness didn't seem to be holding to his script.

"Well, actually, there was no control. Except he can be sure that the link will not be broken."

"Did he ever tell you he wanted any particular type of information?"

"No."

"Did you ever give Mr. Ou any information concerning the United States other than the type you described?"

"No."

"Did you ever give Mr. Ou any military information?"

"No."

"Was any information like that available to you had you wanted to get it?"

"Yes."

Getting to the prosecution's dearth of physical evidence, Stein raised the issue of sample documents the FBI produced during Larry's interview. "Did you affirm that all four were of the type that you saw?"

"Yes."

"Had you transferred any one of those four documents to Mr. Ou as a matter of fact?"

"No."

"Did you ever say to anyone that you wanted Mr. Ou to try and indoctrinate Victoria Lowe for any purpose?" Stein sought to preempt the grilling he expected Larry to take from the prosecution on his effort to have his former FBIS colleague recruited.

"No."

"In your interview with the FBI, did the FBI give you information that you had given to Mr. Ou?"

"That is right."

"What did you say to the FBI when they gave you that information?"

"I said this information you give me could only come from Mr. Ou. So, I told them that was Mr. Ou a defector [*sic*]."

"What did they say?"

"They said they cannot disclose this information."

He then had Larry recall a conversation he'd had with Braegelmann back around 1974 or 1975 when, obviously unaware that he was talking to a spy, Braegelmann, according to Chin's testimony, offhandedly remarked,

"I wish there was a mole so that the Chinese leadership would know the truth about the United States."

For his final question, Stein cautioned Larry that he wanted only a yes or no answer with no elaboration, "Mr. Chin, I am going to read you something which the government and I agree is true. 'In 1972 Larry Chin assisted the Directorate of Operations in its attempt to recruit a potential human asset for a sensitive operation of importance to the CIA.' Did that happen?"

"Yes."[21]

Left out was the certainty that whoever this recruit was, his identity would quickly have been blown to Chinese intelligence and his value to the CIA undermined from the very start. Perhaps this is what some people in a position to know had in mind when they suggested darkly and vaguely, during interviews for this book, that Chin did expose and endanger American assets.

It was getting late in the day, but Aronica would get his cross-examination in before Merhige adjourned court.

Aronica feigned last-minute preparations, shuffling through some papers on the table in front of him in order to have a moment to get his excitement in check before rising to face the defendant. He had been waiting — hoping — for this opportunity.

"We expected Larry to testify. Otherwise, why bother going to trial?" he reasons. Indeed, the contradiction in admitting to the crimes for which he was charged, only to plead not guilty and opt for trial, seems self-evident. Never did Larry argue that the FBI was mistaken, that he was being falsely persecuted, that he had never shared American secrets with agents of the Chinese government. Never did he recant the statement he gave to the FBI. "He obviously had a story to tell."[22]

No other testimony, no exhibit, not even reference to what Larry had admitted to the FBI agents would carry as much weight with jurors as whatever they heard him say to their face. Not in relation to this case, but in a column for a legal magazine, Stein has written, "The law is skeptical of confessions made outside the courtroom. People may confess for reasons known and unknown and be innocent. The temptation to extort confessions is strong."[23] Juries love to hear a confession because it is so apparently clear When a defendant says, *I* did it, they are absolved of the responsibility to declare, *You* did it, in the face of evidence challenged by a staunch denial.

Why, then, did Chin take the stand and eliminate such skepticism by allowing the jury to hear him confess in his own words, qualified not by a repudiation of his actions, but by a justification? Why not just plead guilty and trade cooperation for leniency come sentencing?

"Mr. Chin," Aronica commenced, "the Chinese, you indicated, received and gave great attention to the stolen documents, is that correct?"

"Yes."

"And that is what you had been doing, at least for eleven years, from 1970 until '81, was stealing documents from the CIA and giving them to the Chinese?"

"That is right."

"Each of the times that you are charged with in the indictment, you traveled to Toronto and passed undeveloped roles of classified film, is that right?"

"That is right."

"And that film contained documents that you had stolen out of the CIA, FBIS headquarters in Rosslyn, Virginia?"

"Yes."

"And when you passed these documents that you had stolen out of the FBIS headquarters your intent was to help China, is that correct?"

"My intent was to help China and the United States to reestablish good relations."

"Was your intent to help the Chinese, the People's Republic of China?"

"Yes, in the meantime help the United States, too."

"Answer if you would, Mr. Chin, my question. When you passed the documents, was it your intent to help the People's Republic of China?"

"Yes."

Aronica proceeded to hammer at Larry about the money he was paid by Chinese intelligence. Larry agreed when asked if he was paid well, but hesitated when told he was paid "very well."

"*Well*, it is a relative word," he quibbled, but, as in response to his own lawyer, he didn't try to deny being paid nor the reason for his remuneration. He did claim only to have received less than US$10,000 until Aronica confronted him with deposits he'd made to Hong Kong banks totaling at least US$150,000. He insisted that these were loans.

Aronica's black eyes bore into Chin, trying to make him squirm, but Larry maintained his composure. Even as his arguments faltered, he held steady. Aronica was masterful at structuring his examination to make denials sound false.

He homed in on the Victoria Lowe story. "Did you tell the Chinese that Victoria Lowe had a brother in China?"

"Yes."

"Did you tell them that you thought they could recruit her to carry on the kind of work you had been doing for them?"

"No."

"Did you attempt to get any information about her brother in China?"

"Yes."

"How did you go about doing that?"

"I asked Mr. Ou's assistance to try to locate him."

"Did Mr. Ou oblige you?"

"Yes, he told me finally he found where he was."

"What did you do with that information?"

"Well, then I told Victoria Lowe that her brother was found, not by Mr. Ou, but through an overseas Chinese association."

"Why did you tell her that story?"

"Because I cannot reveal Mr. Ou to Victoria Lowe."

"Why would Ou help you find her brother?"

"This must be a favor for me, because I wanted it."

Even in the face of hostile questioning, Larry couldn't be humble. Aronica asked, "Did you meet with the top leaders of the Chinese government?"

"I was supposed to meet with Deng Xiaoping," Larry boasted, "but he was a busy person and it couldn't be arranged."

"Mr. Chin, you have lied a number of times in the past thirty years." Aronica's tone softened from accusation to regret. "You lied in the secrecy agreement you signed in April of 1970 when you got a top-secret clearance, did you not?"

"I did lie when I signed this secrecy agreement, because I wanted to advance my mission."

"You wanted to advance your mission, Mr. Chin, and you wanted to advance your pocket?"

"Well, that is only a by-product."

"A substantial by-product."

"You can say that, but it is far less than what I earned from FBIS."

Keeping with his disappointed tone, Aronica continued, "And you lied to your fellow employees throughout the thirty years that you worked for the government, operating as a faithful employee and yet supplying the Chinese with information, is that correct?"

"Yes."

"You lied on all your tax returns that you filed?"

"That had to be done. No other way out."

"You even lied to the Chinese when you were trying to get some more money and you gave them the research from *The Puzzle Palace*?" He called attention to the best seller that Larry had tried to pass as secret intelligence.

"Well, that was my way to get their full attention to that."

"To get some more money, too?"

"The money was a by-product," Larry repeated.

"Mr. Chin, for thirty years you have lived a life of lies, isn't that correct?"

"I object." Stein rose.

"Objection sustained, argumentative," Merhige declared. "All right. Any redirect?"

"With respect to the things that you told on the witness stand here today, have you been truthful?" Stein asked.

"Yes."

"No further questions, Your Honor." Stein sat down.

"Any recross?" Merhige asked.

"No, Your Honor," Aronica said.

"Call your next witness," Merhige told Stein.

"We rest."

"I have been at it forty years and it was the first courtroom confession I ever heard. Mr. Chin corroborated every allegation made against him," Merhige reflected,[24] perhaps wondering at the defense's motive in calling him to testify. Larry left nothing to the imagination.

Chin's testimony was disastrous. Moreover, it was avoidable. The law accords the right to protection from self-incrimination, making it strictly the defendant's prerogative whether to testify or not. Stein must have argued vehemently against having him take the stand. If Larry sincerely believed he could win the jury over by explaining his motive, Stein would have tried to disabuse him of the notion. A jury in Alexandria — the government's preferred jurisdiction for trying espionage cases because it generally brings forth a contingent with personal or familial connections to the federal institutions in the vicinity — couldn't be expected to sympathize with even the most well meaning of spies. They probably concluded he was guilty as soon as he conceded passing information to China, hardly awaiting his exculpatory "but" with rapt attention.

Nonetheless, at the end of the day, a defendant also has the right to be heard and, in a matter wherein he is fighting for his life, may overrule the best legal advice and take the chance to explain himself.

On the subject of clients' whims, Aronica shrugs in sympathy with his opposite number and says, "Sometimes you just have to accede to their wishes and play the cards you're dealt."[25]

Larry was sophisticated, attuned to the political realities and attitudes prevailing in and around the DC Beltway, a resident of the very suburb where he was being tried, and a long-standing member of the intelligence fraternity that had pursued him. So why, again, would he insist on testifying?

"He wanted people to know why he did it, that he was a man of honor," Moore suspects. "He was willing to admit to the substance in order to portray his motives as pure."[26]

Perhaps he sought peace of mind from articulating his reasons to the public before whom he stood accused. He would answer his accusers, refute their depiction of him as a venal man without principles. He would present himself, on the contrary, as a man on a selfless mission. Despite the personal risks, even though he was bound to be misunderstood, he persevered, martyring himself for what he knew was right. Ultimately, he was rewarded with the satisfaction of seeing relations between China and the United States flourish, and the knowledge that, were it not for his decisiveness and courage, they would conceivably be at loggerheads. This, he would tell the American people.

*Or* . . . maybe he had another message to communicate to a different audience entirely.

What if Larry had already given up on these proceedings, accepting the establishment of his guilt as a foregone conclusion? Above and beyond what he'd revealed in his statement to the FBI and what they'd found in his diaries and other private papers, he would anticipate that Ou had purchased his defection with physical proof of their relationship. Therefore, proclaiming innocence was futile.

Why not, then, plead guilty and seek leniency in sentencing in exchange for a full accounting of his activities?

Because that would seal his fate. It would leave him no better than the Chinese prisoners who had succumbed to American interrogation in Korea. The ones he had informed upon way back in the beginning.

Larry wasn't surprised when, in their embarrassment, his friends disavowed him publicly. It didn't mean they'd broken faith with him, so long as they believed he'd kept his with them. He understood their suspicion of the media and that they'd disparage anything reported about his case as propaganda.

He needed to communicate directly with Beijing, to convey a message in his own words. To tell them exactly what he'd revealed to his captors — and hence, what he had withheld. Only one forum was available: his trial. Surely the Chinese would have an agent in attendance to faithfully report back on the proceedings.

He could speak in open court, to his friends. Let them know what they'd cornered him into conceding and how he had excused himself, making the whole episode seem so benign. They would hear and they would trust him. They had always trusted him. Chairman Mao, Zhou Enlai had trusted him. Deng Xiaoping had trusted him. Never had he forsaken them. Their man had betrayed him. They knew that. He would remind them. Then, we shall see.

The day after Larry's testimony, the court heard closing arguments.

Aronica began his presentation in low gear, revving himself up with a summary of the evidence presented by the government, becoming more impassioned as he discussed the harm Chin had done to national security.

"Just imagine the documents," he implored. "These documents are being read by the National Security Council, the secretary of state, secretary of defense, Joint Chiefs of Staff, the vice president and the president of the United States. Those same documents are arriving in Beijing and being read by the Central Committee of the Politburo. Incredible."

He went about clearly defining the term *national defense* and how it did not strictly refer to military conditions, but applied more broadly to cover intelligence and national security, which he delineated as referring to "national preparedness." He also specified that the actions of the defendant were criminal if the information he disclosed could be used to the advantage of a foreign nation *or* to the injury of the United States. In other words, if the intelligence related to the Nixon initiative ultimately helped the US in its objective of improving relations with China, as has been suggested, relaying it to the Chinese was still a crime because, the government sought to prove, it had given them an advantage, regardless of its effect on the United States.

"The government does not have to prove the conjunctive," Aronica
stipulated, with a grammatical precision most jurors had been spared since
grade school. "Only the disjunctive, the *or*. And he admitted why he did it.
That was to help the Chinese."

Stein must have risen to deliver his summation with a hollow feeling
in the pit of his stomach — the feeling you get when you pull into an
intersection and realize the car heading toward the red light opposite isn't
going to stop. And there's nothing you can do but brace for impact and
hope that some intervening force will spare you from injury.

He fingered the knot in his tie to ensure it was straight in his collar,
buttoned his jacket, and demurely tapped his toes to sharpen the crease in
his pants. At that moment, he embodied the incongruous mix of grace and
absurdity demonstrated by the musicians aboard the *Titanic* who played
on bravely, impotently, as the ship submerged.

He began by inflating the jurors' sense of responsibility. "It is an important case, important to the administration of justice, and of course very
important to Mr. Chin." There were people on the panel probably unused
to deciding matters of consequence. That they were to determine the
course of the rest of a man's life ought to be, from the defense's point of
view, their first consideration.

He contended, "There is no dead body in this case. And that may
be the reason why it is repeatedly said that Mr. Chin confessed. He
didn't confess. What he is telling you is that the information that was
transmitted was publicly held information."[27] This is a neat example of
a lawyer trying to turn the evident into the dubious. If the jury questioned the confidentiality of the information Chin passed, then a negative becomes a positive, and he is no longer a spy, but a trusted back
channel confirming the reliability of facts China could — *should* — have
picked up on its own.

For good measure, Stein argued that even if Chin did as was alleged, his
motives were pure and the outcome favorable to all concerned. Opening
a dialogue with China "was a supreme objective of the United States . . .
[Chin] wanted to bring the nations together." Indeed, he said with a flour-

ish, had rapprochement not been achieved and China had pursued a closer alliance with the Soviet Union instead, "the whole world would be spinning in a different direction." In other words, far from doing injury to the national security of the United States, he actually succeeded in furthering its foreign policy objective and reinforcing its well-being.

"Motive has an awful lot to do with this case, because you can only look into a person's mind when you understand a person's motives," Stein implored the jurors. "And Mr. Chin's motive is unassailable in this case. . . . I don't think in his testimony, his true value to this country came through."[28]

When I asked Merhige whether Chin's claim that he sought to have a positive effect on Sino–American relations in any way moved him, he replies, "If that was the case, he should have joined the State Department."[29]

Because it bears the burden of proof, given the presumption of innocence with which all trials are to begin, the prosecution has a last opportunity to rebut the defense. In his final remarks, Aronica spoke fervently about the consequences of Chin's actions.

You see, it's all too easy to lose perspective in discussions of divulged secrets. Of trusts violated. Of vows broken. Abstractions, all; formulations that conceal how the calculus applies, like scribbling out the equation for splitting the atom and ignoring the explosions to follow. A secret never feels the bullet rupture the brain. Trust cannot be imprisoned behind dank concrete walls that are impervious to light, but allow all manner of vermin to sweat through its pores. A vow has no face to pummel until the swelling and encrusted blood leaves it unrecognizable.

How to convey the heartbeat within the abstraction?

Aronica had to make the jurors feel a sense of loss more tangible than government secrets or unidentifiable moles in far-off China. He tried to give them flesh-and-blood victims.

"You ought to think about the problems with bringing the Korean War to a conclusion, about people who may have died because of [Chin]. You ought to think, too, about the Vietnam era, what we went through during that time."[30]

With a bit of encouragement from Merhige, Aronica brought his oration to a close. It then fell to the judge to charge the jury with the legal framework within which to arrive at a verdict.

Among his comments, Merhige stated, "Good motive alone is never a defense when the act done or accused is a crime."[31]

Aronica tilts so far back in the swivel chair that I expect him to flip back, heels-over-head, at any time. But his gentle rocking holds him in equilibrium. He is in his early sixties, but he could pass for a good decade younger, with a thick head of black hair, sturdy shoulders, and knotted forearms. His fingers are interlaced behind his head as if complying with an order to surrender, his elbows flapping like the wings of a flightless bird. The collar on his crisp white shirt is open and his sleeves pushed up, as if he only straightens out the uniform of his profession when necessary — to reassure a client or argue in court. He has a booming, affable voice.

He joined the US Attorney's Office in the Eastern District of Virginia in 1979, where he remained until 1994, when he entered private practice in Washington. He now specializes in white-collar criminal defense at a K Street firm.

When a jury returns from deliberating, he purposely avoids eye contact, preferring to await the reading of the verdict rather than trying to guess at it based on body-language games. They look down, it's guilty; they look happy, it's not guilty. Or is it the other way around?

He knew he had a solid case to present, but is almost testy, jolting forward aggressively in his chair when I suggest it was a slam dunk. No such thing, he says shortly.[32] It puts me in mind of the old lawyer's joke, "I wouldn't want to be judged by twelve people who aren't smart enough to get out of doing jury duty."

The jury deliberated less than three and a half hours before returning with a verdict. They pronounced Larry guilty on all seventeen counts.

# — 9 —

# The End

For months, Tom Carson had convinced himself that Larry's conviction would bring him the euphoric sensation of being liberated from captivity. He expected to look over at Larry Chin upon hearing the foreperson call out guilty and see the dragon slain.

He was surprised at the anticlimax of the moment. Perhaps his anticipation had been too fully realized, like someone who has seen the *Mona Lisa* all his life on lunch boxes and T-shirts only to be underwhelmed by the small scale of the real portrait gazing out impassively from behind its gilded cage of bulletproof glass at the Louvre.

He didn't see that smoldering chimera that had once been so elusive as to seem invincible. He just saw a beaten old man, and it had a deflating effect on him. The others at the prosecution table pumped his hand in congratulation. He didn't resist, but neither did he share their ebullience.

He could have his life back. And if he didn't particularly enjoy the triumph, at least he was spared the disappointment of regret. Like toast buttered by a harried short-order cook, the credit would be laid on thick at the center, thin around the edges. Exactly opposite to the way blame is applied.

He could return to the routine of monitoring comings and goings at the Chinese embassy. It's all pensionable time, the experienced hands like to remind themselves when performing tedious duty. The same holds for thankless duty. There's no Christmas bonus or added stock options for running a major operation. No penalty for never catching your spy.

Well, Tom had his spy. As he contemplated returning to normal, he hoped to be able to forget all about Larry Chin.

---

The end of a man's life doesn't necessarily coincide with his death. It comes when his purpose and expectations run out, when he has nothing left to hope for. When there are no more questions he yearns to answer.

For Larry Wu-Tai Chin, life ended that February 7, 1986, in the Alexandria courtroom when the verdict condemned him to the prospect of 133 years in prison and $3.3 million in fines; an oddly symmetrical punishment for the 33 years he'd sold American secrets to the People's Republic of China.

*Stoic* is how observers describe Larry's reaction. He'd been generally expressionless throughout the proceedings, Aronica recalled. Perhaps because he recognized that he'd sealed his fate with his confession or merely in an effort to maintain his dignity in the face of a packed courtroom convened to pass judgment on him.

Aronica heard someone call out, "Oh my God!"[1] at the verdict. Cathy, sitting faithfully in the gallery, broke out in sobs. Larry paused as he was led out of the courtroom, and they looked sadly into each other's eyes. Their marriage had been stormier than most. There had been instances when he'd treated her cruelly. But in his moment of greatest desperation and helplessness, she was by him.

Described by Moore as a loyal American, she may have been as much confused as anything by what he'd done. She had experienced firsthand his capacity for betrayal, so she was unlikely surprised by his perfidy, even if she'd never admitted to how fully it dominated his nature. It's hard to know what a wife who has caught her husband cheating with other women and accused him of assaulting her continues to feel for him in her heart. Is it a boundless forgiveness or weary resignation? Perhaps some people just believe wholeheartedly in for-better-or-worse and that marriage is, ultimately, about acceptance, if not always love, in adversity. Simple acquiescence. Or it could be a practical assessment of need: Cathy was dependent on Larry's income and, subsequently, his pension for support. Probably a complicated mélange of all this along with a tumult of emotions that surge and recede well outside the limits of articulation.

She appeared to be the devoted, suffering spouse. In terms many wives would recognize, she described their married life: "I cooked, cleaned, washed, housekeeping for him, serving him like a king."[2] She claimed to have been unaware of his espionage until learning of it when he was first arraigned.[3]

Judge Merhige set March 17 for Chin's sentencing hearing.

"I'm the wrong guy to be before if you're looking for sympathy here. I cannot understand how an American could betray his country," Merhige is quick to point out. "I'm usually a pretty compassionate guy, but I can't think of anything worse than that. I just can't understand that."

He gives a little combination headshake and shrug. I believe what he says.

Asked how he would have ruled on Chin's fate, he leaves no doubt he would not have been lenient. "I would have adhered to the prescribed guidelines and done my duty."[4]

Larry was sixty-three years old. One way or another, he would die in prison. When and how were the only details to be finalized.

Stein immediately sounded his intention to appeal. He told the press that the judge was in error not to instruct the jury to take the prosecution's failure to produce the informant upon whose information Chin had been investigated as favorable evidence for the defendant.[5] In the meantime, Larry was returned to the Prince William County jail.

## Manassas, Virginia, February 10, 1986

Manassas, Virginia, hasn't attracted much media attention since the great Civil War battles of 1861 and 1862 that etched the name of this quiet community in the blood of American history.

Just days following his conviction, Larry invited reporters from *The Washington Post* and *The New York Times* to a news conference. He had failed to win over a jury of his peers, but there was a wider public to which he could appeal as he awaited sentencing. He was anxious lest China had failed to place someone in the court to hear him out. It was conceivable that they'd assessed a courtroom, with its never-blinking security cameras, its ubiquitous uniformed police presence, and its constant flow of non-uniformed law enforcers as too obvious a trap for an agent. He was confident that reports in both of these outlets would quickly find their way to his friends.

That his capture had left them extra cautious, he understood. Indeed, his own situation would worsen if other agents were arrested, causing the Americans to feel besieged by Chinese spies. It was bad enough that his arrest had coincided with so many other espionage cases, though he could console himself that China still conjured benevolent sentiments where the Soviet Union evoked hostility.

Despite the impatience that left Larry's nerves arthritically gnarled and throbbing, he rationalized that whatever scheme they could devise to help him would inevitably take time. Surely, in private, they accepted responsibility for his predicament. How could Mr. Ou have . . .

"It was worth it. I have nothing to regret," he insisted to the press. "When I think I have accomplished — the improvement of the livelihood of one billion Chinese people — my imprisonment for life is a very small price to pay."

He described himself as a "patriotic American trying to convert a sworn enemy into a trusted ally." While he conceded that the means — stealing classified material — were wrong, he extolled the end. By way of illustration, he recalled the legend of the Chinese statesman Sima Guang, who smashed a jar full of water to save a child drowning within. "By the same token, I broke the law of the United States, like breaking that jar, but I drained away the water of hostility and saved the child of US and China friendship and cooperation and reconciliation."

He was asked if he would accept an offer of asylum in China should one be forthcoming.

"I would have to think it over," he replied, careful not to alienate the American authorities with whom he would have to deal, or the Chinese who may be plotting to liberate him. "I have very good feelings about the United States. This is my country. I want to stay here."[6]

His mood was described as upbeat, and he even compared his cell favorably to the accommodations he'd enjoyed back in his student days at Yenching.[7]

The following week, Larry sat down with Charlie Rose on CBS's *Nightwatch* for what would turn out to be his final videotaped interview. He spoke with the self-possession of a thoroughly briefed statesman, calmly and in even tones, never descending into the shrill bluster of a man who doesn't believe every word he says. He had carefully rehearsed the message he wanted to get across.

"I feel that I was wronged. I think I did a tremendous contribution to the welfare of the United States, as well as the People's Republic of China. Because to turn an enemy into an ally is a tremendous performance that can be done only in a unique position like mine," he asserted. "They convicted me on a technicality because Mr. Aronica said you should convict him if his deed was to the advantage of a third country *or* to the injury of the United States."

Challenged about his loyalties, Larry insisted, "I am a patriot of the United States and of the People's Republic of China," equating them with his father and mother. "You don't distinguish between the two.

"Of course, you can be loyal to several countries. There are things you can do to serve the benefits of a billion people."

When the issue of money was raised, Chin explained, "I was offered the money in a way that would control my association with them." He was, he said, like a kite, and the money was the string: "If there is no string the kite can fly away. I think that is the reason why they gave me money."

Whatever Larry's desire to be paid, there is truth in his analogy. Intelligence officers insist on paying. Satisfying an agent's material needs is so much easier than filling his emotional void, which, at any rate, remains largely beyond fathoming.

He did change his mind on one point. Where he had admitted only a few days earlier that he *might* consider an offer of asylum from China should it be forthcoming, he was now prepared to plead with Deng Xiaoping to initiate a spy exchange on his behalf, adding, in disbelief, "I didn't realize

I was going to be in jail for the balance of my life."[8] In her book, Cathy would claim that Larry encouraged her to approach Deng to personally appeal for his help.[9]

This was a marked departure from the cavalier manner in which he'd dismissed his impending punishment as a worthwhile price to pay for his achievements.

But of course, the price he looked ahead to paying was huge. One he could scoff at during the moments he reveled in the attention of the media, buoyed at having his every utterance recorded, being treated like a man of importance, one who influenced the great affairs of state. However, in those glum hours when a man has only himself to impress — or lie to — he was forced to confront uncertainty over whether his life had been of any value whatsoever.

His family became concerned about his state of mind in the days following his conviction. He had reportedly told a fellow inmate that "if he was given a life sentence, he would not serve it. . . . Instead, the sources said, Chin, a diabetic, said he would induce a coma by eating sugar."[10] On February 11, he was interviewed by medical personnel at the jail and, according to then superintendent Stephan Kaftan, "denied he had any intention of committing suicide." He must have been convincing, for he was never placed under the close supervision of a suicide watch.[11]

His son Homer contacted Larry's attorney and suggested someone should speak with him.

"I told them I thought my dad was depressed," he said. "Outwardly, he was saying things were fine, but I realized deep down that he was not doing well. He is someone who doesn't like to burden other people with his problems."

A member of the firm confirmed calling Chin on the phone on February 20, saying, "I certainly did not see anything that would have alerted me to despondency or any break from his normal circumstances."[12]

Larry was making tentative plans for the immediate future, at any rate. He anticipated passing time by writing his memoirs.[13]

———

On the evening of February 20, Larry sat at the narrow inlaid shelf that ran the length of his cell to compose a letter to Cathy. The stainless steel was cold against his forearms; he could feel every scratch in the surface through his skin. He smoothed his hand over the blank sheet of paper. So many words to find if he was to express what he was going through in that instant. So difficult to state facts that indicated one thing, convey emotions that suggested something totally different.

He wasn't sad and he didn't want her to be, he wrote in Chinese.

He explained how he saw his position. "A letter from lawyer S [presumably a reference to Stein] today, mentioned about an appeal. The reasons for appeal mentioned in the letter were not very strong. It was mentioned also that it will go to the Supreme Court at the end, and it may take a year and a half. . . . Therefore, it is better not to lodge an appeal." He went on, "(7 PM Thursday, Feb. 20th, 1986) After I have decided not to appeal, I feel extremely tranquil."[14]

He proceeded to write more metaphorically,

> This morning I had a dream of a celestial world which makes me comfortable mentally and physically. When I thought of the fact that I don't need to do anything after waking up and can control my own time, and keep on sleeping, it's extremely comfortable.
>
> So, Little Fish [evidently a pet name for Cathy], don't worry about me . . . Isn't it a happy thing in the life? Except that I can't stay with you, I already have everything.

He went on to speak about "retreating to the mountains and forests," and urged Cathy,

> Please rest your heart after you know about this . . . The only thing I'm worried about is you. If you can let me leave, you're freed from suffering, as well as from my psychological

burden. If you can't, please simply imagine I'm not suffering in spite of being imprisoned.[15]

He posted the letter before lights-out for pickup first thing the next morning.

On February 21, 1986, breakfast was served at 6:30 AM. A new day, same as the last, same as the next. Bland institutional food served up on plastic trays, swallowed off blunt plastic utensils. Larry Chin had bacon, pancakes, and juice alone in his cell. His cellmate was napping in the common room.

I imagine he ate deliberately. I wonder, does knowing you're consuming your last meal make your appetite insatiable, or do you have to force every mouthful reluctantly down your arid, cottony throat? Perhaps he savored each bite, the way one does a last look around the landscape on the final day of a memorable vacation. For good or bad, we can only count on passing this way one time. If for that reason alone, departure is at best bittersweet. Reflecting on the finality of what he was about to do must have unleashed complicated emotions he clenched up to control. He took stock.

If he seemed calm as he went about his preparations, it was because he had eliminated uncertainty from his mind. The worst time, after all, is before deciding, when choices swirl indistinctly like glimpses of the bobbing running lights on ships far out in the fog at sea. Which one to swim for when resolve is failing?

He had formulated a simple plan, but it depended on timing. He was well aware of the prison's adherence to routine. Following breakfast, the night-watch guards make rounds and then prepare for shift change. Larry took the initiative of reminding a jail worker that the trash needed to be emptied from the common room prior to inspection. This was done at seven fifteen, and the worker passed Chin a fresh plastic bag.

Instead of placing it in the bin, he surreptitiously took it with him to his cell. He sat on his bed. He removed the laces from the eyelets of the Adidas sneakers he had ordered just a couple of days earlier from the commissary.

Perhaps he was thinking; perhaps he'd succeeded in wringing thought out of his mind. He unfolded the bag, carefully pulling apart the two sides of the open end, expanding it to its full width.

He must have paused to consider what he was about to do — how would it be possible not to? — at least for a moment. Not much more than that, because the day-shift guards would soon be on the block. A last look around, if only to ensure he was unseen. He lowered the bag over his head. He would have gulped a fresh lungful of air. He'd need it to enable him to gather the end of the bag and secure it tightly around his neck with the shoelace. If he tried to hold the bag closed, he'd pass out before he was done, let go, and find himself able to breathe again.

Blindly, he tied the lace tight. He lay back on his bunk and pulled the blanket up over his head so he'd appear to any passerby to be sleeping. He waited rigidly, with fierce determination, his mind likely swinging between resigned and frantic. In a spasm of animal panic, he'd fight reflexively to keep his last gulp of air in his tightening chest, try to draw out one more molecule of oxygen. He'd fail. He'd gasp involuntarily as his body convulsed instinctively to stave off death. If he wanted a second chance, he could claw the bag open with his fingers and take in cool, rich air. He didn't. His chances were up.

At 7:30 AM, he was observed lying on his bed and left undisturbed. He was still in the same position at eight o'clock during a prisoner count, though the guard reported seeing his leg move. Around forty minutes later, an inmate was instructed to rouse Larry. The inmate informed a guard he'd gotten no response to rapping on his door. At eight forty-five, a guard entered the cell and found Larry Chin unconscious. An alarm was sounded. Efforts to revive him were in vain. He was pronounced dead at nine thirty-five.[16]

When you commit suicide by gunshot, you need only summon enough courage for a split irrevocable second. When you overdose on pills or poison yourself with carbon monoxide, you simply settle back into sleep before unconsciousness. Chin's was a hard death, a supreme demonstration of willpower. A clear declaration that he wanted to die more than to live. District medical examiner Dr. Rak Woon Kim said, "The natural instinct to fight for air can be overcome, but that 'it needs determination to die.' It takes five to 10 minutes to become unconscious after the airways are blocked."[17]

The discipline he exhibited was impressive. From his manner of death, perhaps we can draw important inferences about his life. The poet and critic A. Alvarez, himself a failed suicide, wrote of the act, "However impulsive the action and confused the motives, the moment when a man finally decides to take his own life he achieves a certain temporary clarity. Suicide may be a declaration of bankruptcy which passes judgment on a life as one long history of failures. But it is a history which also amounts at least to this one decision which, by its very finality, is not wholly a failure. Some kind of minimal freedom — the freedom to die in one's own way and in one's own time — has been salvaged from the wreck of all those unwanted necessities."[18]

# — 10 —

# The Visit

Suicide, like espionage, is an act of great emotional complexity. You enter one side with nothing but blind faith in how you come out the other. From neither is there any going back. To both there are elements of courage and cowardice. Larry hadn't acted in haste or in a transient moment of depression. He had seized upon a choice.

But why?

"In the beginning was the deed. Not the motive, least of all the word," wrote John le Carré in his novel *A Perfect Spy*, discussing Magnus Pym, a lifelong double who also took his own life. "It was his own choice. It was his own life. No one forced him. Anywhere along the line, or right at the start of it, he could have yelled no and surprised himself. He never did."[1]

Interestingly, beside all the reasons used to explain his espionage can be discovered parallel reasons for his suicide. Thus, here, again, one finds the convergence of the two acts.

From the moment Larry Chin was confronted with his treason, he had clung to a higher purpose for his actions: "Legally I was wrong, but morally I was right," he maintained.[2] No common criminal, motivated by avarice, was he. No, indeed, he was a man of honor. But how to prove this upon being judged a traitor? Certainly not by languishing in prison. It would take an extraordinary statement in order for the world to be convinced of his integrity.

Sincerity is not a commitment to objective truth, but an honest, fiercely held belief. It is, like courage, a quality embedded deep in the heart, produced only when properly demanded by circumstance. So whether Larry was truthful in expressing his desire to help the United States as much as China, he was, one may argue, sincere. Once he was caught, at any rate.

Following his conviction, Larry was left with only one alternative for a public assertion of his integrity — suicide.

Referring to his final letter to Cathy — which, in retrospect, is properly read as a suicide note — Moore concludes, "He was telling her he was not in turmoil. He was setting himself up to be grafted onto this long tradition [of suicide] in Chinese history to demonstrate his sincerity."[3]

At the core of every human culture is a death myth: something to make sense of life and offer hope for afterlife. What they all hold out in common is the conviction that a better place awaits, and that the pain endured here is alleviated, somehow rewarded. By this conception, Chin's suicide fell in line with the classical Chinese culture he so cherished.

The tradition of employing suicide as a way to demonstrate the courage of one's convictions is well entrenched in the Chinese conception of honor. During the Cultural Revolution, for example, many who were about to be struggled threw themselves from windows on the cusp of being interrogated, not for fear of torture so much as to proclaim in the most powerful terms possible that they were wronged. Suicide becomes a response to injustice.

"Larry's was not a remorseful suicide," Moore decides. "This was how to show that you are prepared to die for that which you believe."[4]

Or he had simply fabricated a cover that satisfied his sense of the dramatic, his ego. As he had done in explaining his treason, he created the illusion of sacrificing his own interests to a nobler purpose. He had, to paraphrase Magers, plucked another fig leaf to hang over his actions.

For there was another motive that warranted concealment: a financial consideration. Under law, the United States does not sentence the deceased. Without sentencing, a conviction stands unfulfilled and the entire process hangs suspended in a judicial limbo. This was very significant to Larry because of the massive fines he stood to incur. His assets would be wiped out by the penalty the court was expected to impose. Thus, suicide was a tactic to preserve his estate for his wife and children.

Another legal precedent — that a conviction is not upheld so long as the possibility of appeal is pending — offered a shield to Larry's good name. The principle is meant as protection for those who die before having the opportunity to exhaust all avenues of appeal against wrongful conviction. On February 28, the court acknowledged Larry's death by issuing an order ending the case. Not leaving it at that, the defense filed a motion on March 10 to abate, asking the court to vacate the conviction and dismiss the indictment. In plain English, this means that the entire case is stricken from the books. As if no charges were ever laid. As if no crimes were ever committed.

It's a routine matter — "undisputed," according to the motion — granted with little more thought than it takes the judge to scribble his signature. However, this case was atypical because Larry hadn't died of natural or inflicted causes. He had made a conscious choice to end his life. Moreover, in his last letter, he clearly stated he had no intention of pursuing an appeal, thereby accepting his conviction.

Consequently, the US attorney was not prepared to let the motion pass unchallenged. Filing a memorandum in opposition to the motion, Aronica argued that there was no reason not to leave the matter as it was on the day of Chin's death.

"We do not wish to be ghoulish about this matter, nor to inflict pain on Chin's family," Aronica granted. "At the same time, we are unwilling to surrender Chin's conviction, a conviction fairly obtained before a jury of his peers. The Court should not permit Chin, or those purporting to act in his behalf, to do by his self-inflicted death what he could not do while he was alive."[5]

Citing Larry's letter to Cathy, Merhige agreed that it expressed how he had consulted with counsel and decided against appealing. Of his decision to commit suicide, Merhige wrote, "Chin had a choice: his life or an appeal. Sadly and regrettably, he chose to die and, although he is now unable to present his case on appeal, the Court cannot help but conclude that such a choice was a conscious and deliberate one."[6] Therefore, he decided, motion denied.

The judge's decision set an important precedent on abatement, because he took into consideration whether the defendant intended to appeal the ruling that stood at the time of his death. Since Larry did not, it was illogical to dismiss the indictment; the finding of guilt would stand for all time as the verdict.

Was Larry aware of the legal nuances attending the aftermath of a suicide? Only he could answer. If he was, it constitutes the second instance where, in Rudy Guerin's words, he fell on his sword for that thing he cared about more than he was afraid for himself: his kids. To live would be to waste away in jail, a doddering old man deprived of those rights — freedom, privacy — he'd taken for granted since leaving China, helplessly watching while everything he'd built over a lifetime was dismantled. To die was to preserve his legacy intact.

When news of Larry's suicide reached the Washington Field Office, Tom Carson was on his way back from the US Attorney's Office in Alexandria, where he had been dealing with another case.

Dispatch hailed him on the two-way: "Return to WFO ASAP, see the supervisor."

He 10-4ed and continued down the Beltway. The radios were scrambled, but not so securely that counterintelligence was transmitted in detail. If he was needed at the office, whatever it was could wait until he got there.

He walked in, and a hush descended on the bullpen. He sensed that something was wrong. He was swimming along in calm seas when the shark struck from below.

Schiffer stepped from his office. "Chin committed suicide," he said softly, unsure how Tom would react.

The initial impact brings on a frenzy of confusion. Carson blinked, stunned. Pain comes later.

Johnson grinned and cackled. Fuck him. Guerin didn't bother to look up from the report he was typing. Larry wasn't worth the effort. Tough shit. He wasn't in the habit of wasting pity on traitors, and nothing about Chin moved him to react differently.

The county officers had jurisdiction, but Larry was a federal prisoner, so the FBI was a party to the investigation that is mandatory whenever an inmate dies violently. As the agent of record, Tom had to go out to the jail and find out what happened.

He discovered Larry's corpse still on the cot where he'd taken his last breath. Dazed corrections officers milled about. Detectives from the Prince William County Police took notes and photographs of the crime scene. Though the jailers reported that he'd been discovered lying flat on his back with his arms by his side, as tranquil as if in slumber, Tom saw the body in a wild jumble, like a puppet cut from its strings, by the efforts to revive him. His face was smeared with the vomit that filled the bag when the officers tore it off his head. His shirt had been ripped open and flung off his chest when they'd tried to administer cardiopulmonary resuscitation. His trousers were soiled by the last convulsive purging of bodily fluids.

Carson had seen bodies before. He was always affected by the unseemliness of sudden violence. This was the first time in his career — he couldn't fend off the thought — when his actions had brought on another's death. "It's not guilt, but you do feel sorry." The feeling still lingers.

That night he broke the news to his wife over dinner.

Overhearing, his ten-year-old daughter blurted, "If you hadn't arrested him, he wouldn't be dead."

She didn't miss a beat, plunging her fork into her spaghetti and hungrily filling her mouth.

Tom wasn't sure whether he heard the inflection of a question or the even cool of an accusation. It didn't matter. Whether it sprang from some mystical father–daughter connection or was just the innocent honesty of a child, it was unnerving to have her give voice to his insecurities.

"I thought about it, when you're personally responsible for somebody's death, and I was directly responsible for Chin dying," Carson says ruefully. "But you know, my daughter, she was just a child. She didn't say it maliciously. It was just something a child says."[7]

Carson has a law enforcer's simple belief in having the punishment fit the crime, and he holds to a faith in the moral scale prescribed by the criminal code. He had no dark fantasies about meting out anything more excessive than what the law decided was just. He didn't sympathize with Larry, but the man didn't deserve to die. He doesn't think about the lurid Chin engaging in sticky phone sex with his "niece," nor does he picture him slinking furtively to meet with his handler, or eating voraciously at the infamous banquet held in his honor in Beijing, or gambling greedily. He sees him helpless and defeated, submitting docilely to the cuffs he secured on his wrists. It troubles him that Larry was so tortured and died so agonizingly.

No sleep came that night. He was back in the throes of the worst anxiety he'd known since the peak of the case.

Intelligence officers share strong bonds of mutual dependence based on the secrets and hazards of the job. They relax their guard with one another as they are permitted to with nobody else. They solicit one another's advice on cases. They discuss problems and exchange frustrations. But as with everything else in their lives, there are strands of falsehood embroidered into the fabric. Fear is taboo. Doubt is okay, but only so long as the fat streaks of weakness it implies are trimmed back from the firm meat. Thus, honesty is always held in check, scrambled through a filter that encrypts genuine pain in toughness. Mirth is the sanctioned response to a con's death; remorse is ridiculous. Worse, it is to be ridiculed. So you sandbag it back, like the rising waters of a swollen river, resorting to faith that you won't be swallowed up.

When Tom arrived at work the next morning, Guerin, Johnson, Roth, Schiffer, Carlson, and Wang were all in the office. He got a few curt greetings, but mostly each man seemed engrossed in phone calls or conversation. On his desk was a thick brown envelope. Written in neat block letters, ENCLOSED PLEASE FIND THE LARRY WU-TAI CHIN STRESS RELIEF KIT.

He looked up to see his colleagues grinning; a couple guffawed prematurely. He tore open the envelope and pulled out a large beige trash bag, a replica of the puke-laden one he'd handled the day before in Larry's cell. The other agents broke out in a chorus of laughter. After the slightest hiccup of hesitation, Tom joined them.

---

As director of inmate services, Glendell Hill was charged with investigating Larry's death. His conclusive finding that it was a suicide was backed up by the investigation of the Prince William County commonwealth's attorney and confirmed by the official findings of the northern Virginia state medical examiner. No official dispute with their conclusion has ever been issued. This ought to be the end of the tale.

Every true spy story closes on an unsolved mystery. So be it with this one.

Never far removed from espionage is its shadow, conspiracy. I confess skepticism toward all conspiracy theories. They tend to be convoluted, expansive, and defy most benchmarks of common sense. Yet the more complex, the more fascinating, and, moreover, the more irrefutable: hence, in some quarters, the more convincing. Efforts to contradict conspiracy theories only widen the scope of the plot by suggesting that you, too, might be one of its agents. Such is their seductiveness and insidiousness. Like good gossip, they incorporate just enough fact and plausibility to make people pause and concede, "Yeah, well, maybe."

Cathy suggests that Larry was murdered, presumably by Chinese intelligence. She cites three inconsistencies that preclude the suicide theory. First, the lace he used to secure the bag around his neck was from a size twelve sneaker, whereas Larry wore size nine. Second, prior to being arrested, Larry was being treated for his insulin-dependent diabetes with oral medication prescribed by his son, a physician. While in prison, he was switched to an injection. She wonders whether this was to facilitate poisoning him. And third, the final agonizing moments of asphyxiation are typically accompanied by considerable thrashing, leaving the victim in some disarray. Larry, to the contrary, was found by officers in a very composed state, the blanket, even, still neatly in place over his body.[8]

These are curiosities, in my opinion. They don't eclipse the improbability of unknown agents successfully arranging a murder within a maximum-security lockup. Aside from the organizational intricacy of implementation, the larger question is why they would be disposed to killing him.

Chin had been in custody for three months. China would have to assume the Americans had gotten all they could from him in that time. Killing him made no operational sense. The risks of getting caught should have dissuaded anyone who might contemplate such an action.

But Cathy's is not the last word on the subject.

More intriguing, by far, than her misgivings is the rumor I first learned in a conversation I had with Joe Aronica early in my research.

"Did you hear Larry got a visit at the jail?" he asked.

"No, what visit?"

He thought hard, paddling back through seventeen dense years of memory to be accurate.

"I was told at some point, I don't remember by whom, that Chinese journalists, or some guys posing as journalists, paid a visit to him a few days before his suicide," he recounted slowly. "My suspicion is that these were really Chinese intelligence agents and that they told him to do the right thing."[9]

Larry was, in fact, visited on February 19 by a journalist named Chen Guokun from the Chinese-language newspaper *Zhong Bao*. The interview he conducted seems perfectly legitimate, based upon a transcript Cathy quotes at length in her book.[10] Could this be what Aronica is thinking of? Perhaps.

Would the Chinese, risk-averse as they are in their foreign intelligence operations, designate an agent to go to the jail where he would confront guards, be required to present identification (even if falsified), sign a logbook, and be photographed on security cameras? Might they not have supposed that a conversation in a secure facility would be taped? There seem to be myriad ways such an initiative could go disastrously wrong. I found the story unconvincing, but too promising to ignore.

The obvious place to start was at the Prince William County jail. Unfortunately, this proved to be a dead end. Hill had no recollection whether Chin received any visitors other than his family in the days leading up to his suicide, and visitor logs from the period have long since been destroyed.

Following up on this point became a standard question in my repertoire. I asked it of everybody I interviewed. The problem with inquiring after a rumor is that it's difficult to discern when you've gone from curiously listening to playing a part in reinforcing its validity.

"I remember we checked the records at Prince William County [jail] and we didn't find any evidence," Schiffer replied. "Do I think there was some sort of conspiracy to kill him? Absolutely not. The Chinese government wanted to distance itself from Larry as much as possible. They wouldn't get involved in this thing."[11]

Carson was, likewise, dismissive of the suggestion that Chin was paid a visit.

Roth's memory was different. "There was definitely a Chinese visitor, a reporter. I can't think of any pressure he could have put on Chin. A threat against his family? There's been a lot of speculation that this guy was a Chinese agent and he told Larry it was time to do the right thing."[12]

Guerin said he'd never heard the story, but called any such speculation absurd.

Moore, too, denied hearing the story. "My take on the suicide is that he was behaving in the literary tradition of the righteous man wrongfully condemned. Besides, I'm sure he didn't want to bother with prison life. Far better to demonstrate his sincerity, his higher purpose."[13]

Magers said, "I have a vague recollection of having heard that someone visited him before his suicide. I remember something about that being discussed at the time, whether there was some connection. But I don't think it could have been anyone official. A friend, maybe, someone connected through *guanxi* who was asked to talk with him. It would have been unique, but so was the rest of the Chin case."

Asked how it would have been unique, he replied, "It would have represented an acknowledgment of a relationship. It would have been to take ownership of the problem. I would never say never. I certainly can't disprove it, but I surely don't think any such thing happened."[14]

So I returned to Aronica, armed with all these refutations, and asked him whether he still believed someone paid Larry a visit.

"Absolutely," he insisted. "Why would someone commit suicide under the circumstances? This is not a situation where a guy's been sentenced to life and exhausted all his appeals. Then I could buy in to it. But it ain't that."

As part of pre-sentencing discussions with the government, Larry had agreed to be debriefed by the CIA and to cooperate with its damage assessment. "I have a feeling this visitor was aware he was preparing to talk. I think he suggested that he end it. I believe that's exactly what happened," Aronica concluded.[15]

In his final letter to Cathy, Larry contradicts this, saying he had decided not to speak with the CIA. "At least I maintain the freedom of silence right now," he wrote, "and talking doesn't result in anything and won't help me."[16]

I sought out another expert on the methodology of Chinese intelligence, one of the most knowledgeable men I've ever known on the subject. He had no direct involvement with this case. For reasons of his own, he preferred not to be identified by name.

"I wouldn't read anything into the suicide. It would have been a tremendous loss of face for Chin to be caught. It's possible he just couldn't face what he'd done, or the consequences." He puffed out his lips in thought. "I really can't imagine that the Chinese would send someone to the prison who might be identified later. There would be no reason to want him dead, the story was already out. It isn't in their psyche to want him dead. All they had to do was deny, deny, deny."

He paused. "Unless the bureau really missed something much deeper."[17]

# Coda

Spies are haunted.

They take such pains to disguise themselves as ordinary, all the while aching to be recognized as extraordinary. When spies dream, they are admired; what they've done is admirable, every hard lie they've told protected a vulnerable truth. Upon awakening, misgivings sweep in, like mist over a mountain peak, on some days to dissipate harmlessly, on others to gather into a blackened storm.

Those traits that make a successful spy are the ingredients for a failed human being. The instinct to be false whenever given the opportunity to be honest. To approach every circumstance with apprehension, every person with suspicion. To perceive calculated bad intentions when simple carelessness is at issue. To constantly see the shadow of a scheme outlining happenstance. To withhold the benefit of a doubt in favor of casting aspersions. To feel safer when blanketed in fear because, at least, it forewarns of the expectation that life turns out badly in the end.

Living in anonymity and isolation causes spies to think often of death. They despair of being, in the rather contemptuous thoughts of a Joseph Conrad character in *The Rescue*, "the sort of people that pass without leaving footprints."[1] The fear of being forgotten can lead to mad choices.

The spy envisions his chipped tombstone listing wearily on an untended bed of thirsty grass, his name and the dates bracketing his brief existence eroded by the weather. You want so badly to leave more.

Today you won't find any plastic bags in the Prince William County – Manassas Detention Center. Prisoners wipe down each trash can every day. This is a legacy of Larry Chin.

# Acknowledgments

I owe thanks to those who shared their time and memories and expertise with me. Dr. Paul Moore and T. Van Magers answered my questions on several occasions and commented on an early version of the manuscript. Bob Dixon taught me much during the time I worked for him on the headquarters China desk at the Canadian Security Intelligence Service, never, I suspect, imagining how I might apply those lessons. He, too, read and commented upon the manuscript.

Tom Carson paid me the greatest compliment a subject can pay an interviewer: He seemed to put aside my intention to publish a book and spoke from his heart. I hope I paid him the appropriate respect in return.

For their graciousness and generosity, I thank Joseph Aronica, Rudy Guerin, Glendell Hill, Mark Johnson, James Lilley, the late Robert Merhige, Terry Roth, Ken Schiffer, I.C. Smith, and Howard Spendelow.

I wanted to interview Jacob Stein, because it would have been an opportunity to speak with somebody involved in the case who didn't look upon Larry as an adversary, and because I wanted insight into his strategy, in particular the decision to allow Larry to testify. He refused, saying, "The family wouldn't want me to discuss it."[1]

My sincere thanks to Michael Carin, a reader of infinite patience. If only all criticism could be rendered with such wit, it would be much easier to take. Because of his attention, some of my more embarrassing turns of phrase have been excised and are, therefore, known only to him.

Thanks also to Beverley Slopen, my agent, for all she did to see the manuscript into print, and to Chip Fleischer and everyone at Steerforth Press for believing in the book.

I want to express my heartfelt appreciation to the Canada Council for the Arts for its generous support. I would not otherwise have been able to complete this project.

Once again, I am eternally grateful to my wife, Sally, for enduring the process alongside me.

Obviously, not everyone I spoke with will agree with how I have assembled the information I gathered, nor will they necessarily concur with my conclusions. I, alone, bear responsibility for the contents of this book.

Tod Hoffman

2008

# Author's Note

This book is based on two things: meticulous research and the knowledge I acquired over eight years as an intelligence officer with the Canadian Security Intelligence Service. The latter informs my assimilation and interpretation of the former. There are three passages derived in large part from my background: The descriptions of PLANESMAN's recruitment by the CIA (pages 27–34) and his exfiltration (pages 81–86), and of Larry Chin's recruitment by Chinese intelligence (pages 137–140). The manner in which these episodes unfold and the people who were involved are predicated on fact. The specific details of conversations and the states of mind of these individuals are imagined. I feel comfortable doing this because my experience as an intelligence officer gives me relevant insight into these situations. Several experts who reviewed these sections of the manuscript found them plausible. To omit references to these crucial parts of the story would have left gaping holes in the narrative.

# Selected Bibliography

Alvarez, A. *The Savage God: A Study of Suicide.* New York: Bantam Books, 1971.

Andrew, Christopher. *For the President's Eyes Only: Secret Intelligence and the American Presidency from Washington to Bush.* New York: HarperCollins, 1995.

Bailey, Sydney Dawson. *The Korean Armistice.* New York: St. Martin's Press, 1992.

Bamford, James. *The Puzzle Palace: A Report on America's Most Secret Agency.* Boston: Houghton Mifflin, 1982.

Bearden, Milt, and James Risen. *The Main Enemy: The Inside Story of the CIA's Final Showdown with the KGB.* New York: Random House, 2003.

Blitzer, Wolf. *Territory of Lies: The Exclusive Story of Jonathan Jay Pollard: The American Who Spied on His Country for Israel and How He Was Betrayed.* New York: Harper & Row, 1989.

Byron, John, and Robert Pack. *The Claws of the Dragon: Kang Sheng — The Evil Genius Behind Mao and His Legacy of Terror in People's China.* New York: Simon & Schuster, 1992.

Chin, Cathy. *Death of My Husband: Larry Wu-Tai Chin.* Taipei, Taiwan: Tunghwang, 1998.

Conrad, Joseph. *The Rescue.* Middlesex, England: Penguin, 1920.

Douglas, John, and Mark Olshaker. *Mindhunter: Inside the FBI's Elite Serial Crime Unit.* New York: Pocket Star Books, 1995.

Eftimiades, Nicholas. *Chinese Intelligence Operations.* Annapolis, Md.: Naval Institute Press, 1994.

Faligot, Roger, and Rémi Kauffer. *The Chinese Secret Service: Kang Sheng and the Shadow Government in Red China.* Translated by Christine Donougher. New York: William Morrow and Company, 1989.

Gao Wengian. *Zhou Enlai: The Last Perfect Revolutionary.* Translated by Peter Rand and Lawrence R. Sullivan. New York: Public Affairs, 2007.

Gordievsky, Oleg. *Next Stop Execution.* London: Macmillan, 1995.

Howard, Edward Lee. *Safe House: The Compelling Memoirs of the Only CIA Spy to Seek Asylum in Russia.* Bethesda, Md.: National Press Books, 1995.

Joy, Admiral C. Turner. *How Communists Negotiate.* New York: Macmillan, 1955.

Jung Chang and Jon Halliday. *Mao: The Unknown Story.* New York: Alfred A. Knopf, 2005.

Kissinger, Henry. *Diplomacy.* New York: Simon & Schuster, 1994.

———. *White House Years.* Boston: Little, Brown, 1979.

———. *Years of Upheaval.* Boston: Little, Brown, 1982.

Le Carré, John. *A Perfect Spy.* New York: Alfred A. Knopf, 1986.

Li Zhisui. *The Private Life of Chairman Mao.* Translated by Tai Hung-chao. New York: Random House, 1994.

Lilley, James, with Jeffrey Lilley. *China Hands: Nine Decades of Adventure, Espionage, and Diplomacy in Asia.* New York: Public Affairs, 2004.

MacMillan, Margaret. *Nixon in China: The Week That Changed the World.* Toronto: Viking Canada, 2006.

Mangold, Tom. *Cold Warrior: James Jesus Angleton, The CIA's Master Spy Hunter.* London: Simon & Schuster, 1991.

Nixon, Richard. *In the Arena: A Memoir of Victory, Defeat, and Renewal.* New York: Simon & Schuster, 1990.

————. *RN: The Memoirs of Richard Nixon.* New York: Grosset & Dunlap, 1978.

Richelson, Jeffrey T. *A Century of Spies: Intelligence in the Twentieth Century.* New York: Oxford University Press, 1995.

————. *Foreign Intelligence Organizations.* Cambridge, Mass.: Ballinger Publishing, 1988.

Smith, I.C. *Inside: A Top G-Man Exposes Spies, Lies, and Bureaucratic Bungling Inside the FBI.* Nashville: Nelson Current, 2004.

Sontag, Sherry and Christopher Drew with Annette Lawrence Drew. *Blind Man's Bluff: The Untold Story of American Submarine Espionage.* New York: Harper, 1998.

Spence, Jonathan D. *The Search for Modern China.* Second edition. New York: W.W. Norton, 1999.

————. *The Chan's Great Continent: China in Western Minds.* New York: W.W. Norton, 1998.

————. *Chinese Roundabout: Essays in History and Culture.* New York: W.W. Norton, 1992.

Stein, Jacob A. *Legal Spectator & More.* Washington, D.C.: The Magazine Group, 2003.

Stober, Dan, and Ian Hoffman. *A Convenient Spy: Wen Ho Lee and the Politics of Nuclear Espionage.* New York: Simon & Schuster, 2001.

Toland, John. *In Mortal Combat: Korea, 1950–1953.* New York: William Morrow, 1991.

Tuchman, Barbara W. *Stilwell and the American Experience in China, 1911–45.* New York: Bantam Books, 1971.

Vatcher, William H., Jr. *Panmunjom: The Story of the Korean Military Armistice Negotiations.* New York: Frederick A. Praeger, 1958.

Wadler, Joyce. *Liaison.* New York: Bantam Books, 1993.

Weiner, Tim, Davis Johnston and Neil A. Lewis. *Betrayal: The Story of Aldrich Ames, An American Spy.* New York: Random House, 1995.

West, Philip. *Yenching University and Sino-Western Relations, 1916–1952.* Cambridge, Mass.: Harvard University Press, 1976.

Whiting, Allen S. *China Crosses the Yalu: The Decision to Enter the Korean War.* Stanford, Calif.: Stanford University Press, 1960.

Wise, David. *The Spy Who Got Away: The Inside Story of Edward Lee Howard, the CIA*

*Agent Who Betrayed His Country's Secrets and Escaped to Moscow.* New York: Random House, 1988.

Woodward, Bob. *Veil: The Secret Wars of the CIA, 1981–1987.* New York: Pocket Books, 1987.

Xu Meihong and Larry Engelmann. *Daughter of China: A True Story of Love and Betrayal.* New York: John Wiley & Sons, 1999.

## Author's Interviews

Joseph Aronica

Tom Carson

Rudy Guerin

Glendell Hill

Mark Johnson

James Lilley

Margaret MacMillan

T. Van Magers

Robert Merhige Jr.

Paul Moore

Terry Roth

Ken Schiffer

I.C. Smith

Howard Spendelow

# Notes

## 1. UNSUB

1. Personal interview, April 25, 2005.
2. Tom Mangold, *Cold Warrior: James Jesus Angleton, The CIA's Master Spy Hunter,* London: Simon & Schuster, 1991, 290.
3. *Ibid.,* 139.
4. *Ibid.,* 209.
5. *Ibid.,* 223.
6. See Milt Bearden and James Risen, *The Main Enemy: The Inside Story of the CIA's Final Showdown with the KGB,* New York: Random House, 2003, 26.
7. Personal interview, April 20, 2005.
8. Quoted at www.emergency.com/1999/chinaspy.htm.
9. Personal notes, March 24, 2007.
10. Personal interview, March 20, 2003.
11. Personal interview, April 20, 2005.
12. Personal interview, September 12, 2005.
13. Paul D. Moore, "How China Plays the Ethnic Card," *Los Angeles Times,* June 24, 1999, 9. Also online at http://cjkcreativedesigns.com/paulmoore/How_China_Plays_the_Ethnic_Card.htm.
14. Personal interview, September 12, 2005.
15. The details come from a document released by the Federal Bureau of Investigation through a Freedom of Information request.

## 2. PLANESMAN

1. Daniel Southerland, "China Silent on Reported Defection of Intelligence Official," *Washington Post,* September 4, 1986, A30. The definitive public source on Yu is Roger Faligot and Rémi Kauffer, *The Chinese Secret Service: Kang Sheng and the Shadow Government in Red China,* translated by Christine Donougher, New York: William Morrow and Company, 1989, 443–452. The identification of Yu and his position has subsequently been repeated elsewhere, including: Jeffrey T. Richelson, *Foreign Intelligence Organizations,* Cambridge, Mass.: Ballinger Publishing, 1988, 287; and Nicholas Eftimiades, *Chinese Intelligence Operations,* Annapolis, Md.: Naval Institute Press, 1994, 21.
2. "Chinese Official Said Exposer of CIA Turncoat," *Washington Post,* September 5, 1986, A18.
3. James Lilley, "Blame Clinton, Not China, for the Lapse at Los Alamos," *Wall Street Journal,* March 17, 1999. Also online at www.aei.org/publications/pubID.10211,filter.all/pub_detail.asp.
4. Personal interview, April 25, 2005.

5. James Lilley with Jeffrey Lilley, *China Hands: Nine Decades of Adventure, Espionage, and Diplomacy in Asia*, New York: Public Affairs, 2004, 189.
6. This story was told during a personal interview with the author, February 11, 2003, and is related in *China Hands*, 190–191.
7. Personal interview, February 11, 2003.
8. Faligot and Kauffer, xvi. The authors draw a family tree wherein Yu connects to his father, who links to his former spouse, Jiang Qing, who was once Kang Sheng's lover and Mao's wife.
9. *Ibid.*, 444.
10. *Ibid.*, 444–446.
11. John Byron and Robert Pack, *The Claws of the Dragon: Kang Sheng — The Evil Genius Behind Mao and His Legacy of Terror in People's China*, New York: Simon & Schuster, 1992, 481.
12. *Ibid.*, 90.
13. *Ibid.*, 124.
14. *Ibid.*, 181.
15. *Ibid.*, 225.
16. He describes his posting in Lilley with Lilley, 169–195.
17. Jung Chang and Jon Halliday, *Mao: The Unknown Story*, New York: Alfred A. Knopf, 2005, 518.
18. Jonathan D. Spence, *The Search for Modern China*, 2nd edition, New York: W.W. Norton, 1999, 574.
19. More conservative numbers cited in *ibid.*, 645; higher numbers cited in Chang and Halliday, 547.
20. Personal interview, May 27, 2004.
21. See *The Little Prince* at http://www.odaha.com/littleprince.php?f=English (accessed March 11, 2008).
22. Personal interview, May 28, 2004.
23. The reorganization would take place in 1983.
24. I.C. Smith, *Inside: A Top G-Man Exposes Spies, Lies, and Bureaucratic Bungling Inside the FBI*, Nashville: Nelson Current, 2004, 49–50.
25. Personal interview, April 25, 2005.
26. Personal interview, April 20, 2005.
27. Smith, 42.

## 3. Larry Wu-Tai Chin

1. The trials and tribulations of Director Casey's tenure at CIA are the subject of Bob Woodward, *Veil: The Secret Wars of the CIA, 1981–1987*, New York: Pocket Books, 1987.
2. Document obtained through a Freedom of Information Act request.
3. From a personal interview with Paul Moore, February 14, 2003.
4. See imos.rccb.osis.gov/index.html.
5. George C. Wilson, "Anti-Espionage Efforts Urged Within Government," *Washington Post*, November 22, 1985, A31.

6. All information pertaining to the security investigation of Larry Chin comes from FBI files obtained through a Freedom of Information request.
7. Personal interview, September 12, 2005.
8. Personal interview, April 29, 2005.
9. This came out during the trial, *United States v. Larry Wu-Tai Chin* (85-00263-A).
10. Document obtained through a Freedom of Information Act request.
11. Document obtained through a Freedom of Information Act request.
12. Personal interview, February 14, 2003.
13. Notes received March 24, 2007.
14. Documents obtained through a Freedom of Information Act request.
15. Personal interview, May 28, 2004.
16. Personal interview, February 14, 2003.
17. Personal interview, September 13, 2005.
18. Testimony of Larry Chin, February 6, 1986, *United States v. Larry Wu-Tai Chin.*
19. Ruth Marcus, "Accused Spy Used Hong Kong Banks," *Washington Post,* November 28, 1985, A26.
20. Document obtained through a Freedom of Information Act request.
21. Personal interview, September 13, 2005.
22. *Ibid.*
23. Personal interview, May 30, 2004.
24. Personal interview, February 14, 2003.
25. Chin, Cathy, *The Death of My Husband: Larry Wu-Tai Chin*, Taipei, Taiwan: Tunghwang, 1998, 210–1.
26. Personal interview, April 29, 2005.
27. From a diary page entered into evidence, *United States v. Larry Wu-Tai Chin.*
28. Testimony of Larry Chin, February 6, 1986, *United States v. Larry Wu-Tai Chin.*
29. Personal interview, September 12, 2005.
30. James Bamford, *The Puzzle Palace: A Report on America's Most Secret Agency,* Boston: Houghton Mifflin, 1982, 2.
31. *Ibid.*, 56.
32. *Ibid.*, 61ff, and also 118–119 with respect to the color scheme of badges.
33. *Ibid.*, 91.
34. *Ibid.*, 114–117.
35. See *ibid.*, 197 and 206–208.
36. Testimony of Larry Chin, February 6, 1986, *United States v. Larry Wu-Tai Chin.*
37. Personal interview, February 14, 2003.
38. Personal interview, May 29, 2004.
39. Testimony of Larry Chin, February 6, 1986, *United States v. Larry Wu-Tai Chin.*

## 4. Bernard Boursicot

1. Chang and Halliday, 520.
2. Joyce Wadler, *Liaison*, New York: Bantam, 1993, 94–95.
3. Personal interview, May 27, 2004.
4. Wadler, 170.

5. *Ibid.*, 107.
6. Faligot and Kauffer, 446–447.
7. Wadler, 168.
8. Personal interview, April 25, 2005.
9. *Ibid.*
10. Xu Meihong and Larry Engelmann, *Daughter of China: A True Story of Love and Betrayal*, New York: John Wiley & Sons, 1999.
11. The account of Boursicot's arrest is drawn from Wadler, 5.
12. *Ibid.* Wadler quotes the surveillance as occurring in the winter of 1982; stating that Shi arrived in October 1982 may be carelessness on her part, or an inaccuracy in the DST documents.
13. *Ibid.*, 229.
14. *Ibid.*, 7.

## 5. Eagle Claw

1. Personal interview, April 29, 2005.
2. *Ibid.*
3. "Spy Stories," *U.S. News & World Report*, January 27–February 3, 2003, 51.
4. Sherry Sontag and Christopher Drew with Annette Lawrence Drew, *Blind Man's Bluff: The Untold Story of American Submarine Espionage*, New York: Harper, 1998, 353.
5. Wolf Blitzer, *Territory of Lies: The Exclusive Story of Jonathan Jay Pollard: The American Who Spied on His Country for Israel and How He Was Betrayed*, New York: Harper & Row, 1989, 165.
6. *Ibid.*, 171.
7. *Ibid.*, 93.
8. *Ibid.*, 48.
9. *Ibid.*, xix.
10. *Ibid.*, 64.
11. Oleg Gordievsky, *Next Stop Execution*, London: Macmillan, 1995, 349.
12. Woodward, 525.
13. Bearden and Risen, 38.
14. David Wise, *The Spy Who Got Away*, New York: Random House, 1988, 68.
15. Edward Lee Howard, *Safe House*, Bethesda, Md.: National Press Books, 1995, 143–145.
16. See, for example, Tim Weiner, David Johnston, and Neil A. Lewis, *Betrayal: The Story of Aldrich Ames, An American Spy*, New York: Random House, 1995, 53–54. Also, in the unclassified CIA journal *Studies in Intelligence*, former associate director of operations for counterintelligence Barry G. Royden writes, "There is little doubt that Howard betrayed Tolkachev," adding, "As it turned out, Tolkachev's days would have been numbered even if Howard had not betrayed him. According to overt sources, Aldrich Ames also passed Tolkachev's name to the KGB." Barry G. Royden, "Tolkachev: A Worthy Successor to Penkovsky," *Studies in Intelligence* 47, 2003, www.cia.gov/csi/studies/vol47no3/

articleo2.html. Milt Bearden, former chief of the CIA's Soviet/East European Division, says that Tolkachev was already in KGB custody when Ames would have passed over his name, in Bearden and Risen, 16.

17. Personal interview, May 29, 2004.
18. Personal interview, February 14, 2003.
19. Smith, 40–41, and personal interview, April 20, 2005.
20. Personal interview, September 12, 2005.
21. Personal interview, May 28, 2004.
22. Personal interview, April 29, 2005.
23. Personal interview, February 14, 2003.
24. Personal interview, September 13, 2005.
25. John Douglas and Mark Olshaker, *Mindhunter: Inside the FBI's Elite Serial Crime Unit*, New York: Pocket Books, 1995, 193.
26. Personal interview, April 29, 2005.
27. Personal interview, May 29, 2004.
28. Personal interview, April 25, 2005.
29. Personal interview, September 13, 2005.
30. Personal interview, April 29, 2005.
31. Personal interview, February 14, 2003.
32. Personal interview, September 13, 2005.
33. Personal interview, April 29, 2005.
34. Personal interview, April 29, 2005.
35. Personal interview, September 13, 2005.
36. Personal interview, April 29, 2005.
37. *Ibid.*
38. Personal interview, April 29, 2005.

## 6. A Very Long Story

1. Personal interview, April 29, 2005.
2. *Frontline: From China with Love*, "Interview: T. Van Magers," June 4, 2003, www.pbs.org/wgbh/pages/frontline/shows/spy/interviews/vanmagers.html.
3. Personal interview, February 14, 2003.
4. Rather than referencing every quote and detail in this account of how the interview transpired, I will state that it is drawn from personal interviews with all three of the FBI agents who participated as well as others in a position to know exactly what happened, plus transcripts of court testimony given by Mark Johnson, Terry Roth, and Larry Chin.
5. Personal interview, April 29, 2005.
6. Personal interview, April 28, 2005.
7. Personal interview, March 20, 2003.
8. Personal interview, November 6, 2004.
9. Personal interview, April 28, 2005.
10. Personal interview, February 14, 2003.
11. Personal interview, March 20, 2003.

12. Personal interview, March 14, 2003.

13. Personal interview, April 29, 2005.

14. Philip West, *Yenching University and Sino-Western Relations, 1916–1952,* Cambridge, Mass.: Harvard University Press, 1976, 84.

15. Personal interview, April 25, 2005.

16. West, 148.

17. *Ibid.,* 145.

18. *Ibid.,* 214.

19. Quoted in Jonathan D. Spence, *The Chan's Great Continent: China in Western Minds,* New York: W.W. Norton, 1998, 85.

20. Personal interview, May 28, 2004.

21. Over the course of several interviews, February 14, 2003, April 25, 2005.

22. Personal interview, May 28, 2004.

23. Personal interview, April 29, 2005.

24. Personal interview, April 28, 2005.

25. Personal interview, September 13, 2005.

26. Chang and Halliday, 347–348.

27. *Ibid.,* 356–357.

28. Allen S. Whiting, *China Crosses the Yalu: The Decision to Enter the Korean War,* Stanford, Calif.: Stanford University Press, 1960, 46.

29. John Toland, *In Mortal Combat: Korea, 1950–1953,* New York: William Morrow, 1991, 237.

30. Chang and Halliday, 358.

31. *Ibid.,* 360.

32. Toland, 463.

33. Testimony of Larry Chin, February 6, 1986, *United States v. Larry Wu-Tai Chin.*

34. Admiral C. Turner Joy, *How Communists Negotiate,* New York: Macmillan, 1955, 103.

35. William H. Vatcher Jr., *Panmunjom: The Story of the Korean Military Armistice Negotiations,* New York: Frederick A. Praeger, 1958, 143–144.

36. Chang and Halliday, 368.

37. Testimony of Larry Chin, February 6, 1986, *United States v. Larry Wu-Tai Chin.*

38. *Ibid.*

39. *Ibid.*

40. Quoted in Sydney Dawson Bailey, *The Korean Armistice,* New York: St. Martin's Press, 1992, 89.

41. Personal interview, April 29, 2005.

42. Testimony of Larry Chin, February 6, 1986, *United States v. Larry Wu-Tai Chin.*

43. Chang and Halliday, 374.

44. Personal interview, April 29, 2005.

45. Joseph Aronica, opening statement, February 4, 1986, *United States v. Larry Wu-Tai Chin.*

46. The account of Larry's introduction to Ou Qiming is drawn from his testimony, February 6, 1986, *United States v. Larry Wu-Tai Chin.*

47. Related in a personal interview with Ken Schiffer, April 29, 2005.
48. Testimony of Larry Chin, February 6, 1986, *United States v. Larry Wu-Tai Chin*.
49. Joseph Aronica, opening statement, February 4, 1986, *United States v. Larry Wu-Tai Chin*.
50. Personal interview, April 25, 2005.
51. *Ibid*.
52. Personal interview, April 28, 2005.
53. *Ibid*.
54. Personal interview, April 29, 2005.
55. Byron and Pack, 338.
56. FBI, New York Field Office document dated February 11, 1970, obtained through a Freedom of Information Act request.
57. Personal interview, April 25, 2005.
58. Jacob Stein, closing argument, February 7, 1986, *United States v. Larry Wu-Tai Chin*.
59. Testimony of Larry Chin, February 6, 1986, *United States v. Larry Wu-Tai Chin*.
60. *Ibid*.
61. Document obtained through a Freedom of Information Act request.
62. Testimony of Larry Chin, February 6, 1986, *United States v. Larry Wu-Tai Chin*.
63. Quoted in Jonathan D. Spence, *The Search for Modern China*, 539.
64. *Ibid.*, 544.
65. Chang and Halliday, 417.
66. Personal interview, May 29, 2004.
67. Chang and Halliday, 503.
68. Dr. Li Zhisui, *The Private Life of Chairman Mao*, translated by Tai Hung-chao, New York: Random House, 1994, 398.
69. Personal interview, April 25, 2005.
70. Quoted in Henry Kissinger, *Diplomacy*, New York: Simon & Schuster, 1994, 721.
71. *Ibid.*, 27.
72. Richard Nixon, *In the Arena: A Memoir of Victory, Defeat, and Renewal*, New York: Simon & Schuster, 1990, 29.
73. Henry Kissinger, *White House Years*, Boston: Little, Brown, 1979, 177–178.
74. Kissinger, *Diplomacy*, 722–723.
75. Li, 514.
76. Kissinger, *Diplomacy*, 725.
77. Li, 515.
78. Kissinger, *White House Years*, 684.
79. Nixon, *RN: The Memoirs of Richard Nixon*, New York: Grosset & Dunlap, 1978, 545.
80. Quoted in Kissinger, *White House Years*, 712.
81. Nixon, *In the Arena*, 288.
82. Kissinger, *Diplomacy*, 22.
83. Chang and Halliday, 579.

84. Nixon, *In the Arena*, 327.

85. Kissinger, *White House Years*, 724.

86. Nixon, *RN*, 559.

87. Chang and Halliday, 581.

88. *Ibid.*, 583.

89. Personal interview, April 25, 2005.

90. Testimony of Larry Chin, February 6, 1986, *United States v. Larry Wu-Tai Chin*.

91. Personal interview, April 29, 2005.

92. Kissinger, *Years of Upheaval*, Boston: Little, Brown, 1982, 66.

93. Personal interview, May 27, 2004.

94. Personal interview, April 29, 2005.

95. Margaret MacMillan, *Nixon in China: The Week That Changed the World*, Toronto: Viking Canada, 2006, 163.

96. Personal interview, November 12, 2006.

97. Personal interview, May 27, 2004.

98. MacMillan, 329.

99. Li, 514.

100. Personal interview, February 14, 2003.

101. Testimony of Larry Chin, February 6, 1986, *United States v. Larry Wu-Tai Chin*.

102. Chang and Halliday, 349.

103. *Ibid.*, 70.

104. Li, 258.

105. Gao Wenqian, *Zhou Enlai: The Last Perfect Revolutionary*, translated by Peter Rand and Lawrence R. Sullivan, New York: Public Affairs, 2007, 3–4.

106. All of the above quotes are drawn from court transcripts, testimony of Larry Chin, February 6, 1986. *United States v. Larry Wu-Tai Chin*.

107. Personal interview, April 29, 2005.

108. Personal interview, May 28, 2004.

109. Personal interview, May 30, 2004.

110. Testimony of Larry Chin, February 6, 1986, *United States v. Larry Wu-Tai Chin*.

111. Personal interview with Terry Roth, November 6, 2004.

112. Peter Perl, "Chin's 'Good Fortune' Debated," *Washington Post*, November 25, 1985, A16.

113. Caryle Murphy, "Accused Spy Says He Meant to Promote U.S. China Ties," *Washington Post*, February 7, 1986, A11.

114. Personal interview with Mark Johnson, April 29, 2005.

115. *Ibid.*

116. Personal interview, April 29, 2005.

117. Personal interview, September 13, 2005.

118. *Ibid.*

119. Personal interview, April 29, 2005.

120. Personal interview with Mark Johnson, April 29, 2005.

121. Personal interview, September 13, 2005.

# 7. The Preliminaries

1. Personal interview, February 10, 2003.
2. Personal interview, September 13, 2005.
3. The account of State's contact with Chinese embassy officials comes from a telex dispatched to the American embassy, Beijing, November 24, 1986, under the subject, "Arrest of Larry Wu-Tai Chin." Obtained through a Freedom of Information request.
4. Ruth Marcus, "Accused Spy Used Hong Kong Banks," *Washington Post*, November 28, 1985, A1 and A26.
5. From Trial Memorandum, filed by the US attorney in the US District Court for the Eastern District of Virginia, Alexandria Division, February 3, 1986.
6. *Ibid.*
7. The above comes from Superseding Indictment filed with the US District Court for the Eastern District of Virginia, Alexandria Division, January 2, 1986.
8. Personal interview, September 13, 2005.
9. The above comes from Supplemental Memorandum of Points and Authorities in Support of Defendant's Motion to Suppress Statements filed with the US District Court for the Eastern District of Virginia, Alexandria Division, January 2, 1986.
10. Trial Memorandum.
11. Supplemental Memorandum.
12. Personal interview, March 19, 2003.
13. Testimony of Larry Chin, January 3, 1986, *United States v. Larry Wu-Tai Chin*.
14. Personal interview, April 29, 2005.

# 8. The Trial

1. Personal interview, April 29, 2005.
2. Patricia Sullivan, "Federal Judge Robert R. Merhige Dies," *Washington Post*, February 20, 2005, C8.
3. Bill Lohmann, "The Face of Justice," *University of Richmond Magazine*, fall 1998, 12.
4. Opening statement, Joseph Aronica, February 4, 1986, *United States v. Larry Wu-Tai Chin*.
5. Opening statement, Jacob Stein, February 4, 1986, *United States v. Larry Wu-Tai Chin*.
6. Personal interview, September 14, 2005.
7. Caryle Murphy, "Top CIA Official Gives Chin Jurors a Lesson in Intelligence Gathering," *Washington Post*, February 6, 1986, A32.
8. Documents obtained through a Freedom of Information Act request.
9. Personal interview, September 14, 2005.
10. Personal interview, April 29, 2005.
11. *Ibid.*
12. The comment was made during the abatement hearing at *United States v. Larry Wu-Tai Chin*, October 3, 1986.
13. Murphy, "Top CIA Official," A32.

14. *Ibid.*
15. Testimony of Carl Walter Ford Jr., February 7, 1986, *United States v. Larry Wu-Tai Chin.*
16. Murphy, "Top CIA Official," A32.
17. Testimony of Carl Walter Ford Jr., February 7, 1986, *United States v. Larry Wu-Tai Chin.*
18. Personal interview, April 24, 2005.
19. Closing argument, February 7, 1986, *United States v. Larry Wu-Tai Chin.*
20. Personal interview, April 24, 2005.
21. Testimony of Larry Chin, February 6, 1986, *United States v. Larry Wu-Tai Chin.*
22. Personal interview, April 29, 2005.
23. Jacob A. Stein, *Legal Spectator & More,* Washington, DC: The Magazine Group, 2003, 71.
24. *United States v. Larry Wu-Tai Chin,* October 3, 1986.
25. Personal interview, April 29, 2005.
26. Personal interview, February 14, 2003.
27. Closing arguments, February 7, 1986, *United States v. Larry Wu-Tai Chin.*
28. *Ibid.*
29. Personal interview, February 12, 2003.
30. Closing arguments, February 7, 1986, *United States v. Larry Wu-Tai Chin.*
31. Engelberg, "Ex-CIA Aide Convicted in Spy Case," *New York Times,* February 8, 1986, 8.
32. Personal interview, March 14, 2003.

## 9. The End

1. Personal interview, April 4, 2003.
2. Testimony of Cathy Chin, October 3, 1986, *United States v. Larry Wu-Tai Chin.*
3. Chin, *The Death of My Husband,* 31.
4. Personal interview, February 12, 2003.
5. Caryle Murphy, "Jury Convicts Chin of Spying for Chinese," *Washington Post,* February 8, 1986, A11.
6. Reports of the interview were very similar in Caryle Murphy, "Chin: Nothing to Regret," *Washington Post,* February 11, 1986, A5; and "CIA's Security Was Lax, According to Convicted Spy," *New York Times,* February 11, 1986, A29.
7. Engelberg, "Spy for China Found Suffocated in Prison, Apparently a Suicide," *New York Times,* February 22, 1986, A1.
8. Interview with Charlie Rose, CBS *Nightwatch.*
9. Chin, *The Death of My Husband,* 341–3.
10. Caryle Murphy, "Spy Larry Chin Dies in Apparent Suicide," *Washington Post,* February 22, 1986, A1 & A6.
11. Caryle Murphy, "Chin's Death Ruled a Suicide," *Washington Post,* February 23, 1986, A10.
12. Engelberg, "Spy for China Found Suffocated in Prison, Apparently a Suicide," *New York Times,* February 22, 1986, 1 & 7.

13. Murphy, "Chin's Death Ruled a Suicide," A10.

14. Memorandum from US District Judge Robert Merhige Jr., April 24, 1986, *United States v. Larry Wu-Tai Chin*. The letter in question has been under seal in the interest of protecting privacy. The passage quoted herein is the only portion to have been entered verbatim in the public record.

15. Chin, *The Death of My Husband*, 386.

16. Caryle Murphy, "Chin's Last Letter to Wife Ordinary Note, Son Says," *Washington Post*, February 25, 1986, B5.

17. Murphy, "Chin's Death Ruled a Suicide," A10.

18. A. Alvarez, *The Savage God: A Study of Suicide*, New York: Bantam Books, 1971, 83.

## 10. The Visit

1. John le Carré, *A Perfect Spy*, New York: Alfred A. Knopf, 1986, 273.

2. "Confessions of a 'Mole,'" *U.S. News & World Report*, February 17, 1986, 9.

3. Personal interview, February 14, 2003.

4. Personal interview, April 25, 2005.

5. Memorandum in Opposition to Motion to Abate Criminal Proceedings, US District Court for the Eastern District of Virginia, March 13, 1986.

6. Memorandum, US District Court for the Eastern District of Virginia, April 4, 1986.

7. Personal interview, September 14, 2005.

8. Chin, *Death of My Husband*, 441–2.

9. Personal interview, April 4, 2003.

10. Chin, *Death of My Husband*, 370ff.

11. Personal interview, April 29, 2005.

12. Personal interview, November 6, 2004.

13. Personal interview, February 14, 2003.

14. Personal interview, May 30, 2004.

15. Personal interview, April 29, 2005.

16. Chin, *Death of My Husband*, 385.

17. Personal interview with anonymous source, March 22, 2003.

## Coda

1. Joseph Conrad, *The Rescue*, Middlesex, England: Penguin, 1920, 315.

## Acknowledgments

1. Telephone conversation, December 10, 2002.

# Index

Vadim Daniel Photography

Tod Hoffman is the author of three previous books, including *Le Carré's Landscape* and *Homicide: Life on the Screen*. An eight-year veteran of the Canadian Security Intelligence Service, Hoffman served for a period on the Counter-Intelligence: China desk. He attended the Institut d'etudes politiques de Paris and earned a master's degree in political science from McGill University.